The Ultimate History of the
Sports Car

This is a Parragon Publishing Book

First published in 2005

Parragon Publishing
Queen Street House
4 Queen Street
Bath BA1 1HE, UK

Copyright © Parragon 2005

ISBN: 1-40543-870-3

A copy of the CIP data for this book is available from the British Library upon request.

The rights of Andrew Noakes to be identified as the author of this work have been asserted in accordance
with Section 77 of the Copyright, Designs and Patents Act of 1988.

Created, designed, produced, and packaged by Stonecastle Graphics Ltd

Designed by Paul Turner and Sue Pressley
Edited by Philip de Ste. Croix

Printed and bound in China

The author and publishers have made every reasonable effort to contact all copyright holders. Any errors that may have
occurred are inadvertent and anyone who for any reason has not been contacted is invited to write to the publishers so that
a full acknowledgement may be made in subsequent editions of this work.

Photographic credits:

Andrew Noakes: page: 183(bl)

Pictures © Neill Bruce's Automobile Photolibrary by:
Neill Bruce and others: pages 8-9, 10(b), 13(t), 15(t), 16(t), 17(t), 18-19, 22(b), 24(t), 24(b), 25(t), 26(b), 28(b), 29(r), 33,
34(b), 36, 38-39, 40(t), 41, 42, 43(b), 44(r), 45, 46, 47(t), 47(b), 48(t), 50-51, 54(tr), 56(br), 57(tl), 60, 62(b), 63(br), 66(t),
67, 68(t), 69, 70-71, 72(r), 73(t), 74(b), 75(l), 77(b), 76(b), 77(t), 78(t), 78(bl), 79(b), 80, 81(b), 82(t), 83(b), 84(br), 85(t),
86(b), 87(t), 88(b), 89, 92(l), 93(t), 93(b), 95, 96(t), 96(b), 98(t), 98(b), 100, 101(t), 102(t), 102(b), 105(tr), 106, 107(t),
107(bl), 108-109, 110(b), 112(t), 113(t), 113(b), 114(b), 116(t), 116(b), 117(t), 118(b), 119(t), 122(t), 123(b), 124(t),
124(b), 125(tr), 125(b), 126, 127(b), 130(t), 132(t), 135, 136(b), 137(t), 138(t), 144-145, 146(b), 147(t), 150(t), 157(cl),
157, 158(b), 159(t), 160(t), 160(b)

Ian Dawson: page 136(t)

Geoffrey Goddard: pages 11(t), 29(l), 30, 43(t), 48(b), 62(t), 92(r), 99, 115(b), 127(t), 140(l), 161(tl)

Christian Gonzenbach: page 37(t)

Trevor Legate: pages 90-91, 94, 103(t)

Richard Meinert: pages 122(b), 184(t)

F Naef: page 142

Jorg Petersen: page 177(b)

All other photographs are manufacturers' press pictures supplied from The Peter Roberts Collection c/o Neill Bruce, and
from the author.

Please note: prices shown in US dollars are a current conversion of original
prices, calculated in UK pounds sterling, and are intended only to give an
approximate indication of values.

The Ultimate History of the
Sports Car

FROM EARLY ENTHUSIASTS' RACERS TO PERFORMANCE SUPERCARS

ANDREW NOAKES

p

Contents

Introduction   **6**

1   What is a Sports Car?   **8**

2   Pre-War: The Right Crowd   **18**

3   1945-49: Austerity in Action   **38**

4   1950s: Success Breeds Success   **50**

5   1960s: Sports Cars for All   **70**

6   1960-69: The Age of the Supercar   **90**

7   1970s: Safe at Any Speed   **108**

8   1980-89: The Roadster Reborn   **128**

9   1990s: Widening the Choice   **144**

10   Today's Sports Cars   **162**

11   Toward Tomorrow   **178**

Index   **192**

Left: *Light, strong, and very fast –*
Porsche's fabulous Carrera GT.

Introduction

Just about everyone wants a sports car. Maybe you wish you could drive a classic Jaguar E-type or a big Healey, or you lust after a vintage Bentley or the latest high-tech BMW roadster. Maybe you're lucky enough to have one of those machines in your garage, but even if everyday practicality forces you to get behind the wheel of a more mundane motor car, you cannot help but be stirred by some of the machinery to which the beguiling sports car label has been applied over the years. *The Ultimate History of the Sports Car* tells the story of these fascinating cars, and the people behind them.

The sports car's roots lie firmly in motor sport, the very earliest machines having been conceived as dual-purpose road and racing cars. Aston Martin, Bentley, MG and a host of others would quite happily have sold you a car not too far removed from their own 'works' racing machines, provided you had the money to pay for it. And as a well-heeled young man you would have been likely to race your car at the weekends and then drive it on the road during the week – to show people you were a 'sporting motorist.'

That attitude survived, to some extent, until the 1960s. Then, as racing cars became more highly specialized, sports cars diversified: at the affordable end were MG's best-selling roadsters and recently-arrived rivals from Austin-Healey and Triumph, all of them based on simple if effective engineering and mass-made components. At the other end of the scale there appeared a new breed of ultra-rapid 'supercars' boasting sophisticated, technically advanced design and astounding, space-age styling, led by the Italian marques Lamborghini, Maserati, and Ferrari.

Between those two extremes were dozens of other marques. From Italy there were roadsters and rapid coupés from Fiat, Lancia, and Alfa Romeo. From Britain, the Jaguar XK series and then the astonishing E-type, plus specialist marques such as Lotus, TVR, and Reliant. France had its own specialists: Alpine's Renault-based sports cars would become successful in rallying. In the US the Chevrolet Corvette became ever faster and more well-developed, while in Germany Porsche quietly refined its 911 series until, by the 1970s, it was a genuine supercar.

The true sports car faced twin threats in the 1970s. First, safety legislation seemed poised to ban open roadsters for good. Second, the sports sedans of the 1960s – chief among them the Mini Cooper and Lotus Cortina – gave way to a new breed of 'hot hatch,' typified by the fuel-injected VW Golf GTI. But the sports car survived.

In the 1980s came a resurgence, with Mazda's Miata roadster and Toyota's mid-engined MR2. Today, a revised Miata is still in production and Toyota's third-generation MR2 is enjoying considerable success. More and more manufacturers are adding machines like these to their product ranges. There's never been a better time to celebrate the sports car.

Left: *Porsche Boxster, one of the world's*
most desirable sports cars.

What is a Sports Car?

Your idea of what a sports car should be is likely to depend on how old you are, or at least on how old you feel. If your memories stretch back to Bentley's multiple Le Mans wins or MG's myriad successes in motor sport during the 1920s and 1930s, then you'll see a sports car as a very different machine to someone born after the end of World War II. But even though 'sports car' means different things to different people, there are many common threads that run from the very earliest sporting machines to the high-tech sports cars of today.

In its earliest days, the sports car was a machine which was capable of winning races and hillclimbs at the weekend, but which could act as swift and secure transport on the poor roads of the day during the week. Wilhelm Maybach's 35hp Mercedes, often described as the first real sports car, could even be provided with a dual-purpose body which turned it from a racing machine to a road car in minutes.

The dual-purpose sports car became the car of choice of clubman racers. Marques such as Mercedes, Bentley, Vauxhall, Alfa Romeo, and MG would sell you a machine which bore a striking resemblance to their own works racers, though usually without the latest tuning tweaks – the higher-compression cylinder head, for instance, or larger carburetors.

But as motor sport developed, so the needs of racing teams dictated that the cars they used became more and more sophisticated – and at the same time took them further and further from the ideal for a roadgoing car. By the 1930s the Mercedes-Benz and Auto Union Grand Prix teams were racing not just for the respective manufacturer's honor, but also for the glory of Hitler's Reich, which subsidized them both to some extent – and the money that Germany poured into its racing teams raised the professionalism of motor sport to heights never before seen.

Racing road cars

There was still a place for the sports car. Outside the rarified world of Grand Prix racing, mildly-tuned roadgoing cars still formed the bulk of the entry in several classes of motor sport. But already many buyers of sports cars intended to use their machines exclusively as road cars, leaving competition up to the manufacturers. Success at the Brooklands track or the Shelsley

Previous page: A gleaming example of the impressively powerful AC Shelby Cobra 427. This is a 1966 model.

Above: In the 1930s Germany dominated Grand Prix races with cars such as this Mercedes-Benz W154.

Below: The MG TC was a huge export success in the 1940s.

Left: Early sports cars like this TT-Replica Frazer Nash were designed for dual roles – on the road and in motor sport.

Below: Bernd Rosemeyer and the rear-engined Auto Union were tough to beat in pre-war Grands Prix.

Walsh hillclimb served to build the cars' reputations, and gave the enthusiastic owners of roadgoing versions a plausible reason to justify their purchases.

To many, though, sports cars needed no justification. As motor cars became more sophisticated, so they became more refined and more comfortable and easier to drive, but some drivers felt that there was a price to pay for this increased tractability. Sports car enthusiasts relished the instant feedback from the machine, and prided themselves in displaying the driving skill that these cars demanded. The sense of involvement was key to the sports car's appeal, and the sheer satisfaction to be had from a spirited drive of a sporting machine was unequalled. Sports cars, in short, were fun.

It was this that led American servicemen returning from Europe after World War II to seek out Stateside dealers for MG sports cars, turning the hastily-conceived MG TC into one of the British motor industry's few export successes of the time. In some ways the TC was cruder and cheaper than some of its forebears, and was the brainchild more of Morris Motors' accounts department than MG's racing workshop. But that didn't matter: it worked, it was available at a good price, and it had that magic 'fun' ingredient that was lacking in so many cars of the 1940s, on both sides of the Atlantic.

The basic sports car recipe called for a chassis which carried its masses low to the ground, to give the car a low 'center of gravity' and thus improve its handling and roadholding. On top sat a lightweight body which generally offered little space and only a small measure of weather protection for the two occupants – a driver and a 'riding mechanic' if the car was entered in a race, but more likely the driver and his girlfriend out on the road. By the 1920s a skimpy canvas roof was often provided, though hardened sports car drivers rarely used them, except when the car was parked. In racing they were only used when the regulations demanded it, such as at the early Tourist Trophy races. There, the races were intended to be for 'touring cars' rather than out-and-out racers, and to prove their cars' status drivers were required to complete two laps of the demanding 14-mile (23km) Newtownards circuit with their roofs erected, before stopping to fold them down.

A sports car engine could be of virtually any size depending on the size or 'class' of car – from the 847cc Wolseley engine in the M-type MG Midget on the one hand to monsters like the 6½-liter Bentleys on the other. But in every case the engine would be tuned for a high power

Above: The XK120 Drophead Coupé was far more civilized than previous sports cars.

Below: Jaguar's D-type competition car is one of the most famous automotive shapes of all.

output, often with two (or more) carburetors. In the majority of sports cars the power unit was front-mounted and drove the rear wheels through a propeller shaft and live rear axle – though there were oddities such as the chain-drive Frazer-Nash and the front-wheel-drive Alvis. This distribution of major masses, with the engine at the front, gearbox and passengers in the center, and the heavy driven axle at the back, helped to even out the load on the tires and give the car a better handling balance.

As technology improved, so sports cars became quicker and more sophisticated. Early cars had brakes on the rear wheels only, but front-wheel brakes gained popularity on sporting machines in the 1920s. Engine outputs improved, and huge improvements in tire and suspension technology gave sports cars better roadholding than ever before.

Meanwhile, public interest in speed reached new heights with the battle for the Land Speed Record between such drivers as Malcolm Campbell and Henry Segrave, while a myriad of class speed records were contested by George Eyston, 'Goldie' Gardner and others. The aerodynamic shapes essential for these record-breaking cars fired public imagination, and 'streamlining' became a fashion that was applied beyond the world of motor racing. The express locomotives of the London and North Eastern Railway (LNER) and the London, Midland and Scottish Railway (LMS) in Britain appeared in the 1920s with innovative, low-drag shapes and high speed potential.

The same aerodynamic thinking led to the production of low-drag 'fastback' coupés based on open sports cars, such as the Airline Coupé version of MG's P-type Midget. For the first time, the traditionalists who looked upon a sports car as having an open top had a dilemma: the P-type was clearly a sports car, and yet with the Airline body it suddenly became dangerously close to

Left: The glassfiber-monocoque Lotus Elite derived speed from light weight rather than high power.

Below: Porsche developed the 356 from humble, VW-based origins into a fast and fine-handling sports car.

looking like a sedan. As sports cars became more refined and sporting sedans became quicker, the line between the two would become harder to draw.

The distinctions were blurred again after World War II by a significant new arrival from Jaguar. The 1948 XK120 shared its engine and much of its chassis with the MkV sedan: there was nothing wrong with the engine, a lusty twin-overhead-cam in-line six, but the independent front suspension was a novelty for sports car enthusiasts used to beam front axles. If the diehards doubted the Jaguar's sporting credentials, few of them expressed any concern, because the car was sensationally beautiful and capable of an unprecedented 120mph (193km/h) – unheard of for a production car of the time. Three years later the XK120 was made available in a fixed-head coupé guise, giving the open roadster enthusiasts more to think about…

Sophisticated sports cars

Throughout the 1950s and 1960s, the idea of the hard-riding, unrefined roadster was overtaken by sporting machines revealing a new level of sophistication. Ferrari introduced roadgoing sports cars which learned lessons from its racing machinery. Jaguar's E-type blended the racing know-how of the Le Mans-winning C- and D-type with advanced independent suspension, making it rapid but also refined and easy to drive. Lotus used innovative materials and design to offer high performance from a small-engined car, with the fixed-head Elite and later the Elan – available both as a fixed-roof coupé and an open roadster. Also available in both guises was Porsche's rapid 356, but its successor, the 911, would initially only be available in fixed-roof form.

Traditional roadsters were still being bought in their thousands, some of the most popular being Triumph's successful TR series. But road drivers were becoming more demanding of their machinery. Sports cars still had to be fast and fun to drive, but increasingly they had to be comfortable and easy to live with – and even though they were seen as road cars rather than racers, they were expected to use the latest technology that had been developed with racing in mind. So disc brakes appeared on the otherwise conventional TRs, followed later by mechanical fuel injection. Independent suspension, too, gained wider acceptance.

Above: Lamborghini emerged in the 1960s to challenge Ferrari.

Above: The fun Fiat X1/9.

As the 1960s progressed, a new alternative to the sports car threatened its very existence. Sedan cars were now competing in their own racing classes, often producing close, exciting racing that captured the imagination of motor racing enthusiasts. As car makers battled for supremacy, performance sedans were developed to make production sedans more competitive. Jaguar's compact sedans were naturally competitive, using the same six-cylinder engines as the XK sports cars. John Cooper slotted a Formula Junior-spec engine into a BMC Mini to produce the Mini Cooper, which proved to be a formidable weapon on the race track and an equally big success in rallying, where its tidy handling and front-wheel drive gave it an advantage in adverse conditions. Meanwhile Lotus and Ford joined forces to produce the Lotus-Cortina, using a Lotus-developed twin-cam engine harnessed to Colin Chapman's ideas on suspension. With drivers of the caliber of Jim Clark and Sir John Whitmore, the Lotus-Cortina proved to be another sedan car success on the track.

Both threatened to make the sports car irrelevant. The Mini Cooper, in particular, turned many drivers away from the spartan open sports car. With its practical shape and astonishing roadholding, a well-prepared Mini (and particularly the quicker 1275cc Cooper S of 1964) was a match for many roadsters on a twisty road – and no less fun to drive. The Mini was more fashionable, too, but even that couldn't persuade every enthusiast to give up his Austin-Healey or Triumph TR.

Where sports cars had once been the kings of the road, now there were other machines that were potentially quicker. The smaller-engined sports cars could be outclassed by a hot Mini, particularly in poor weather conditions and on bad roads, and the pace of the bigger roadsters was being threatened by effective sports sedans like the 3.8 Jaguar. On top of that, a whole new breed of sports car – the ultra-fast supercar, epitomized by Ferrari, Lamborghini, and Aston Martin – was taking roadgoing performance to new levels and introducing innovative technology to the sports car genre.

Mass management: the dynamics of the sports car

Sports cars vary in layout, but in every case the engineers will have faced a common problem – that of arranging the major masses in the car to achieve the best balance and cornering power. The key factors are the weight distribution, the 'polar moment of inertia,' and the height of the 'center of gravity.'

A front-engined, front-wheel-drive car will tend to carry its weight at the front of the car, and this tends to promote straight-line stability at the expense of crisp handling. The other extreme, a rear-engined, rear-drive car like the Porsche 911, will turn in swiftly but can then be subject to oversteer as the heavy masses at the rear try to swing around. The classic front-engined, rear-drive layout distributes the mass evenly around the car, giving it an even handling balance.

The polar moment of inertia is a measure of how much weight is carried away from the center of the car – more weight further away means a higher moment of inertia. Cars with a high polar moment turn in sluggishly, but are stable in a corner; with a low polar moment turn-in is swift, but the car can feel nervous. Sporting machines tend to have low polar moments, and this is the reasoning behind mid-engined layouts: concentrate the heavy mass of the engine and transmission near the center of the car and you reduce the polar moment, giving the car swifter and sportier handling.

The key factor in the sports car's feel is the height of its center of gravity. If the main masses of the car, such as the engine, transmission, fuel tank, and passengers are concentrated as low down as possible, the center of gravity will be low. This reduces weight transfer onto the more heavily-loaded outer tires in a corner, allowing the tires to work more effectively. Roadholding improves, and handling is sharper. Throughout the sports car's evolution, a low center of gravity has been every automobile designer's aim.

An Italian thoroughbred

Ferrari's fastest road cars had been built very much with competition in mind, but the challenge of the new Lamborghini marque in the 1960s swung the emphasis toward the creation of spectacularly fast cars intended solely for road use. Lamborghini's 1966 Miura used the mid-engined layout that was becoming the norm for endurance racing cars, as typified by Ford's multi-million dollar GT40, but applied it to a road machine to derive unparalleled speed and eye-catching looks. Ferrari responded with a line of front-engined, V12 coupés before it too took the mid-engined route in the early '70s.

At the end of the '60s most sports cars still stuck to a relatively traditional formula with, in particular, an open roof. In this form the cars were popular in the United States and particularly in California, with its affluent economy and fine weather. However, now safety legislation threatened to take away that essential ingredient of a sporting machine, the folding roof, because it was too dangerous.

The car makers responded. VW and Porsche teamed up to produce the VW-Porsche 914, with its fixed roll-over bar and removable roof panel. In Italy, Bertone and Fiat created the X1/9 with a similar roof arrangement. Both cars departed from the traditional sports car layout in their engine location, the VW-Porsche with a rear-mounted unit and the Fiat with its 1.3-liter engine mid-mounted. Both were very different machines from the traditional front-engined, rear-drive open roadsters and yet both clearly possessed the essential ingredients that defined a sports car.

Above: *Ford's GT40 Le Mans challenger.*

Below: *Toyota's mid-engined MR2.*

Right: The Mazda Miata (MX-5) led a revival in open-top sports cars in the 1980s.

Sports sedans and hot hatches

Another threat emerged in the mid-1970s. First, Ford developed the 'Rallye Sport' range of Escorts based on its considerable success in rallying, and then Volkswagen's swift, fuel-injected version of its new Golf family hatchback (known as the Rabbit in the USA) created a whole new type of car, the 'hot hatch.' Again sporting sedans rather than sports cars became the machines of the moment, and other manufacturers jumped on the bandwagon. In Britain, for decades a leading sports car producer, while uncertainty over safety rules about open cars persisted and the economy was in turmoil, few new sports cars were emerging. That left the old guard, like MG's ageing Midget and MGB, to fly the sports car flag – but compared to the efficient, modern hot hatches they were simply outclassed.

Even so, the sports car did not roll over and die. It simply evolved yet again. Toyota's mid-engined MR2 developed the X1/9 theme still further, and then the whole roadster movement was revitalized by the appearance of the Mazda Miata – a Japanese reinterpretation of the classic Lotus Elan. BMW branched out into open roadsters with the Z1, Lotus launched a new Elan with front-wheel drive, and in the 1990s MG sports cars were revived – first with the MG RV8, and then the mid-engined MGF. Porsche, Mercedes, Renault, Honda, and many others launched new

Below: BMW's Z1 was the first of a new generation of roadsters from Munich.

sports cars, making the true sports machine the hottest property at the motor shows and out on the road. A new generation of drivers realized that little could match the fun factor inherent in a roadster or a close-coupled two-seater. And anyway, it was much easier for other people to see and admire the driver of an open car…

Today there are more sports cars on the market than there have been for years, and there is more variety in their designs than ever before. Buyers today can choose a fixed or folding roof, and the latter can be anything from a simple drop-down canvas affair to the fully-powered folding hardtop of the Mercedes-Benz SL and SLK. There's a choice of front-, rear- or mid-mounted engines, from four to 12 cylinders, with power outputs ranging from under 100bhp to over 500bhp and manual or automatic gearboxes. But all sports cars have something in common. Every one is rewarding to drive. However, the essence of the sports car goes even deeper than that. Whatever the design, whatever the power output or the cost or the age of the car, all sports cars share the philosophy that the driving experience is the most important aspect of the car and everything else – practicality, ease of maintenance, sometimes even reliability and durability too – takes a back seat. Like no other car, a sports car is built around its driver.

Arguments have raged, almost since the beginning of motoring, about the exact definition of a sports car. To some, a sports car is only worthy of the term if it was built for, and then successfully used in, competition. For others a sports car is a not a racing car, but a roadgoing machine – and yet it is one which offers the kind of performance and feedback that would be essential for a racer. Some enthusiasts maintain that a true sports car must be an open roadster, while there is yet another group who happily admit hot hatches and sporting sedans to the genre. To some extent, they are all right.

Above: MG returned to sports cars with the striking MGF.

Below: The Mercedes-Benz SLK featured a clever, folding hard top.

Pre-War: The Right Crowd

Previous page: By the late 1930s Aston Martin were producing fine road cars like this 15/98.

Above: Emil Jellinek, who coined the name Mercedes for the Daimler cars he sold in France.

Right: Maybach's 35hp Mercedes made its debut at the Nice 'speed week' in 1901.

Pioneers of motoring were mostly concerned with making their 'horseless carriages' run reliably, but as the fledgling motor industry found its feet each car maker wanted to demonstrate to the public that its machine was the best. So motor racing was born.

The early motoring innovations took place in mainland Europe, particularly in Germany and France, and these countries were at the forefront of the earliest competitions. Reliability trials were the earliest forms of motor sport, but these soon developed into road races from town to town, often over hundreds of miles of poorly-made road. The first real motor race, run as early as June 1895, was from Paris to Bordeaux and back.

The cars that took part in these early races were not built for racing – they were simply a constructor's normal product, such as was available to any well-heeled customer. But it was clear to many racers that purpose-built speed machines would stand a much greater chance of success, and so the quest for performance began. The concept of the performance car really arrived with the 35hp Mercedes of 1901, a car built in Germany by the Daimler company (one of the original pioneers of the motor car) but inspired by a very different source.

Emil Jellinek, a German-born businessman living in Nice in the south of France, was fascinated by technology and in particular by motor cars, which by the turn of the century were becoming a fashionable accessory for the wealthy. Jellinek recognized that there was a ready market for Daimler's motor cars in France, if only they had a less Germanic name: anti-German feeling, a remnant of the 1870 war, was still rife in France. Jellinek solved the problem by using the name of his ten-year-old daughter, Mercédès.

Convinced that motor racing was a vital sales tool, Jellinek persuaded Daimler to build two high-performance cars based on its rather ungainly front-engined Phoenix model. Fitted with 28hp four-cylinder engines, they were entered – under the name Mercedes – at the La Turbie hillclimb in March 1900. The cars were prepared by Daimler Motoren Gesellschaft, and

Left: *Henry Segrave won the 1923 French Grand Prix in a Sunbeam, but British GP success was rare.*

Mercedes 35hp	
Manufacturer:	Daimler Motoren Gesellschaft (Cannstatt, Germany)
Production years:	1901
Engine location:	Front
Configuration:	In-line four-cylinder
Materials:	Aluminum crankcase
Bore x stroke:	116x140mm
Capacity:	5786cc
Valve operation:	T-head side-valve with twin camshafts
Fuel system:	Twin carburetors
Power:	Approximately 35hp at 1000rpm
Gearbox:	Four-speed manual
Driven wheels:	Rear, with chain drive
Chassis/body:	Pressed steel ladder chassis with separate body
Suspension:	Front: leaf-sprung beam axle Rear: leaf-sprung beam axle
Brakes:	Mechanically operated rear drums and transmission foot brake
Wheels/tires:	Wooden 'artillery' wheels
Top speed:	55mph (89km/h)
Acceleration:	Not recorded

accompanied by Daimler's plant foreman Wilhelm Bauer, an accomplished driver. Bauer took the wheel of one car, but tragedy struck almost at once: at the first bend the Mercedes crashed, and Bauer died from his injuries the following day. Already the Daimler company was mourning its founder, Gottlieb Daimler, who had died earlier in the month at the age of 65.

Undeterred, Jellinek returned to Daimler with a request for a more competitive car, and in the process laid down the foundation for the design of sports cars for many years to come. Jellinek wanted an even more powerful engine, with lighter weight for better acceleration. To improve roadholding the new car had to have a longer wheelbase, wider track, and lower center of gravity. And, said Jellinek, it would be called a Mercedes. To emphasize the seriousness of his intentions, he placed a major order, for 36 of these cars – but stipulated a delivery date of October 15. Daimler's design chief, Wilhelm Maybach, had just eight months to design a new car that had to be more advanced than anything yet seen.

Maybach's Mercedes

Maybach's design bristled with new technology. For the first time, the engine's crankcase was made from aluminum, reducing the weight of the engine by almost a third, to 507lb (230kg). Conventional 'atmospheric' intake valves, sucked open by the vacuum created in the cylinder as the piston dropped on the intake stroke, were eschewed in favor of mechanical valves operated by a camshaft. Another new feature was that the four-cylinder engine had not one, but two, carburetors to improve power and smoothness. Cooling was by a new 'honeycomb' radiator which used more than 8000 tubes, each 6mm square, soldered together with an integral reservoir provided at the top. Despite the engine's greater cooling requirements, the honeycomb design's efficiency meant that the amount of water carried could be cut from 18 liters (4.75gal) to just nine, saving weight and space.

The chassis, too, was innovative. The main chassis members were pressed from sheet steel to allow a more integrated design: previously the engine had been mounted on a subframe, but on the new car Maybach narrowed the chassis members at the front and bolted the engine directly to them. The car's overall weight was reduced as a result, and the center of gravity was lowered. As

Below: *Wilhelm Maybach was Daimler's right-hand man.*

Right: *Laurence Pomeroy at the wheel of the 'Prince Henry' Vauxhall that he designed, at Lynmouth in 1911. The Prince Henry was one of the first true sports cars.*

Jellinek had specified, the wheelbase and track dimensions were increased, and wheels of almost equal size used front and rear. The braking system was improved, with 12in (300mm) diameter drum brakes on the rear wheels, activated by a hand lever, and a pedal-operated transmission brake.

The first test runs of Maybach's new machine took place on November 22, 1900, a little over a month after the original October 15 deadline. Jellinek took delivery of the first 35hp cars on December 22. In the hands of Wilhelm Werner the new Mercedes dominated the speed trials at Nice in March 1901, prompting Paul Meyan of the French Automobile Club to declare, 'We have entered the age of the Mercedes.'

Below: *Vauxhall's E-type 30/98 was one of the best sporting cars of its day, and a true Bentley rival.*

Swifter 40hp and 90hp Mercedes models followed, their greater power outputs being just one part of a package that included more accomplished chassis designs and more effective, water-

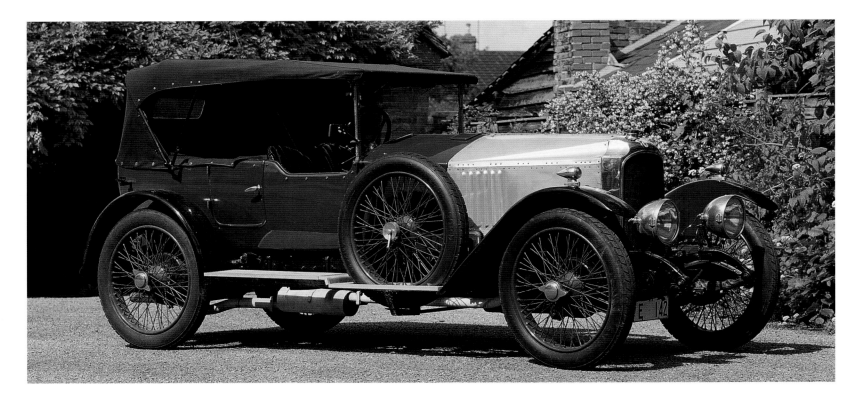

cooled brakes. But before long the needs of motor racing at the highest level began to dictate a change in the way the cars were constructed. The French 'Grand Prix' became the biggest race of the year, attracting purpose-built racing machines with ever-larger engines – often aero-engines, as in the case of Count Louis Zborowski's famous and ill-fated *Chitty Chitty Bang Bang*. As a spectacle, there was little to match these enormous Grand Prix machines, but the cost of racing was so high that interest among manufacturers dwindled. A 'voiturette' class was introduced for smaller cars, but even these were purpose-built at enormous cost and bore little resemblance to the machines that the public could buy.

The answer was to introduce a new class of racing for 'touring cars' – motor cars built for road use, though they would be carefully prepared for racing. Costs for this class of racing were much lower than for the Grands Prix, and the events were popular with manufacturers because their customers could see a car win a race at the weekend, and then could go out and buy something very similar the following week. If they were wealthy enough, that is: even the purchase of a Model T Ford or Austin Seven showed that you had a little money, and a sports car could easily cost ten times as much.

Racing Britons

In this era only two British makes – Sunbeam and Vauxhall – attempted to compete at Grand Prix level. Sunbeam achieved some success, Sir Henry Segrave winning the French GP in 1922, but Vauxhall's Grand Prix campaign was less effective. In 1922 Vauxhall had built a brand new 3.0-liter Grand Prix car, only to find that the Grand Prix formula had that year changed to 2.0-liters…

Vauxhall's roadgoing machines, however, were very impressive. The Laurence Pomeroy-designed Vauxhall C-type of 1911 was known as the 'Prince Henry,' after prototype cars performed well in the Prince Henry Trials in Germany. The high-revving 3.0-liter side-valve engine of the Prince Henry had, unusually, five main bearings for reliability and drove through a

Vauxhall 30/98 E-type	
Manufacturer:	Vauxhall Motors (Luton, England)
Production years:	1913-22
Engine location:	Front
Configuration:	In-line four-cylinder
Bore x stroke:	98x150mm
Capacity:	4525cc
Valve operation:	Single camshaft, overhead-valve
Fuel system:	Zenith updraft carburetor
Power:	95bhp at 3000rpm
Gearbox:	Four-speed manual
Driven wheels:	Rear, with shaft drive
Chassis/body:	Pressed steel ladder chassis with separate body
Suspension:	Front: leaf-sprung beam axle Rear: leaf-sprung beam axle
Brakes:	Mechanically operated, rear wheels only
Wheels/tires:	Center-lock wire-spoke wheels
Top speed:	80mph (129km/h)
Acceleration:	Not recorded

Left: Bentley won the Le Mans 24-hour race at its second attempt. Here drivers Frank Clement (left) and John Duff (right) meet W.O. Bentley after the race.

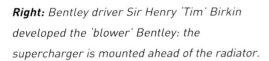

Right: Production of the 3.0-liter, four-cylinder Bentley began in 1921.

Bentley 3-liter

Manufacturer:	Bentley Motors (London, England)
Production years:	1919-29
Engine location:	Front
Configuration:	In-line four-cylinder
Bore x stroke:	80x149mm
Capacity:	2996cc
Valve operation:	Four valves per cylinder, single overhead camshaft with rockers
Fuel system:	Smiths or Claudel-Hobson carburetor
Power:	85bhp at 3500rpm
Gearbox:	Four-speed manual
Driven wheels:	Rear, with shaft drive
Chassis/body:	Pressed steel ladder chassis with separate body
Suspension:	Front: leaf-sprung beam axle Rear: leaf-sprung beam axle
Brakes:	Mechanically operated rear drums (mechanical front brakes added in 1924)
Wheels/tires:	Center-lock wire-spoke wheels
Top speed:	85mph (137km/h)
Acceleration:	Not recorded

multi-plate clutch rather than the typical leather-lined cone clutch of the time. As well as being innovative, it was distinctive: all Vauxhalls of the period had a fluted top to the radiator cowling, said to have been inspired by the detailing on a wardrobe owned by one of the company's directors.

The Prince Henry built up a considerable sporting reputation, with a win in the tough Swedish Winter Trial against much more powerful opposition and in 1913 alone Prince Henrys won 35 hillclimbs, 23 Brooklands races, and 14 trials. That same year, Vauxhall announced its seminal E-type, better known as the '30/98' – though quite why is unclear, as the figures don't relate to the car's RAC rating or actual power output. The 30/98 was born almost by accident, when Joseph Higginson approached Pomeroy in March 1913 with the idea of building a faster Vauxhall to

Right: Bentley driver Sir Henry 'Tim' Birkin developed the 'blower' Bentley: the supercharger is mounted ahead of the radiator.

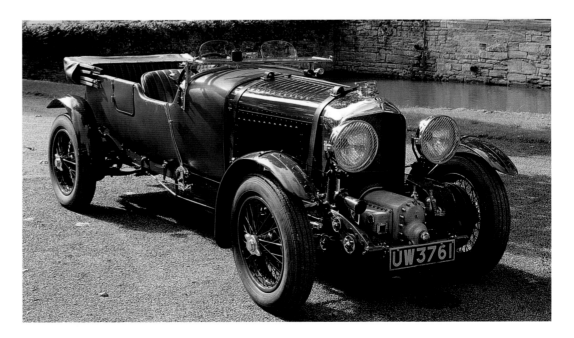

compete at the famous Shelsley Walsh hillclimb in June – just 13 weeks away. Pomeroy took up the challenge, expanding the C-type's engine from 3.0-liters to 4.5-liters, and building a new lightweight, aluminum body. At Shelsley Walsh a few weeks later, Higginson beat all comers and sliced eight seconds from the hill record, becoming the first person to climb the hill in less than 60 seconds – an average speed of 34.09mph (54.86km/h).

Though 13 cars were built before the war, serious production had to wait until after the cessation of hostilities. Then the 30/98 quickly proved to be one of the best sports cars of its era, with numerous wins in hillclimbs and speed trials during the 1920s. Despite the sporting successes, 'The car of Grace that sets the Pace,' as Vauxhall described it, was always too fast for its brakes. Laurence Pomeroy had departed for America in 1919, so it was his erstwhile assistant Clarence King who added front-wheel brakes and also a more powerful, 120bhp overhead-valve engine to produce the OE-type of 1922. Production continued in small batches even after General Motors bought Vauxhall for $2.5million in 1924, but finally came to an end in 1927. It would be more than 70 years before sports cars would again take to the road bearing the famous Vauxhall griffin badge.

Sports car racing was by now well established. It had become popular at the Brooklands race track in Surrey, England and after a successful six-hour sports car race, the Brooklands 'Double 12' (two consecutive 12-hour stints forming a 24-hour race) became an annual event. But the biggest British sports car race was the 'Tourist Trophy' or 'TT,' initially held in the Isle of Man and run to regulations which required the cars to be four-seaters available to the public, and limited to a fuel consumption of 25mpg. In the 1920s the TT moved to the Ards circuit in

Above: W.O. Bentley preferred the 6.0-liter 'Speed Six' to the supercharged car. This is the special Speed Six which Woolf Barnato used to beat the Blue Train across France.

Above: A driver-selectable supercharger gave the Mercedes-Benz SSK colossal power, but only for a few seconds at a time.

Above: Alfa Romeo's straight-six sports cars won the famous Mille Miglia in 1929 and 1930.

Below: Vittorio Jano was responsible for Alfa Romeo cars from 1923. This is the 6C 1750 from 1930.

Northern Ireland, a 14-mile (23km) triangle of roads between the towns of Newtownards, Comber, and Dundonald which was described as the greatest road circuit of its time. In the first Ards race in 1928, the cars' 'touring' credentials were ensured by requiring the drivers to complete the first two laps with their roofs erected, before stopping to fold them down. The following year the cars were lined up for the start with the roofs raised, and the drivers had to stow them before starting off.

Bentleys at Le Mans

Belgium, too, had a 24-hour race, and the most famous 'round the clock' event of all began in 1923, near the French village of Le Mans. To compete in the 'Grand Prix d'Endurance' cars had to have full weather equipment and road-type lights, they had to run on normal gas (unlike the special brews by then being used in Grands Prix cars) and all the spares and tools required during the 24 hours had to be carried in the car. The race was dominated by French cars in its first year, but the sole foreign entry showed a good deal of promise. The car was a 3.0-liter Bentley, owned by John Duff and driven by Duff and Frank Clement. Clement recorded the fastest lap at an average speed of more than 66mph (106km/h), and the Bentley came home equal fourth. The potential showed by the Bentley was realized the next year, when Duff and Clement (again the only non-French entry) won, despite some wheel-changing difficulties alleged to be the result of sabotage.

W.O. Bentley had set up in business in 1912 as a distributor of the French DFP cars. After World War I Bentley started to design his own sporting car, which was announced to the public in the magazine *The Autocar* in March 1919. Production of the 3.0-liter Bentley began in 1921, the car incorporating a number of very modern features including four valves per cylinder, a 'crossflow' layout with the carburetor on one side of the engine and the exhaust system on the other. The engine drew some inspiration from that of the 1914 Grand Prix Mercedes, which Bentley had examined in 1915, and the car was also influenced by Peugeot and Humber racing machinery. Built to be strong and reliable, the Bentley was in its element at Le Mans, but the green cars would not quickly repeat their 1924 triumph on French soil.

In 1925 the Duff/Clement car caught fire, while an accompanying 'works' entry for Bertie Kensington Moir and Dr Dudley Benjafield retired after a miscalculation caused it to run out of fuel half-way through its 19th lap. The following year three works entries failed with mechanical

Above: Jano's eight-cylinder 8C 2300 was innovative and effective.

Alfa Romeo 8C 2300

Manufacturer:	Alfa Romeo (Milan, Italy)
Production years:	1930-34
Engine location:	Front
Configuration:	In-line eight-cylinder
Bore x stroke:	65x88mm
Capacity:	2336cc
Valve operation:	Twin overhead camshafts
Fuel system:	Twin Weber carburetors, Roots-type supercharger
Power:	142bhp at 5000rpm
Gearbox:	Four-speed manual
Driven wheels:	Rear, with shaft drive
Chassis/body:	Pressed steel ladder chassis with separate body
Suspension:	Front: leaf-sprung beam axle Rear: leaf-sprung beam axle
Brakes:	Mechanically operated drums on all four wheels
Wheels/tires:	Center-lock wire-spoke wheels
Top speed:	Approximately 115mph (185km/h)
Acceleration:	0-60mph (97km/h): approx. 11sec

Brooklands: No Crowding

Hugh Fortescue Locke-King opened the world's first purpose-built racing circuit in 1907 on his own estate at Brooklands, near Weybridge in Surrey. The main track (or 'Outer Circuit') was 2.76 miles (4.44km) long and about 100ft (30.5m) wide, consisting of two essentially straight sections connected by two banked curves. A road circuit and a test hill were later added.

Though Brooklands looked simple to drive, it had some idiosyncrasies which kept competitors on their toes. The two sections of banking were subtly different, the Home banking near the clubhouse being tighter and higher than the Byfleet banking at the far end. One of the straightaways incorporated a gentle curve which became trickier as the cars got faster, and was made all the more

difficult by the wind rebounding from the nearby Vickers aircraft works. The all-time lap record was held by John Cobb, in the Napier-Railton, at 143.44mph (230.84km/h).

Cars raced at Brooklands from 1907 to 1914, then from 1918 to 1939. While the circuit was operational it was one of the most important racing venues in the world, even though it did not test its competitors in as many different ways as a road circuit such as Ards or Le Mans. The Brooklands 'Double 12' was said by some to be tougher even than the Le Mans 24 hours.

Brooklands was also a center for aviation, with Hawker as well as Vickers producing aircraft at factories on the estate. During World War II hangars were erected and the circuit camouflaged, and later building work

encroached onto the track. Today two sections of banking still remain, and the thriving Brooklands Museum has restored some of the original buildings. In 2002 DaimlerChrysler announced its intention to buy much of the Brooklands site and turn it into a heritage center.

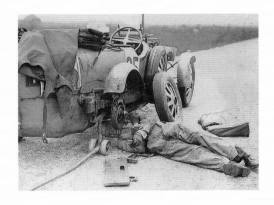

Above right: Many considered the Brooklands 'Double 12' to be tougher even than the Le Mans 24-hour race. In 1930 Earl Howe stopped in answer to a signal to find a rear wheel about to part company with his Bugatti.

Right: The 1921 Bugatti Type 13, first of an illustrious line of cars from the Molsheim marque.

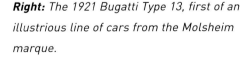

trouble, but the team's luck changed in 1927. Two 3.0-liter works cars were joined by a brand new 4½-liter, set to become Bentley's next production model and featuring a bigger-bore four-cylinder engine with twin SU 'sloper' carburetors to develop 110bhp. All three cars joined the wreckage hidden around the White House corner early on the Saturday evening, but Sammy Davis extricated his battered Bentley (the famous 'Old Number 7,' owned by Benjafield) and made what repairs he could to keep running. A 3.0-liter Aries led the race, but to the joy of the Brits it expired with barely an hour of the race remaining, leaving the Davis/Benjafield Bentley to return as the victors.

Success after success

The 4¹/₂-liter Bentley showed its mettle the following year, when Bentley director Woolf Barnato brought his car home ahead of a 5.0-liter Stutz despite a failing chassis frame. While Bentley driver Sir Henry 'Tim' Birkin prompted development of a supercharged 4¹/₂-liter for 1929, W.O. Bentley worked on a high-performance version of the six-cylinder Bentley engine that had been revealed in 1925. The resulting 'Speed Six' is the archetypal vintage Bentley, and at Le Mans in 1929 it was clocked at an easy 115mph (185km/h) in practice, and then won the race in the hands of Barnato and Birkin. The latter indulged his habit of carrying a supply of oranges with him in the car and sucking them for sustenance as he went along. Birkin swapped to a 4¹/₂-liter supercharged Bentley for the 1930 race, but it was Barnato in the Speed Six who would win again, to chalk up Bentley's fifth success in the French 24-hour race.

Birkin's 'blower Bentleys' never achieved the success that was hoped for them, but other manufacturers did make supercharging effective. The idea of using an engine-driven pump to force extra air into the cylinders, and thus produce more power, had been introduced to racing cars on the American Chadwick, the German Mercedes, and the Italian Fiat. The shriek of a supercharger became a familiar sound in motor racing, and a spin-off was that the supercharger became common on European roadgoing sports cars. In 1926 the two German manufacturers Daimler and Benz merged, and the Mercedes-Benz range of cars included the enormous SSK, developing up to 275bhp from its supercharged 7.1-liter engine – though using the driver-selectable supercharger for long periods was apt to cause engine damage, about 15 seconds being the safe maximum. Owners of the big Mercedes included Sir Malcolm Campbell, and Sherlock Holmes' creator Sir Arthur Conan Doyle. The car was the work of Ferdinand Porsche, who had already produced the 27/80 Austro-Daimler that won the Prince Henry Trial in 1910. Porsche would become a much bigger part of the sports car story after World War II.

Bugatti Type 35A	
Manufacturer:	Bugatti (Molsheim, France)
Production years:	1924-30
Engine location:	Front
Configuration:	In-line eight-cylinder
Bore x stroke:	60x88mm
Capacity:	1991cc
Valve operation:	Three valves per cylinder, single overhead camshaft with 'finger' rockers
Fuel system:	Twin Solex or Zenith carburetors
Power:	100bhp at 5000rpm
Gearbox:	Four-speed manual
Driven wheels:	Rear, with shaft drive
Chassis/body:	Pressed steel ladder chassis with separate body
Suspension:	Front: leaf-sprung beam axle Rear: leaf-sprung beam axle
Brakes:	Mechanically operated drums on all four wheels
Wheels/tires:	Cast-alloy with integral brake drums
Top speed:	Approximately 100mph (161km/h)
Acceleration:	0-60mph (97km/h): approx. 10sec

Above: Bugatti's Type 35A was the roadgoing version of the straight-eight Type 35 racer.

Left: The larger-engined Bugatti Type 57 was created as a result of new racing requirements.

Above: LM18 was one of the works Aston Martins which won the team prize at the TT in 1935.

Aston Martin Ulster

Manufacturer:	Aston Martin Motors (Feltham, Middlesex, England)
Production years:	1934-35
Engine location:	Front
Configuration:	In-line four-cylinder
Bore x stroke:	69.3x99mm
Capacity:	1494cc
Valve operation:	Single overhead camshaft
Fuel system:	Twin SU carburetors
Power:	85bhp at 5250rpm
Gearbox:	Four-speed manual
Driven wheels:	Rear, with shaft drive
Chassis/body:	Pressed steel ladder chassis with separate body
Suspension:	Front: leaf-sprung beam axle
	Rear: leaf-sprung beam axle
Brakes:	Mechanically operated drums on all four wheels
Wheels/tires:	Center-lock wire-spoke wheels
Top speed:	Approximately 100mph (161km/h)
Acceleration:	0-50mph (80km/h): approx. 12sec

Straight-eight Alfas

The engineer responsible for Fiat's supercharged Grand Prix car, Vittorio Jano, moved to the new Alfa Romeo company in 1923. His first job was to create an Alfa Grand Prix car, the supercharged straight-eight P2, which won first time out and went on to dominate Grand Prix racing. A line of roadgoing six-cylinder sports cars developed from the P2 began with the 6C 1500 of 1925, and by 1930 a bigger capacity, twin-cam, supercharged 6C 1750 Gran Sport was available with 85bhp and the potential for 95mph (153km/h). Works racing versions with more than 100bhp and lightweight bodywork won the Mille Miglia, the famous 1000-mile (1609km) sports car race around Italy, in 1929 and 1930.

A 1.9-liter version of the 6C engine followed, but Alfa Romeo's sights were set much higher. In 1930 Jano created a new eight-cylinder engine with an innovative design – instead of the camshaft and accessory drives being at one end of the engine, they were in the center, making the straight-eight effectively a pair of in-line fours coupled together. Straight-eights were inevitably long engines and that meant they had long crankshafts and camshafts, which tended to be 'whippy' because they could not be made stiff enough along their length. The torsional vibrations of the crankshaft wore out the bearings, and the 'winding up' of the long camshafts upset the valve timing. Jano's split straight-eight had two short crankshafts, and four short overhead camshafts, giving it a healthy power output and at the same time delivering the reliability essential in a production car. The new 8C 2300, in fact, delivered much the same power output as the old P2 Grand Prix car, and works racing versions with bigger valves and higher compression developed 155bhp. They went on to win the Targa Florio on 1931, and the Mille Miglia in 1932. Alfa Romeo's road cars were regarded as some of the finest available between the wars.

Left: Cecil Kimber's M-type MG Midget brought sports car motoring to a whole new market.

MG M-type Midget

Manufacturer:	MG Car Company (Abingdon, Berkshire, England)
Production years:	1928-32
Engine location:	Front
Configuration:	In-line four-cylinder
Bore x stroke:	57x83mm
Capacity:	847cc
Valve operation:	Single overhead camshaft
Fuel system:	SU carburetor
Power:	27bhp at 4500rpm
Gearbox:	Three-speed manual
Driven wheels:	Rear, with shaft drive
Chassis/body:	Pressed steel ladder chassis with separate body
Suspension:	Front: leaf-sprung beam axle Rear: leaf-sprung beam axle
Brakes:	Mechanically operated drums on all four wheels
Wheels/tires:	Bolt-on wire-spoke wheels
Top speed:	65mph (105km/h)
Acceleration:	Not recorded

Another marque which became highly respected during this period was Bugatti, which produced numerous sports road cars based on its competition machinery. Ettore Bugatti was an Italian engineer who set up in business to produce his own car in 1909, at Molsheim in Alsace-Lorraine. Bugatti's first car, the 1.3-liter Type 13, was well received and a line of fine sporting cars followed. The best known was probably the straight-eight Type 35 of 1924, which was available in normally-aspirated and supercharged racing versions, and as a roadgoing sports car (the Type 35A). In 1926 a 1.5-liter four-cylinder engine was introduced in the same chassis, to create the Type 37 sports car and soon this was available in supercharged form as the Type 37A.

Left: The C-type Midget won the Brooklands 'Double 12' in 1931. Note the radiator cowling designed to reduce drag.

The Type 51 of 1931 was a development of the Type 35 fitted with a twin overhead camshaft engine, and this sired the handsome Type 55 sports car. Competition requirements then led Bugatti to produce a 3.3-liter racing car, the Type 57, which itself was to lead to a series of road cars, the ultimate development being the supercharged Type 57SC. Though Bugatti's designs were often interesting and effective, and the marque had many supporters, efforts to revive automobile production after World War II were only partially successful and once Bugatti himself had died, in 1947, the company was doomed to follow him into extinction.

Sporting lightweights

Most of Bugatti's best designs had been for lightweight cars with small engines. In Britain numerous manufacturers were building sports cars to a similar philosophy, including Riley, Alvis, Lagonda, AC, and Aston Martin. The latter was built by Lionel Martin, who had sold Singer cars and run modified Singers successfully in hillclimbs. Though early Aston Martins were well

received, Martin was more interested in racing than production – and the marque nearly sank without trace. Fortunately it was rescued, and with Italian engineer A.C. Bertelli in charge Aston Martin developed successful racing cars and respected, if expensive, road cars. One of the company's biggest competition successes of this era came in the Ards Tourist Trophy of 1934, where the Astons finished third, sixth, and seventh to win the team prize. To capitalize on this success a high-performance 'Ulster' production model was introduced, developing 80bhp and guaranteed to be good for 100mph (161km/h). There were few better sporting cars available in the mid-1930s.

But not everyone could afford an Aston Martin. Cecil Kimber, who ran Morris Motors' own servicing outlet, Morris Garages, realized early on that there was a market for tuned and special-bodied versions of the inexpensive Morris light cars. Soon these became production sports cars in their own right, under the name 'MG.' For 1928 Kimber introduced an even cheaper sports car, based on the new Morris Minor sedan. The 847cc overhead-camshaft engine was tuned and the chassis fitted with a simple, fabric-covered lightweight body: the result was the M-type MG Midget, which could exceed 65mph (105km/h) and cost just £175. It rapidly became MG's – and the world's – best-selling sports car. It was successful in racing too: Midgets won the team prize in the 1930 Brooklands 'Double 12.'

MG was already planning a new Midget. It formed the basis for a 743cc speed record car which became the first 'three-quarter liter' machine to achieve 100mph (161km/h), in the hands of Captain George Eyston. A racing version, the C-type or 'Montlhéry Midget' (named after the

Above: Under the name Swallow, William Lyons built sidecars and then special bodies for cars such as the Austin Seven. Swallow would become SS and then Jaguar.

Below: *Like Kimber, Lyons kept a firm hand on the styling of his company's products. The rakish good looks of the SS Jaguar 100 were one fine result.*

Below: *BMW's Dixi was a license-built Austin Seven. Years later BMW would take control of the Rover Group, owners of the Austin marque.*

track in France where the record had been achieved) was rapidly created and the untried car not only won the 'Double 12' in 1931, but also brought home the team prize once again. A production car based on the C-type's chassis and a modified version of its engine appeared in 1932, in two forms – the J1 tourer and the J2 sports two-seater. A supercharged J3 and racing J4 followed.

Speed and style

The J-type's trump card was its spectacular good looks, in which Cecil Kimber played a major part. Largely the car's style derived from the successful racing MGs, with a double-humped scuttle panel aping the C-type's scuttle-mounted wind deflector, and the cutaway body sides that had first appeared on the 'Double 12' M-types of 1930. The 'boat tail' shape of the early cars was gone, replaced by the truncated tail used on later C-types, with a simple slab fuel tank and exposed spare wheel. The J-type's shape combined grace and functionality, and it would be repeated on the larger K-series Magnette and then on the bigger, more robust P-type Midget of 1934. The same lines would continue to echo through MG's sports cars well into the 1950s.

Styling was to play an important part in the success of another famous British marque, SS. William Lyons and his partner William Walmsley had founded Swallow Sidecars in Blackpool, in the north of England, in 1922. After five years of building motorcycle sidecars, Swallow diversified into motor car coachwork: Lyons' eye for good lines meant that Swallow's rebodied

Austin Seven proved popular. The company moved to Foleshill, near Coventry, the following year and in 1931 Lyons announced his first complete car design – to be called the SS1. Sales of the Standard-based 2½-liter SS1 and a 1.1-liter SS2 were good despite the growing Depression, because the cars were remarkably good value. Tuned versions followed and in 1936 Lyons introduced the SS Jaguar 100, a 2½-liter sports car with near-100mph (161km/h) performance and dashing looks. A 3½-liter version followed in 1938, and showed William Lyons to be a car maker worth watching in the post-war years.

Another manufacturer with Austin connections was BMW, which had built aero engines and motorcycles in the 1920s before turning to car production in 1929 with the Dixi, a version of the Austin Seven built under license. By 1934 they had produced a sports car, the six-cylinder Type 315/1, which developed just 40bhp from 1.5-liters but had excellent aerodynamics and a light twin-tube chassis with independent front suspension that delivered tidy handling for its time. The touring Type 326 of 1936 had a 2.0-liter engine with more power, but also had a significantly heavier (if stiffer) chassis.

Above: An innovative engine, crisp handling, and fine braking made the BMW 328 one of the finest pre-war sports cars.

America's Early Sports Cars

Steam played a much greater role in the United States than it did in Europe, and the majority of cars sold in the US in the early part of the 20th century were steam powered. One of the biggest manufacturers was Stanley, run by the brothers Francis and Freeland, who included some of America's earliest sports cars in their range. The 1906 Model H and its successor the Model 10 were known as the 'Gentleman's Speedy Roadster,' and were capable of 68mph (109km/h). The popularity of steam, however, was short-lived and later American sports cars were powered by gasoline-fueled internal combustion engines. The best known of the sporting machines of this era were the Mercer Raceabout and Stutz Bearcat.

The Mercer (from Mercer County, New Jersey) was introduced in 1911, using a 4.9-liter engine built by Continental – a large, slow-revving four-cylinder engine of 'T-head' design, where the inlet valves sit on one side of the cylinders and the exhaust valves on the other. To keep weight to a minimum there was very little bodywork, just a pair of seats with a bolster fuel tank behind them, simple wings, and a tiny monocle screen – there was little protection from the weather or from flying dust and stones, and the sporting motorist had to resort to extravagant coats, hats, and goggles instead. The Raceabout, developing 58bhp at 1700rpm, was guaranteed to achieve 70mph (113km/h). Gradually the design became more practical and more efficient, even moving on to a six-cylinder engine in 1923, but the character of the car had been lost and by 1926 the Mercer was dead.

Better known and more successful was the Stutz, built in Indianapolis, Indiana. Like the Mercer it used a bought-in engine, but this time made by Wisconsin and developing 60bhp at 1500rpm. The three-speed gearbox was built into the rear axle, an unusual design at the time and one that would return later in the sports car story. Stutz would go on making glamorous motor cars until the 1930s, when it was claimed by the Depression.

Above right: Mercer produced some of the best-known early American sports cars. This example is a 1913 T35J Raceabout.

Opposite below: The 328 coupé had light bodywork by Touring of Milan, based on their successful Superleggera principle.

Racing power

Rudolf Schleicher, the engineer responsible for the original design of the six-cylinder engine and now BMW's engineering chief, turned to racing practice to derive yet more power. A new cylinder head was designed, with two big valves with an included angle of 90 degrees in each of its hemispherical combustion chambers. The camshaft was left in its original position, low down on the right-hand side of the engine as viewed from the front of the car. Pushrods transferred the action of the cams to the inlet valves on the right, and tiny transverse pushrods crossed from one side of the engine to the other to operate the exhaust valves. Three downdraft Solex carburetors fed the cylinders from the top, through short intake tracts, and thanks to the engine's excellent volumetric efficiency it developed 80bhp. The 328 had a lightweight tubular chassis like the 315, and aerodynamically advanced body shape with faired-in headlights. Another improvement over the earlier cars was the adoption of hydraulically-operated brakes, and the result was a superb all-round sports car.

By June 1937 the BMW was available in Britain, with right-hand drive, as a 'Frazer Nash-BMW' – H.J. Aldington of AFN, the owners of the Frazer Nash name, having imported BMWs to Britain since 1934. The 328 dominated sports car events all over Europe. A very special works racer was built up, with a high-compression 125bhp engine and a fixed-head Superleggera ('Superlight') body by Touring of Milan, the body weighing just 92lb (42kg). This car finished first in its class at Le Mans in 1939 and then won the shortened Mille Miglia at Brescia in 1940 – just as the continent was plunged into war.

Above: BMW became the first non-Italian winners of the Mille Miglia in 1940 with this special 328 coupé.

BMW 328

Manufacturer:	Bayerische Motoren Werke (Munich, Germany)
Production years:	1937-39
Engine location:	Front
Configuration:	In-line four-cylinder
Bore x stroke:	66x96mm
Capacity:	1971cc
Valve operation:	Overhead valve, single camshaft with vertical and transverse pushrods
Fuel system:	Triple Solex carburetors
Power:	80bhp at 4500rpm
Gearbox:	Four-speed manual
Driven wheels:	Rear, with shaft drive
Chassis/body:	Tubular steel chassis with separate body
Suspension:	Front: independent, wishbones and transverse leaf spring Rear: leaf-sprung beam axle
Brakes:	Hydraulically operated drums on all four wheels
Wheels/tires:	Pressed-steel disc wheels
Top speed:	Approximately 95mph (153km/h)
Acceleration:	Not recorded

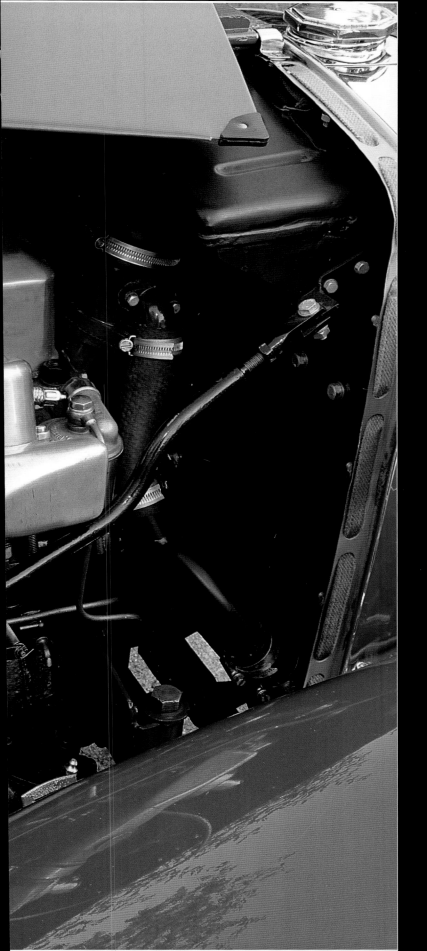

1945-49: Austerity in Action

Previous page: The 1250cc four-cylinder engine of the MG TC lacked the sophistication of earlier MG engines.

Above: MG's famous slogan 'Safety Fast' promoted many of its sedans and sports cars.

Below: The short-lived TA was created by engineers at Morris rather than MG.

War work replaced normal production for European car manufacturers on both sides of the conflict during 1940. Some turned over their production to military vehicles, others used their engineering skills to produce aircraft, engines, or armaments. At Luton, Vauxhall built Bedford trucks and the Churchill tank. The tiny Morgan company made parts for aircraft undercarriages, while the huge Longbridge plant that was the home of Austin made everything from tin hats and jerry cans to Bristol Pegasus engines and Lancaster bombers. Jaguar built military sidecars and trailers, and designed two lightweight personnel carriers that were built to be dropped by parachute. In Germany, Daimler-Benz built cars and trucks along with aero engines – but, like BMW and Auto Union, its factories were almost completely destroyed by Allied bombing.

Cecil Kimber had gone out and found war work for MG as soon as it became clear that normal car production would have to cease, and amongst many other jobs, MG took on the construction of the main section of the Armstrong-Whitworth Albemarle bomber – known to all at Abingdon as the 'Marble.' Having successfully devised a method of constructing the complex assembly, MG then found out that several companies, some of them aircraft manufacturers, had turned down the contract because the job looked too difficult.

Ironically, MG's rapid conversion to war work incurred the wrath of Sir Miles Thomas, head of the parent company the Nuffield Organization, who had decreed that all wartime production in Nuffield factories was to be co-ordinated centrally. Cecil Kimber, the man who had created MG and done so much to turn it into a well-respected sports car maker, was asked to leave the company.

MG's post-war output, as with so many other manufacturers, was based heavily on its immediate pre-war designs. Despite the success of the P-type Midget, it had been summarily replaced in 1936 by the T-type. The two cars looked much the same, but the T-type was very different under the skin. In some areas it was an advance on its predecessors – the four-wheel brakes were now hydraulically operated, for instance, and the PB's friction dampers had been replaced by hydraulic lever-arm units. A larger body gave the T-type a bit more room inside, and a bigger engine gave it more power. But it wasn't all good news. That larger engine was a Morris

pushrod unit, a much more pedestrian design than the sophisticated Wolseley-based overhead-cam engines of previous Midgets, and its 38 percent increase in capacity delivered only a 16 percent increase in power output. The brakes were 9in drums, much smaller than the 12in drums on the PB, and the clutch was an old-fashioned Morris unit with cork linings running in a bath of oil.

Cowley's MG

The TA, as the first T-type became known, was designed not at Abingdon but at the Morris headquarters at Cowley, under the watchful eye of Len Lord. William Morris, by now elevated to the peerage as Lord Nuffield, had installed Lord to reorganize the Morris companies to improve efficiency, and Lord made sweeping changes at MG. Racing was curtailed and the autonomous MG design office was closed, the staff being transferred to Cowley. The new MG sports car was designed to replace both the PB Midget and the larger N-type Magnette, to save the expense of building two new cars, and the components used in the new car were shared with other Morris products to cut costs still further. A revised T-type, the TB, came in 1939 complete with a new Morris XPAG engine, considerably lighter than the old unit (coded MPJM). With a shorter stroke, it was freer-revving and slightly more powerful, but more importantly it had a much better head design and yielded considerably more torque. A modern, Borg & Beck dry-plate clutch was fitted, but otherwise the TB was little changed.

When thoughts started to return to car production in 1944, it was quickly decided that MG should concentrate on sports car production, and that meant a car based on the TB. One of the shortcomings of the T-type had been its narrow cockpit, so the body was widened slightly – by 4in (102mm) MG said, though measurements taken in contemporary road tests suggest it was somewhat less. The only other major complaint had been the regular greasing required by the sliding trunnions on the rear springs, so these were replaced by conventional swinging shackles to cut down on maintenance. The new car, the TC, went into production in the fall of 1945.

Above: Thousands of TC Midgets were taken home by returning American servicemen after the war, and the car became a major export success for Britain.

MG TC	
Manufacturer:	MG Car Co (Abingdon, Berkshire, England)
Production years:	1945-49
Engine location:	Front
Configuration:	In-line four-cylinder
Bore x stroke:	66.5x90mm
Capacity:	1250cc
Valve operation:	Overhead valve, single camshaft with pushrods and rockers
Fuel system:	Twin SU carburetors
Power:	54bhp at 5200rpm
Gearbox:	Four-speed manual
Driven wheels:	Rear, with shaft drive
Chassis/body:	Pressed steel chassis with separate body
Suspension:	Front: leaf-sprung beam axle Rear: leaf-sprung beam axle
Brakes:	Hydraulically operated drums on all four wheels
Wheels/tires:	Center-lock wire-spoke wheels
Top speed:	73mph (117km/h)
Acceleration:	0-60mph (97km/h): 21sec

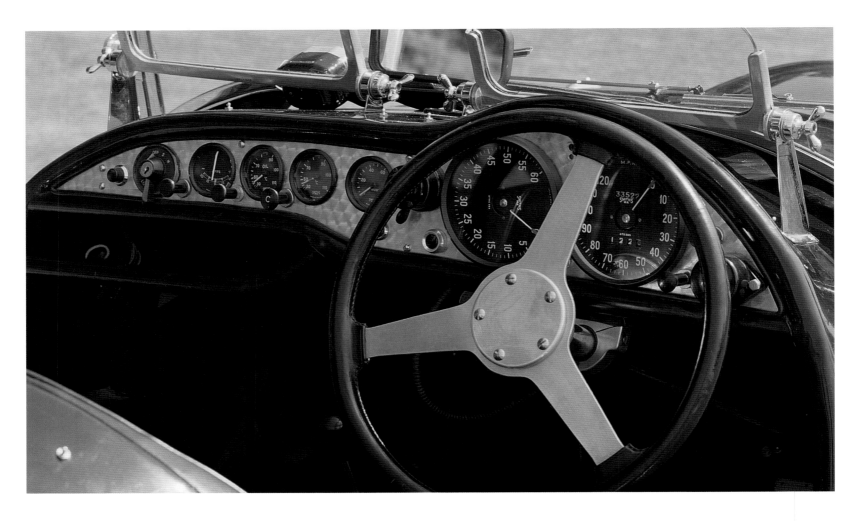

Frazer Nash Le Mans Replica

Manufacturer:	AFN (Isleworth, Middlesex, England)
Production years:	1948-56
Engine location:	Front
Configuration:	In-line six-cylinder
Bore x stroke:	66x96mm
Capacity:	1971cc
Valve operation:	Overhead valve, single camshaft with vertical and transverse pushrods
Fuel system:	Triple Solex carburetors
Power:	120bhp at 5200rpm
Gearbox:	Four-speed manual
Driven wheels:	Rear, with shaft drive
Chassis/body:	Tubular steel chassis with separate aluminum body
Suspension:	Front: independent, wishbones and transverse leaf spring
	Rear: leaf-sprung beam axle
Brakes:	Hydraulically operated drums on all four wheels
Wheels/tires:	Center-lock pressed-steel disc wheels
Top speed:	130mph (209km/h)
Acceleration:	0-60mph (97km/h): 7.5sec

Demand for the new MG, and in fact for any new car, was strong – and the majority of production was exported to earn Britain vital dollars. Many American servicemen who had been stationed in Europe during the war returned home with memories of European sports cars, these being much smaller and more wieldy than the products of the US motor manufacturers. The TC reminded American drivers that motoring could be fun.

MG was relatively lucky that its factory had escaped significant bomb damage: little was left of Coventry, the heart of the motor industry in Britain, and in Europe many car makers had to contend with major damage. Demand for new cars was strong, but output was relatively slow. In Britain, too, manufacturers had to contend with all sorts of shortages. Fuel rationing was still in force, power-cuts were common and on top of that manufacturers were supplied with materials based on their potential for earning foreign currency through exporting their products, so the vast majority of the cars that were produced were earmarked for foreign markets. British motorists waited for their new cars, or paid over the odds for second-hand ones. In the circumstances, it mattered little that most of the new cars available were based on pre-war designs.

BMW and Bristol

Bristol also started with a pre-war design, but not one of its own. Instead it acquired the designs of BMW's pre-war cars as part of the spoils of war, and brought over BMW's Dr Fritz Fiedler to continue development of the engine. Bristol employed better materials and close attention to detail in its re-engineered version of the cross-pushrod engine, and combined it with a reworked

Left: *The Frazer Nash Fast Tourer used Bristol's BMW-derived engine.*

BMW chassis and body to create the Bristol 400 of 1946. The Bristol was a properly engineered fast sedan rather than a sports car, but H.J. Aldington of AFN – importers of BMWs to Britain before the war – took Bristol's engine and installed it in a 328-derived chassis. Clothed with full-width bodywork, this became the Frazer Nash Fast Tourer; a tuned version with 40bhp more and a lightweight body was called the High Speed. In 1949 one of these cars finished third overall in the Le Mans 24-hour race at an average of 78.53mph (126.38km/h). Aldington, rarely slow to spot a marketing opportunity, now called the cars 'Le Mans Replicas.' Subsequent versions of the touring model were named after other famous races and circuits – Mille Miglia, Targa Florio, and

Below: *Aston Martin developed the Atom prototype during the war. Though impressive, the car would not see production in this form.*

Right: *Aston Martin's post-war production begun with the 2-liter Sports.*

Above: *The Jaguar XK120 made its debut at the London Motor Show in 1948.*

Jaguar XK120

Manufacturer:	Jaguar Cars (Coventry, England)
Production years:	1948-54
Engine location:	Front
Configuration:	In-line six-cylinder
Bore x stroke:	83x106mm
Capacity:	3442cc
Valve operation:	Twin overhead cam
Fuel system:	Twin SU carburetors
Power:	160bhp at 5000rpm
Gearbox:	Four-speed manual
Driven wheels:	Rear, with shaft drive
Chassis/body:	Pressed steel chassis with separate steel or aluminum body
Suspension:	Front: torsion bars and wishbones Rear: leaf-sprung beam axle
Brakes:	Hydraulically operated drums on all four wheels
Wheels/tires:	Center-lock wire-spoke wheels or pressed-steel disc wheels
Top speed:	Approximately 120mph (193km/h)
Acceleration:	0-60mph (97km/h): 12sec

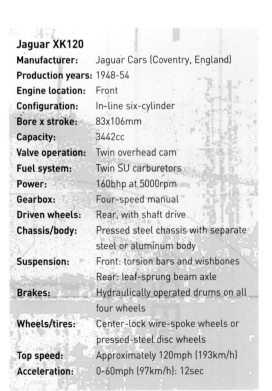

Sebring. Though spectacularly fast and successful on the race track, the Frazer Nash appealed only to a small clientele: it was very expensive.

During the war some manufacturers had managed to make progress toward new models, alongside their more pressing war work. In 1939 Aston Martin had built a prototype sporting sedan, the Atom, and during the war the owner of the company, Gordon Sutherland, had used the car extensively. The only problem was that Aston Martin didn't have the money to develop the Atom into a production possibility, and Gordon Sutherland was forced to sell the company on to someone with deep enough pockets to put the new model into production. That person was industrialist David Brown, who was impressed by the Atom but felt that Aston Martin's next model needed to be an open-topped car. Using a development of the Atom's chassis, together with the new engine designed for it by Aston Chief Designer Claude Hill and a stylish body by Frank Feeley, Brown created the new Aston Martin 2-liter Sports – later known as the DB1. But the changes took time, and the car would not be ready until the Earls Court Motor Show of 1948.

The DB1 had much to commend it, but at Earls Court that year it was overshadowed by two other debutants. One, the Alec Issigonis-designed Morris Minor, was an innovative small car that would go on to become one of Britain's favorites and sell more than a million examples. The other notable machine at the show, in many ways about as different a car from the Minor as it was possible to get, would have a far-reaching influence on the development of the sports car.

That car was the latest product from William Lyons, whose company SS had changed its name to Jaguar Cars in 1945 – 'SS' by then being an unfortunate reminder of the Nazi secret police, the *Schutzstaffel*. During the war the important industrial city of Coventry, where Jaguar was based, had endured countless air raids, and teams from the Jaguar factory took turns at 'fire watching' during the night. Lyons and his design team – William Heynes, Claude Baily, and Walter Hassan – had spent their fire-watching sessions talking about the cars and, in particular, the engines that they would produce when the conflict ended. Finally it was decided that Jaguar would produce a range of four- and six-cylinder engines, which would be closely related so they could share the same production tooling, keeping costs to the minimum. As it turned out, only the six-cylinder engine would be built, based around a cast-iron block with a seven-bearing crankshaft. At the top sat a light-alloy cylinder head with hemispherical combustion chambers, and opposed valves operated by twin overhead camshafts. This 3442cc straight six was originally fed by two SU carburetors, and in this early form it developed 160bhp.

This 'XK' engine was intended to power a new luxury sedan, based on a chassis design by Heynes which incorporated torsion bar independent front suspension and was fitted with a modern full-width body supplied by Pressed Steel. The lead time for producing the tooling for this new body was so long that Jaguar was left with a fine new chassis and engine ready to go, but no bodywork to begin production. As a compromise, Lyons fitted a more traditional body made in the old-fashioned SS way, by assembling lots of small metal pressings in-house. This car, the MkV Jaguar, would be powered by the pre-war pushrod engine so that new unit could make its debut in something altogether more exciting.

XK120 astonishes

Before the war the SS100 had garnered valuable publicity for William Lyons, even if relatively few examples had been sold. Now Lyons wanted to produce another low-volume sports car to do the same job all over again – and this would use the new XK engine, to publicize it and to give Jaguar useful early experience of the unit before it went into large-scale production for the sedans. Heynes' MkV sedan chassis was shortened, and a lightweight body constructed from light-alloy panels over a wooden frame: the skilled labor involved in building the body was no problem, as the new car was only intended for low-volume production. The decision to produce the car was taken early in 1948, and at that first post-war London Motor Show in October 1948 the result was revealed: the Jaguar XK120. Press and public alike were astounded.

The new Jaguar's sweeping, aerodynamic shape left 'austerity-bound' Britain's motorists open-mouthed. Like the pre-war BMW the wings and body were merged to form a much more cohesive shape which was as attractive as it was efficient. There was an effective roof, and the chassis – derived from a luxury sedan, remember – offered secure handling and the kind of ride quality never before seen in a sports car. The engine looked much like a pre-war racing unit, but it combined those impressive looks with both power and docility. Jaguar said the car would happily exceed 120mph (193km/h), and seven months later they proved it at Jabbeke in Belgium. Runs at nearly 127mph (204km/h) with top erected and a rousing 133mph (214km/h) with the full-width windshield and roof replaced by an aeroscreen and tonneau cover proved the XK120's potential. In the hands of Leslie Johnson that same car won the Production Car Race at the 1949 *Daily Express* Silverstone meeting.

Nobody was prepared for the impact the new Jaguar had – not even Jaguar. Faced with enormous demand, Lyons realized that the XK120 was far more than just a publicity machine, it was a real sales winner. When production began in earnest the following year, Coventry was unable to keep up with demand, and a steel body had to be quickly engineered to make production easier and quicker. In Britain, buyers could hardly believe that the XK120's basic price was under £1000 ($1750), but Lyons had deliberately pitched it at that level to avoid the double Purchase Tax imposed on more expensive cars. Not that many British motorists could get their hands on an XK120 anyway, as 92 percent of production was exported. One British driver who did manage to get behind the wheel was Stirling Moss: on his 21st birthday, Moss won the 1950 Ulster TT at Dundrod in Tommy Wisdom's alloy-bodied XK120, with two more XK120s in second and third places.

Above: Sydney Allard's cars blended simple chassis and often stark bodywork with powerful V8 engines.

Healey Silverstone

Manufacturer:	Donald Healey Motor Co (Warwick, England)
Production years:	1949-50
Engine location:	Front
Configuration:	In-line four-cylinder
Bore x stroke:	80x120mm
Capacity:	2443cc
Valve operation:	Twin cam, pushrod overhead valve
Fuel system:	Twin SU carburetors
Power:	104bhp at 4500rpm
Gearbox:	Four-speed manual
Driven wheels:	Rear, with shaft drive
Chassis/body:	Box-section steel chassis with separate aluminum body
Suspension:	Front: independent, trailing arms and coil springs
	Rear: coil-sprung live axle
Brakes:	Hydraulically operated drums on all four wheels
Wheels/tires:	Center-lock wire-spoke wheels or pressed-steel disc wheels
Top speed:	105mph (169km/h)
Acceleration:	0-60mph (97km/h): 11sec

Sporting Allards

Sydney Allard also produced sports cars that were competitive in motor sport, but in this case the accent was on sport rather than sophistication. Allard had built a trials special before the war based on a Ford V8 sedan, retaining the transverse leaf front spring but splitting the axle in the center so that the wheels were suspended independently. Small-scale production began in 1938 but stopped during the war. The Allards reappeared in 1946 with the K-type, which still used the 3.6-liter side-valve Ford V8 but had full-width bodywork with a very distinctive 'waterfall' grille. In 1949 the transverse leaf spring was replaced by coils and the brake system upgraded to hydraulics.

Allard's next model returned to a more competition-oriented style. The J2 had a light, simple body with separate cycle wings, the same Ford engine but with more power thanks to an Ardun-Mercury overhead-valve conversion, and de Dion rear suspension. For export, Allard also offered big V8s from Cadillac, Chrysler, and Oldsmobile. If the J2 was too stark for you, then there were other Allards, including the four-seater L and the P-type sedan that Sydney Allard himself would use to win the Monte Carlo Rally in 1952 (the only driver ever to win in a car bearing his own name). But by then Allard's cars looked crude and expensive compared to the new Jaguar, and sales were slow: the last cars were built in 1960, after which Allard concentrated their efforts on tuning Ford sedans.

Another sports car with a competition flavor was the Healey Silverstone. Donald Healey had begun building cars under his own name in 1946, with the 2.4-liter Riley-engined Elliott sedan and Westland tourer. Though fast, they were also expensive, and the Silverstone was designed to

Opposite: The Healey Silverstone was an ideal dual-purpose road and racing car.

Left: Bristol's fast sedans developed from pre-war BMW designs were more than a match for many sports cars.

Below: Morgan's 4/4 used a variety of engines throughout its long production run, and proved a successful competition car.

The First Ferraris

Enzo Ferrari was a driver for the works Alfa Romeo racing team in the 1920s, and had helped to bring the talented engineer Vittorio Jano to Alfa in 1923. He established his own racing team, Scuderia Ferrari, in 1929 and this represented Alfa Romeo on the track in the 1930s while Ferrari also dabbled in motorcycle racing. The first car built by the Scuderia was an Alfa, the monster *Bimotore* which had a pair of supercharged straight-eight Alfa P3 engines, one at each end of the car. It was built for anything-goes Formula Libre racing, as an attempt to win something against the might of the big-budget Mercedes-Benz and Auto Union Grand Prix teams. It also set records for the flying mile and flying kilometer at average speeds around 200mph (322km/h) in the hands of Tazio Nuvolari, on a blustery day in 1935.

Two Mille Miglia cars under the name Vettura followed in 1940, and then after the war Ferrari started building cars under his own name. The first of them was the 125, designed by Gioacchino Colombo and fitted with a 1497cc, 60-degree V12 engine, with a

single overhead camshaft on each bank of cylinders and a Roots-type supercharger. The '125' designation came from the capacity of one cylinder in cc.

At the 1948 Turin Show Ferrari introduced his first road car, the 166 Inter. The V12 engine was bored out to displace 1995cc, and the cars were bodied by the great Italian coachbuilders of the time – some of them quietly pretty, while others were fussy and ugly. Touring's open-top Barchetta, on the

same chassis, was well proportioned and attractive. A fixed-head 166 won the 1948 Mille Miglia, after which the model was known as the '166 MM.' Bigger engines would follow in the 212 and 195 models, mainly for racing, but Ferrari's significant road cars would have to wait until the 1950s.

Above: *Ferrari's 166 Spider from 1948.*
Below: *Twin-engined Alfa Romeo Bimotore of 1935.*

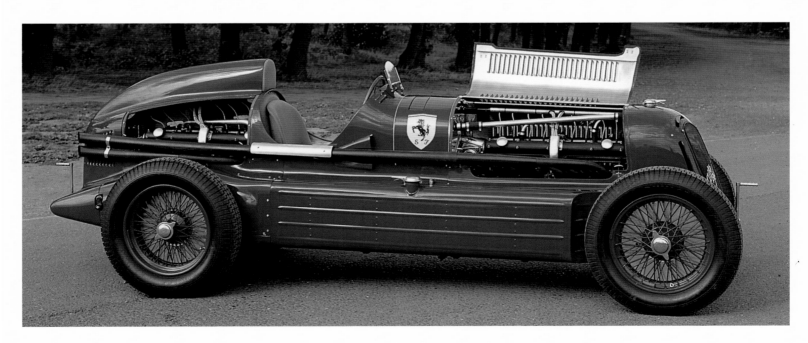

offer similar performance at a lower cost by fitting a simpler, more spartan body – creating a car that was ideal for sports car racing. Even so, building Healeys was little more than a cottage industry and just 105 Silverstones were built before production ended in 1950. By then, Donald Healey had his sights set much higher, and the results would emerge early in the 1950s.

Not far from Healey's Warwick factory, at Malvern, Morgan had been building touring cars and sports cars since 1910 – first with three wheels and then, from 1935, with the four-wheeled 4/4. The 4/4 had put up many a stirring performance in the 1100cc class, and for even greater performance a 1267cc Standard engine had also been available, but Standard ended production of that engine shortly after the war. By 1950 Morgan had fitted one of their cars with the new 2088cc Standard Vanguard engine instead, the chassis still being essentially the same as the 1935 model. It would stay much the same for years to come, but the Vanguard-engined Plus 4, with 68bhp, would prove to be fast and good value.

Like the Healeys and Morgans, early Porsches were built only in small numbers. The Porsche family had moved to Gmünd in Austria to avoid Allied bombing of Germany, and there work began on the 356 in 1947. The original concept used Volkswagen running gear in a spaceframe chassis, but for production a cheaper steel platform chassis was designed and fitted with aluminum alloy bodywork penned by Erwin Kommenda, who had been responsible for the shape of the Volkswagen. Though a roadster was available, the 'standard' Porsche was a fixed-roof sedan – Porsche called it a 'Limousin' – because most customers, it was thought, would prefer the greater comfort and better aerodynamics of the closed car. Small-scale production began in 1948 and those early Porsches were well-received – even if, at this stage, the flat-four Volkswagen-based engine was developing only 40bhp – and the 356 would be consistently developed through the decade to come. Production of Porsches would move to Germany in 1950, and Stuttgart would become the base for a long line of Porsche sports cars that would achieve success on road and track.

Porsche 356

Manufacturer:	Porsche Konstruktionen (Gmünd, Austria)
Production years:	1949-51 (Stuttgart production – 1951-65)
Engine location:	Rear
Configuration:	Air-cooled flat four-cylinder
Bore x stroke:	73.5x64mm
Capacity:	1131cc
Valve operation:	Pushrod overhead valve
Fuel system:	Twin Solex carburetors
Power:	40bhp at 4000rpm
Gearbox:	Four-speed manual
Driven wheels:	Rear wheel drive
Chassis/body:	Steel platform chassis, steel body
Suspension:	Front: independent, trailing arms and transverse torsion bars. Rear: independent, trailing arms and transverse torsion bars
Brakes:	Cable-operated drums on all four wheels
Wheels/tires:	Pressed-steel disc wheels
Top speed:	87mph (140km/h)
Acceleration:	0-60mph (97km/h): approx. 20sec

Below: Porsche's 356 continued a move toward hard-top coupés.

1950s: Success Breeds Success

P orsche's 356 had attracted much favorable comment, but even with its low-drag Erwin Kommenda shape there was only so much that it could do with its paltry 40bhp. Production began in earnest in 1950 when the company returned to its old base of Zuffenhausen, a suburb of Stuttgart in Germany, and soon 356 buyers were given the option of more power with new engine options including a 1286cc unit with twin carburetors. Even so, Porsche customers clamored for more. The answer was a bigger-capacity engine, but that presented Porsche with a problem.

The existing 1286cc engine already utilized the maximum 80mm cylinder bore. Increasing the stroke didn't appear to be possible, because the greater throw of a longer-stroke crankshaft would cause the big-end bolts to hit the single camshaft, located at the bottom of the engine. A redesigned crankcase could have solved that, but was ruled out because of its high cost. Instead, Porsche found a way to incorporate the longer stroke inside the original Volkswagen crankcase: the bottom end of the engine was redesigned using roller bearings and a built-up crankshaft, which meant there were slimmer, one-piece big ends with no big-end bolts. This in itself was an expensive solution, though not as expensive as tooling up for a new crankcase. The engine had drawbacks in use too, as it needed to be warmed up carefully before it could be used in anger and it required regular oil and filter changes so the bearings always ran in clean oil. But it was effective: the 1488cc engine developed 70bhp, and made the 356 1500S a 100mph (161km/h) car.

Porsche 356 Speedster 1500S	
Manufacturer:	Dr Ing hc F Porsche AG (Zuffenhausen, Germany)
Production years:	1954-57
Engine location:	Rear
Configuration:	Air-cooled flat four-cylinder
Bore x stroke:	80x74mm
Capacity:	1488cc
Valve operation:	Pushrod overhead valve
Fuel system:	Twin Solex carburetors
Power:	70bhp at 5000rpm
Gearbox:	Four-speed manual
Driven wheels:	Rear wheel drive
Chassis/body:	Steel platform chassis, steel body
Suspension:	Front: independent, trailing arms and transverse torsion bars
	Rear: independent, trailing arms and transverse torsion bars
Brakes:	Hydraulically operated drums on all four wheels
Wheels/tires:	Pressed-steel disc wheels
Top speed:	100mph (161km/h)
Acceleration:	0-60mph (97km/h): approx. 10sec

Above right: For racing Porsche introduced the 550, which became the 550/1500RS with the addition of a 110bhp four-cam engine.

Previous page: The Triumph TR3 took on competitors from Austin-Healey and MG.

Right: Open versions of the Porsche 356 were popular, though their aerodynamics were inferior to the hard-top coupé.

Professor Porsche died in January 1951, but by then his son Ferry was playing a central role in the development of the company. Already preparations had begun for the 1951 Le Mans race and three special cars were being built to compete in the 1100cc class. Accidents claimed two of the Porsches before they had even reached Le Mans, but the third car – in the capable hands of Auguste Veuillet and Edmond Mouche – won the class and finished 20th overall. Further successes in sports car racing and rallying with the 1300 and 1500 cars added still more to Porsche's reputation.

Above: The tubular-framed XK120C or 'C-type' was built for competition use where the XK120 was too heavy.

Porsche expands

A proper sports-racing car would be the next step. Porsche enthusiast Walter Glöckler had already raced a Porsche-powered, ladder-chassis sports car with some support from Zuffenhausen. Porsche built an 'official' version in 1953, fitting it with a tuned 1500 pushrod engine. The aluminum alloy bodywork was by Wiedenhausen, and at Le Mans the works 1500 appeared with a hardtop that proved to be aerodynamically efficient but very claustrophobic. Richard von Frankenberg and Paul Frère won the 1500cc class. Later that year a four-cam engine with twin camshafts for each cylinder bank was fitted to create the 550/1500RS, a 110bhp car capable of over 130mph (209km/h). It was one of these desirable cars that American movie actor James Dean bought in 1955, after racing an MG special and a 356 Speedster. On the evening of September 30, 1955 Dean was driving the new Porsche to a race meeting in California when a 1950 Ford pulled out in front of him at a junction: Dean died in the collision.

The 356 range continued to expand. However, they were expensive cars, and many other British and European marques were producing sports cars that sold for less. So in 1954 Porsche introduced a low-priced roadster, the Speedster, designed to take on the cheaper marques in their biggest export market – the USA. The lightweight Speedster proved popular, and became an effective weapon in production sports car racing: with the optional 70bhp engine and close-ratio

Above: NUB120, Ian Appleyard's rallying XK120 is one of the most famous of all Jaguars.

Roadsters versus fixed roofs

Both the Porsche 356 and the Jaguar XK120 gave sports car traditionalists plenty to think about. They had independent suspension – at the front only on the Jaguar – which demonstrated that the days of the sporting machine as nothing but a hard-riding roadster were rapidly coming to an end. Both were available with roofs, too: hard-top 356s were listed right from the start of production, and a fixed-head XK120 was added to the range in 1951, mixing the open roadster's phenomenal performance with the extra luxury of a wood-trimmed interior. As if to underline the fixed-head sports car's important role, Stirling Moss, Jack Fairman, Bert Hadley, and Leslie Johnson used LWK707, a fixed-head XK120, to average

more than 100mph (161km/h) for 17 days and nights, at Montlhéry in 1952.

Sports car makers had been flirting with fixed-head cars since the 1930s, when MG had produced 'Airline' fastbacks based on the P-type and T-type Midgets, while SS had built a few fastback sedans and a hard-top SS100 for the 1938 Motor Show. In Europe there had been grand hard-top sports cars from the likes of Bugatti, but the open roadster had always been regarded as the ultimate sporting machine.

Later in the decade the Lotus Elite was built only with a fixed roof – necessary to maintain rigidity because of its glassfiber monocoque construction – and the important MGA could be bought in both roadster and coupé guises. The rarer AC Ace also had a hard-top twin, the Aceca. Though Triumph and Austin-Healey still stuck to the traditional roadster format, their rally cars would invariably be seen sporting glassfiber hard tops: an open car was no longer the only kind of sports car.

Above: *Sir Stirling Moss with LWK707, the fixed-head XK120 which broke records at Montlhéry in 1952.*

Above right: *AC's Ace sports car had a hard-top cousin, the Aceca.*

gear set, few things could keep up with a Speedster from a standing start. Even quicker was a 100bhp four-cam 356 introduced in 1956, named the Carrera after the famous Carrera Panamericana road race.

The Jaguar XK120, too, had been building itself quite a reputation in motor sport. Stirling Moss had headed a Jaguar 1-2-3 in the TT in 1950, and that year another alloy-bodied XK120 had finished a creditable 12th at Le Mans. Belgian band-leader Johnny Claes won the Liège-Rome-Liège Rally in his XK in 1951, at the same time becoming the only driver ever to finish the event with no road penalties. In the US there had been grumblings about the XK120's reliability, but Claes' performance in the Liège – 3000 hard-driven miles (4800km) that reduced a field of 126 to just 58 by the finish – proved that there couldn't be much fundamentally wrong with Coventry's finest. The same year, Ian Appleyard won his first Alpine Rally *coupe*, awarded for an unpenalized run. Appleyard and his XK120, the famous NUB120, repeated the performance in 1952 and 1953 to earn themselves a rare *Coupe d'Or* or Gold Cup, for winning *coupes* in three successive years.

On the track, the XK120 had proved effective enough against the right opposition but clearly couldn't compete against the purpose-built racing sports cars built by Ferrari, Cunningham, and Talbot Lago. With Brooklands gone, the Le Mans 24-hour sports car race had quickly become a favorite and with an assault on this event in mind, Jaguar began work on a competition sports car.

Jaguar at Le Mans

The XK120C – 'C' for competition – soon became known simply as the C-type. Where the XK120 had been based on a shortened, lightened version of the MkV sedan chassis, the C-type had a much lighter and stiffer steel tube chassis clothed in light-alloy panels. As a result the C-type was around 750lb (340kg) lighter than the alloy-bodied XK120, which in turn was about 60lb (27kg) lighter than the steel-bodied production car. Power came from high-compression XK engines developing around 200bhp. Three C-types were entered at Le Mans in 1951. Fast in practice, they led the race convincingly with Stirling Moss posting the fastest lap of the race until failing oil pressure put two of the cars out before half distance, the Moss/Jack Fairman car being one of them. The third car, in the hands of Peter Walker and Peter Whitehead, went on to win, with a privately-entered XK120 finishing 11th.

Already Aston Martin had proved its mettle at Le Mans with a DB1 finishing 11th and a prototype fixed-head Aston powered by the same 2.0-liter four-cylinder engine finishing seventh in the 1949 race. Shortly after he rescued Aston Martin, David Brown also bought what remained of Lagonda, mainly because Lagonda had a new 2.6-liter twin-cam engine that had been designed under the eye of W.O. Bentley. Brown slotted this powerful and proven Lagonda six into the new Aston to create the DB2 production car.

Above: Aston Martin's DB2 blended the Atom-derived chassis with the proven Lagonda six-cylinder engine.

Below: For racing Aston Martin developed the DB3, but it was not as light as the team had hoped.

Three DB2s were built for Le Mans in 1950, but one didn't even get as far as the circuit. In those days the cars were all road-legal and the British teams often drove their race cars to the event. On this occasion one of the DB2s ended up in a ditch at night and in heavy rain, and the damage was too great for it to race. Its place was taken by 'Sweatbox,' one of the prototype DB2s from 1949, which broke its crankshaft early on during the 24 hours. But the other two DB2s finished fifth and sixth, winning their class and the 'Index of Performance.'

Like Jaguar, Aston Martin realized its touring cars weren't going to be competitive against purpose-designed racing sports cars and intended to field one of its own, the DB3, in 1951. Professor Robert Eberan von Eberhorst, who had been Chief Engineer with the pre-war Auto Union Grand Prix team, was brought in to design the car, but development was slow. As an interim measure two lightened DB2s were built, and these ran at Le Mans in 1951 alongside VMF64, the car that had been fifth at Le Mans in 1950 and had since been used by David Brown as his personal transport. While the C-type Jaguar was winning the race, Lance Macklin and Eric Thompson were bringing home VMF64 in third, with the two lightweight cars fifth and seventh. Two privately-entered DB2s also finished, in 10th and 13th places, to complete a successful race for British entrants.

The battle for Le Mans

Jaguar and Aston Martin both fielded new cars at Le Mans in 1952. The DB3 Aston was now running, but had proved to be too big and heavy to make it a major improvement on the lightweight DB2s. Meanwhile, Jaguar had created a long-nose, long-tail C-type in an effort to reduce aerodynamic drag – the long Mulsanne straightaway at the Le Mans circuit gave a clear advantage to a low-drag car. But the race was a disaster for Jaguar, as the C-type's streamlining caused the cars to run hot and they all retired.

The beneficiaries were the Mercedes-Benz team, who had brought along a new racing coupé with curious 'gullwing' doors that opened upward. Chief Engineer Rudolf Uhlenhaut and Technical Director Fritz Nallinger had followed essentially the same route as Jaguar, designing a

Above: *Mercedes-Benz won at Le Mans in 1952 with the 300SL racer.*

Mercedes-Benz 300SL 'Gullwing'	
Manufacturer:	Daimler-Benz (Stuttgart, Germany)
Production years:	1954-57 (Roadster 1957-61)
Engine location:	Front
Configuration:	In-line six-cylinder
Bore x stroke:	85x88mm
Capacity:	2996cc
Valve operation:	Single overhead camshaft
Fuel system:	Bosch direct fuel injection
Power:	215bhp at 5800rpm
Gearbox:	Four-speed manual
Driven wheels:	Rear wheel drive
Chassis/body:	Tubular steel spaceframe with alloy or steel body panels
Suspension:	Front: independent, wishbones and coil springs
	Rear: independent, swing axles and coil springs
Brakes:	Hydraulically operated drums on all four wheels
Wheels/tires:	Center-lock pressed-steel disc wheels
Top speed:	150mph (241km/h)
Acceleration:	0-60mph (97km/h): approx. 9sec

Right: *The first 300SL road car, like its racing cousin, had to use gullwing doors because of the design of its high-sided spaceframe chassis.*

Left: The 300SL Roadster was developed from the Gullwing, with a revised chassis allowing more conventional doors.

lightweight sports car to use existing production engines and running gear. The engine for the Mercedes was an overhead-cam in-line six from the 300S sedan, developing just 115bhp in its original form but tough and capable of significant development – the racing engines delivered 170bhp. The light tubular spaceframe chassis had horizontal tubes along the sides of the car which had to be as high up as possible to give the car sufficient stiffness. This would have made conventional doors too small. The gullwing doors barely extended downward any further than waist height, but were cut into the roof to make entry and exit easier.

Called the SL – standing for *Sport Leicht*, or 'lightweight sports' – the new car made its debut in the Mille Miglia, finishing second to Ferrari, and at Le Mans it finished first and second as the Jaguars expired. More wins followed at the Nürburgring and in the Carrera Panamericana road race, by which time the body had been revised so that the door openings extended a little lower. But curiously the SL racing cars did not reappear the following season – because Daimler-Benz had opted to concentrate on single-seater formulae rather than sports car racing, a decision perhaps influenced by Enzo Ferrari's promise to take the fight to Mercedes in 1953.

Above: Mercedes-Benz deliberately styled the 190SL to look like the 300SL to take advantage of the faster car's image.

But that wasn't the end of the SL. Max Hoffman had a flourishing business based in Park Avenue, New York, which imported European cars including Porsche, Healey, Jaguar, and Alfa Romeo in addition to Mercedes-Benz. Hoffman was convinced that a roadgoing version of the SL sports racer would sell well, and wasted no time in making Daimler-Benz aware of his views. Uhlenhaut had already been planning a 1953 SL racing car, and these ideas went instead into the roadgoing 300SL that made its debut early in 1954 at, significantly, the New York Auto Show.

Alongside it was a prototype version of a new sports car, the 190SL roadster. Deliberately similar in looks to the 300SL, the 190SL was based on the humble 180 sedan and producing just 105bhp from its four-cylinder engine it was in an entirely different performance class to the 300SL. It was also much cheaper, of course, and offered a useful alternative for drivers who wanted something a little more civilized than a Porsche. Just under 26,000 190SLs were sold by 1963.

With the 190SL selling well, Max Hoffman suggested that a roadster version of the 300SL would be a good idea, and this arrived in 1957. A redesigned chassis allowed for conventional doors, while the coupé's swing-axle rear suspension was revised to make the handling a little less tricky. Like the coupé before it, the roadster became the car to be seen in: famous names who owned them included film stars Tony Curtis and Sophia Loren, British comedian Tony Hancock, and the Canadian jazz pianist Oscar Peterson.

Fastest of the '50s

Though the 1950s saw Ferrari find its feet as a road car manufacturer, the fastest cars on the roads came from a different company. Mercedes-Benz Chief Engineer Rudi Uhlenhaut used the SLR racing cars as the basis for a pair of roadgoing supercars which were known as Competition Coupés – essentially SL-style bodies with gullwing doors, using the racing SLR engine and running gear.

Not just an intelligent engineer, Uhlenhaut was also a capable driver: when racing drivers complained about his cars he would go out and drive the car himself to identify the problem. He had also proved he could set lap times in Mercedes-Benz Grand Prix cars which were little shy of the greats of the Mercedes team, including the legendary Juan Manuel Fangio. The Competition Coupé was capable of over 170mph (274km/h), making it the fastest road car anywhere in the world, and Uhlenhaut regularly used one of them to attend races where the Mercedes works team was running.

Sadly the Competition Coupé never made it into production as its racing ancestry made it far too expensive and far too noisy, and just two were built – but Uhlenhaut's creation is still owned by Mercedes and regularly seen at historic car events all over the world.

Above right: Rudolf Uhlenhaut's stunning Competition Coupé, based on the 300SLR racing car, was probably the fastest car on the road in the 1950s.

BMW 507	
Manufacturer:	BMW (Munich, Germany)
Production years:	1955-59
Engine location:	Front
Configuration:	V8
Bore x stroke:	82x75mm
Capacity:	3168cc
Valve operation:	Pushrod overhead valve
Fuel system:	Twin Solex carburetors
Power:	150bhp at 5000rpm
Gearbox:	Four-speed manual
Driven wheels:	Rear wheel drive
Chassis/body:	Box-section chassis, steel body
Suspension:	Front: independent, wishbones and torsion bars
	Rear: torsion bar-sprung live axle
Brakes:	Hydraulically operated drums on all four wheels, servo assisted
Wheels/tires:	Pressed-steel disc wheels
Top speed:	125mph (201km/h)
Acceleration:	0-60mph (97km/h): approx. 9sec

Sporting BMW

BMW had restarted car production in 1951 with a development of the pre-war 326, called the 501, and this led to V8-powered 502 and 503 models. BMW then shortened this chassis by 16in (406mm) to create a sporting version which was clothed in a lithe body styled by freelance designer Count Albrecht von Goertz. A neatly integrated removable hardtop meant it could offer open-air motoring or snug protection from the elements, and fitted with a 3.2-liter, 150bhp version of the V8 it had performance in the same class as the Mercedes SL. But just 250 of these cars were built before production ended in 1959, as BMW struggled to avoid bankruptcy. The company would live to fight on, just, and BMW sports cars would return.

At this point in its history BMW was nowhere near the force in motor racing that Mercedes-Benz was. The Stuttgart concern was back at Le Mans in 1955 with its latest racing machine – the straight-eight SLR. For Le Mans the SLR was fitted with a large flap at the back to act as an air-brake – Uhlenhaut's response to the disc brakes which had been introduced on the Jaguars in 1952. It was an unhappy race for Mercedes, as Pierre Levegh's car left the road after only a couple of hours racing. The car broke up and parts flew into the crowd opposite the pits, leaving Levegh and dozens of spectators dead. It remains to this day the worst accident in the history of motor racing.

Jaguar went on to win with the D-types which had been introduced in 1954. The D-type was a specialist Le Mans car, built to achieve the highest possible speeds on the Mulsanne straightaway, so aerodynamicist Malcolm Sayer had designed a striking low-drag body with an optional vertical fin behind the driver's head. The car's construction was interesting, too, because it owed more to aircraft practice than conventional racing car design. A stressed-skin 'tub' riveted together from aluminum and magnesium alloys formed the strong, stiff central structure which housed the driver's and passenger's seats. A tubular subframe carried the engine and front suspension, and fed the suspension loads back into the main tub. Another stressed-skin structure formed the tail, inside which the fuel was housed in aircraft-style bag tanks.

The following year, 1956, proved less successful for Jaguar's works entries at Le Mans. The D-types of Paul Frère/Desmond Titterington and Jack Fairman/Ken Wharton both crashed out early in the race, while the 1955 winners Mike Hawthorn and Ivor Bueb struggled to the finish in sixth place, suffering from Lucas fuel injection problems. But a D-type still won, in the hands of Ninian Sanderson and Ron Flockhart, driving for David Murray's Ecurie Ecosse team. They would win again in 1957, when D-types would fill the first four places.

On the road Jaguar had been developing the XK120 theme, introducing the more powerful and better-handling XK140 in 1954. In 1957 the disc-braked XK150 appeared, its wider and heavier body demonstrating that the XK was becoming less of a sports car and more of a 'GT' or Grand Touring car. Clearly sporting, though, was the XKSS which was introduced in the same year: essentially a roadgoing, two-seater version of the D-type, with a rudimentary top. Like the C-type, the D-type had been a real production car – built in small numbers to be sure, but nevertheless a car you could buy without having to wait for a second-hand ex-works racer to become available. Sales, though, had not reached expectations and that meant some unused D-type tubs were left in stock. They were used up building the XKSS, which also turned out to be an ideal weapon for American production sports car racing. It was to be one of the last of the old-school sports cars that could be competitive in racing or sprinting, but could then be driven home and used on the road during the week. Fate dealt it a cruel blow when a factory fire at Jaguar halted production after just 16 were built. But the D-type's influence would continue to be felt in the next generation of Jaguar sports cars, which would make their debut early in the 1960s.

In 1958 the Le Mans regulations changed to outlaw bigger engines, leaving the door open for Aston Martin and their 3.0-liter DBR1, which won the race and the World Sports Car Championship in 1959. By then Aston Martin's road cars had developed from the DB2, via the DB Mark III to the DB4 with its brand new twin-cam straight-six engine and aluminum bodywork constructed using Carrozzeria Touring's lightweight Superleggera system. Like Jaguar,

Above: Though it could not quite match the 300SL for performance, the BMW 507 certainly had equally eye-catching looks.

Below: Jaguar developed the XK120 into the more powerful XK140 in 1954.

Left: The D-type Jaguar was built to win at Le Mans. Works D-type OKV3 retired from the 1954 race with gearbox failure.

Above: *The rare XKSS was no less than a roadgoing D-type. This example was owned by American film star Steve McQueen.*

Jaguar XKSS

Manufacturer:	Jaguar Cars (Coventry, England)
Production years:	1957
Engine location:	Front
Configuration:	In-line six-cylinder
Bore x stroke:	83x106mm
Capacity:	3442cc
Valve operation:	Twin overhead cam
Fuel system:	Triple Weber carburetors
Power:	250bhp at 5750rpm
Gearbox:	Four-speed manual
Driven wheels:	Rear wheel drive
Chassis/body:	Monocoque tub with tubular front subframe
Suspension:	Front: independent, wishbones and torsion bars
	Rear: trailing links and torsion bars, live axle
Brakes:	Hydraulically operated, discs all round, servo assisted
Wheels/tires:	Center-lock light-alloy wheels
Top speed:	150mph (241km/h)
Acceleration:	0-60mph (97km/h): approx. 5.5sec

Aston Martin had also built 'production' versions of its racing sports cars, the DB3 and DB3S, a few of which were turned into road cars.

Ferrari, the British teams' biggest competitor in sports car racing in the 1950s, took the reverse route and concentrated on building racing cars rather than roadgoing machines. The V12 engine of the 125 of 1948 was gradually increased in size to become a 166, then a 195 and a 212, signifying an increase in engine capacity from 1500cc to 2544cc. Even bigger versions followed, and after much detail development this engine became the 3.0-liter 250. In between Aurelio Lampredi, who had replaced Gioacchino Colombo as Ferrari's technical chief, drew up a 4.5-liter V12 which replaced the supercharged 1.5-liter V12 in Ferrari's Grand Prix cars. A development of this 'long block' engine went into a new roadgoing Ferrari, the 340 America, which received larger and larger engines until in 1955 Ferrari launched the 410 Superamerica – though only a handful of each type was built.

A much longer production run, lasting from 1956 to 1960, would see almost 500 Ferrari 250GT models built. Again it was powered by a V12, this time based on the old Colombo engine but so thoroughly re-engineered as to be essentially new. Here was another production car with motor sport potential, as Stirling Moss proved by winning the Tourist Trophy at Goodwood in a 250GT bearing the blue and white colors of Rob Walker.

No less sophisticated, though considerably cheaper, were some of the products of the specialist sports car manufacturers such as Lotus. Colin Chapman started buying and selling cars when he was an engineering student. Legend has it that he simply couldn't sell one dilapidated Austin Seven that he had picked up, so he turned it into a trials car which he called a 'Lotus.' Racing followed and by 1951 he had confounded Seven racers by adding strips of metal to 'desiamese' the Seven engine's intake ports, thereby allowing the gas flow into the engine to be improved and so generating more power.

The birth of the Lotus Company

In 1952 the Lotus Company was founded, and Colin Chapman created his first production car, the Mk6, based around a light tubular frame and powered by Ford or MG engines. The Lotus Seven – its 'mark' number became its name – was more of the same, but with a more sophisticated chassis and the availability of a Coventry-Climax racing engine to make it both a lively road car and an effective club motor sport tool. It was relatively cheap, too, partly because it was supplied in kit form for the owner to build himself.

The Coventry-Climax engine had originally been intended as a stand-alone power source for fire pumps, so it was designed to be very light in weight, and to run to peak revs from cold without damage. By the late 1950s this small four-cylinder engine was also powering many club racing cars, and in 1958 Lotus used it in the Elite, a small and astonishingly beautiful hard-top sports car. The fixed-head design was an essential part of the Elite's specification, because it used a glassfiber monocoque body – there was no steel chassis underneath to provide extra strength. Light weight and easy production were the main advantages, but to gain sufficient stiffness the car had to be designed with a fixed roof.

Though the Elite was Lotus' first attempt at a civilized road car, it was a racer at heart and was soon in service on Britain's race tracks – the most famous examples being Les Leston's car (registered DAD10) and Graham Warner's (LOV 1). The Scottish Border Reivers team also had an Elite, and it was performances in this car that brought Jim Clark to the attention of Colin Chapman: Clark would go on to win two Formula 1 World Championships for the Lotus works team in the 1960s.

Glassfiber was still a new and relatively untried material in the motor industry, and the few cars that had used it for body panels retained a stout steel chassis underneath. One of these was America's only true production sports car of the 1950s, the Chevrolet Corvette, which had been born as a home-grown rival to Britain's Jaguars on the one hand and the Anglo-American sports cars like the Allards on the other.

Above: The XK150 was heavier and more refined than earlier XK models.

Left: Stirling Moss in an Aston Martin DB3S. Though the Aston Martins could not match the bigger-engined Jaguars for straight-line speed, they had a distinct handling advantage.

Above: During the 1950s Ferraris became available with bodies better suited to roadgoing use, like this 410 Superamerica.

Automatic-only Corvette

General Motors' master stylist Harley Earl created the concept in 1952 – spurred on, perhaps, by Briggs Cunningham's specialist sports racing cars. The Corvette had a new chassis, designed by English engineer Maurice Olley, but used suspension systems at both ends that were common to existing Chevrolet sedans. The engine, too, was an existing unit, evolved from a 1940s Chevrolet truck engine: for the Corvette this in-line six-cylinder unit gained triple Carter carburetors, new exhaust manifolds, and higher compression to boost power from 115bhp to 150bhp. Chevrolet's Chief Engineer Ed Cole wanted the car to have a manual gearbox, but to keep costs low an existing transmission had to be used and that meant the decidedly unsporting two-speed Powerglide automatic.

Earl had planned to show the Corvette at GM's Motorama events in 1953 and build the production car for 1954, and the short development time available led the engineers to build the

Right: The 250GT and later the GTO led Ferrari's challenge in 'GT' racing. The 250GT SWB pictured was raced by Stirling Moss and Mike Parkes.

Left: Colin Chapman with the Lotus Seven, a fast and relatively affordable car for road or club motor sport.

Lotus Elite	
Manufacturer:	Lotus Components (Cheshunt, England)
Production years:	1958-63
Engine location:	Front
Configuration:	In-line four-cylinder
Bore x stroke:	76.2x66.6mm
Capacity:	1216cc
Valve operation:	Single overhead camshaft
Fuel system:	Twin SU carburetors
Power:	85bhp at 6300rpm
Gearbox:	Four-speed manual
Driven wheels:	Rear wheel drive
Chassis/body:	Unitary glassfiber body
Suspension:	Front: independent, wishbones and coil springs with anti-roll bar Rear: independent, Chapman strut and trailing arm
Brakes:	Hyrdaulically operated discs on all four wheels, inboard at rear
Wheels/tires:	Center-lock wire wheels
Top speed:	120mph (193km/h)
Acceleration:	0-60mph (97km/h): 10.5sec

first body from glassfiber. The plan was to revert to steel for production, but after considerable thought glassfiber was retained because it was cheaper in small volumes, and the lead time required to tool up for a steel body was much longer.

At Motorama the show car was wired up with microphones to record visitors' comments, which were resoundingly positive. But American drivers found it a curious mixture: a price of well over $3000 made it more expensive than an XK120, yet it was significantly slower and thanks to the humble origins of its suspension, its handling couldn't compete. 'America's Sensational Sports Car!' had typical sports car features, such as removable side screens rather than winding windows and a lack of external door handles, so it struggled to appeal to the luxury-conscious country club set – the people who could afford it – even though it had the convenience of automatic transmission. As if that wasn't enough, the Corvette was available only in one color, Polo White, and build quality was very variable.

In 1954 the Corvette was given a major performance boost with the addition of a V8 engine. It was a timely move, as Ford's V8 Thunderbird 'personal car' – another attempt at making an American XK120 – arrived the same year and comprehensively outsold the Corvette. But GM had an answer in the shape of a revised 1956 car. This time Earl's styling studio had derived its inspiration not from Coventry but from Stuttgart: the new Corvette had the stance and style of the Mercedes-Benz 300SL, if not its gullwing doors. Wind-up windows were added, new colors came on stream, a manual gearbox became available and the handling was sorted by Zora Arkus-Duntov, a creative engineer who would play a major role in the Corvette's evolution for some years to come.

The revised Corvette proved to be successful in SCCA sports car racing, the main drawback being brakes that weren't up to the V8's performance. Bigger brakes eventually solved the problem but also made the car significantly heavier, so more horsepower had to be employed to maintain the car's performance. It was the first step down the road to the muscle cars of the 1960s.

Above: The glassfiber Lotus Elite was successful in club racing thanks to its light weight and Coventry-Climax power. This example was the Team Elite car.

Right: The Chevrolet Corvette was GM's answer to the XK120, but at first it was too slow and too expensive.

Below: Ford's 'personal car,' the Thunderbird, became less and less a sports car with each successive generation.

While GM's engineers had been creating the Corvette, several British manufacturers had been working on sports cars of their own – no doubt with one eye on the export success of the MG TC and the TD and TF that followed it. The Rootes Group had enjoyed considerable success in the Alpine Rally with its Sunbeam-Talbot 90 sedans, and decided to build a two-seater sports car based on the 90, to be called the Sunbeam Alpine. With just 80bhp in standard trim it wasn't the fastest sports car, though a 97bhp 'Special' version was available and the works rally cars boasted well over 100bhp from their ERA-tuned engines. But the Alpine was consistent and reliable, and that stood it in good stead on the tough Alpine Rally, where drivers included Grand Prix stars

Stirling Moss and Peter Collins, and Leslie Johnson of ERA. The Alpines competed in two Alpine Rallies, in 1953 and 1954, Moss completing three consecutive *coupes* in 1954 to win a coveted *Coupe d'Or*. The Sunbeam's handsome lines made it a natural for the silver screen, and it appeared in a memorable car chase in Alfred Hitchcock's *To Catch a Thief*, starring Grace Kelly and Cary Grant.

Britain's new sports cars

The Triumph 1800 Roadster had been the sporting offering from Sunbeam's near-neighbors Standard-Triumph in the 1940s. With the advent of the Standard Vanguard engine (as supplied to Morgan for the Plus 4 and also used in Ferguson tractors), a new line of sports cars was planned, and work began in 1950. The original ideas included a very modern full-width body and pop-up headlamps, but the definitive prototype was a more conventional-looking, white Manx-tailed sports car called the 20TS, seen at the London Motor Show in 1952. It was an attractive car, but Standard-Triumph had a problem: the same show saw the debut of Donald Healey's latest sports car, and it took the show by storm.

Healey had realized that the only way to build an affordable sports car was to base it as closely as possible on existing production components, and had created an attractive-looking sports car based on the mechanical parts from the Austin A90 sedan. It was called the Healey Hundred, and on the first day of the show Healey was besieged by customers for it. Austin boss Leonard Lord quickly stepped in to ensure that the Healey could be made in quantity. The timing was opportune: Austin had dipped a toe in the sports car pool with the A40 Sports, an alloy-bodied car designed and built by Jensen as a quid-pro-quo for Austin's assistance with the Jensen Interceptor. Then Austin had built the A90 Atlantic sports sedan to launch an attack on the American market, though even breaking 63 national stock car speed records in the car at Indianapolis failed to win over Stateside buyers. A true sports car had then been mooted as a replacement for the A90 Atlantic, but Lord didn't need to develop his own roadster when Donald

Sunbeam Alpine Special	
Manufacturer:	Rootes Group (Coventry, England)
Production years:	1953-55
Engine location:	Front
Configuration:	In-line four-cylinder
Bore x stroke:	81x110mm
Capacity:	2267cc
Valve operation:	Pushrod overhead valve
Fuel system:	Twin-choke Solex carburetor
Power:	97bhp at 4500rpm
Gearbox:	Four-speed manual
Driven wheels:	Rear wheel drive
Chassis/body:	Ladder chassis, steel body
Suspension:	Front: wishbones and coil springs
	Rear: leaf-sprung beam axle
Brakes:	Hydraulically operated drums on all four wheels
Wheels/tires:	Pressed-steel disc wheels
Top speed:	100mph (161km/h)
Acceleration:	0-60mph (97km/h): approx. 20sec

Below: The Rootes Group's Sunbeam Alpine proved to be a tough rally car.

Right: The fold-flat windshield on the Austin-Healey 100M was intended for racing use.

Austin-Healey 100

Manufacturer:	British Motor Corporation (Longbridge, England)
Production years:	1952-56
Engine location:	Front
Configuration:	In-line four-cylinder
Bore x stroke:	87x111mm
Capacity:	2660cc
Valve operation:	Pushrod overhead valve
Fuel system:	Carburetors
Power:	90bhp at 4000rpm
Gearbox:	Three-speed manual with overdrive
Driven wheels:	Rear wheel drive
Chassis/body:	Pressed-steel chassis with steel body
Suspension:	Front: independent, wishbones and coil springs, anti-roll bar
	Rear: leaf-sprung live axle
Brakes:	Hydraulically operated drums on all four wheels
Wheels/tires:	Center-lock wire wheels
Top speed:	105mph (169km/h)
Acceleration:	0-60mph (97km/h): 10.5sec

Healey's Austin-based machine had so much potential. Literally overnight Donald Healey's car was rebadged, his Motor Show stand was given an Austin makeover, and a new marque was born: Austin-Healey.

The rapturous reception for the Austin-Healey 100 was a headache for Standard-Triumph. In comparison the 20TS looked a little old-fashioned from some angles, and the 1991cc car would struggle to match the 2660cc Austin-Healey for outright pace. After a serious rethink, the Triumph emerged in a much-modified form at the Geneva show as the TR2, with more power, more space inside, and neater styling. To prove its performance Standard-Triumph did the fashionable thing and sent it to Jabbeke in Belgium, where the Jaguar XK120, Sunbeam Alpine, and Austin-Healey 100 had all been speed tested. There, a modified TR2 reached 124mph (200km/h).

More powerful Austin-Healey 100M and 100S models were introduced, and in 1956 the four-cylinder engine was replaced with a six-cylinder motor, again of Austin origin and of similar capacity – slightly smaller, in fact, at 2639cc. This new '100/6' model was claimed to deliver 102bhp, about half way between the original 100 (now often known as the '100/4') and the tuned 100S. In 1959 a 2912cc, 124bhp six-cylinder engine was fitted and the car became the Austin-Healey 3000. It was good for nearly 120mph (193km/h), so Girling disc brakes were wisely adopted. With a useful blend of performance and strength the 'big Healey' was an effective rally

Right: The TR production car line had begun with the attractive TR2 in 1953.

car for BMC's formidable works team in the hands of Pat Moss (Stirling's sister), Don and Erle Morley, and 'flying Finn' Timo Makinen.

The TR was a formidable rallying weapon, too, though its evolution was less dramatic. Shorter doors and stronger sills were introduced late in 1954, and then in 1955 Triumph unveiled a more radically revised model, the TR3. Cosmetic changes included a new grille, fitted flush across the cooling air intake rather than recessed, and the addition of sliding windows into the sidescreens. Larger carburetors improved the power output slightly, and during 1956 more efficient cylinder heads were introduced, the combined effect being to raise the TR3's power output to around 100bhp. In 1958 a full-width grille announced the arrival of the TR3A, which incorporated numerous minor improvements and the availability of a 2138cc engine as an option.

New MGs

With two important new rivals, MG could hardly afford to stand still. The TC, essentially a pre-war design, had given way to the TD in 1950. Superficially similar to its predecessor, the TD was very different under the skin, with a sturdy box-section chassis derived from the Y-type sedan. The Y-type's rack-and-pinion steering was carried over, along with its independent front suspension – which had been designed for Morris by Alec Issigonis back in the 1930s. At the back, the chassis rails were swept upward over the rear axle rather than underneath it as on the TC, giving the TD the potential for greater rear suspension travel and lower spring rates for a smoother ride. The TC's engine was retained unmodified to keep costs down, and for the same reason the traditional wire-spoke wheels were abandoned in favor of pressed-steel wheels.

The TD was warmly received on both sides of the Atlantic, but particularly in America. It was spectacular value in the USA because sterling had been devalued against the dollar, and that meant the new TD was cheaper than the outgoing TC. In addition the TD with all its refinements was the first Midget available with left-hand drive.

Triumph TR2

Manufacturer:	Standard Triumph (Coventry, England)
Production years:	1952-55
Engine location:	Front
Configuration:	In-line four-cylinder
Bore x stroke:	83x92mm
Capacity:	1991cc
Valve operation:	Pushrod overhead valve
Fuel system:	Twin Solex carburetors
Power:	90bhp at 4800rpm
Gearbox:	Four-speed manual
Driven wheels:	Rear wheel drive
Chassis/body:	Unitary steel body
Suspension:	Front: independent, wishbones and coil springs
	Rear: leaf-spring live axle
Brakes:	Hydraulically operated drums on all four wheels
Wheels/tires:	Pressed-steel disc wheels
Top speed:	107mph (172km/h)
Acceleration:	0-60mph (97km/h): 12sec

Below: The TR3A was a much-improved car, despite its resemblance to earlier models.

Above: By the 1950s the T-series MGs (this is the TD) were looking very old-fashioned.

Above: Austin-Healey introduced the tiny 'Frogeye' or 'Bugeye' Sprite in 1958.

By the time Triumph and Austin-Healey revealed their new sports cars at the London Motor Show in 1952, MG had come up with a replacement for the T-series Midgets. *Autosport* photographer George Phillips had raced a special-bodied TC at Le Mans in 1949 and 1950, and MG collaborated with him on a TD-based car for the 1951 race, complete with a low-drag shape to get the highest speed down the long Mulsanne straightaway. Though this car, EX172, was unsuccessful at Le Mans the body shape clearly worked, except that the TD chassis sat the driver too high. By the end of 1951 a new chassis had been built with wider-spaced side members to lower the driving position, and this was turned into a prototype road car coded EX175. Sadly for MG, the Austin and Morris companies combined in 1952 to create BMC, the British Motor Corporation, with Leonard Lord at the helm. When MG bosses asked Lord for approval to put EX175 into production, Lord pointed to the new Austin-Healey 100 and told them he didn't need another sports car…

Instead, Abingdon had to be content with a restyling job on the TD, to produce the TF late in 1953. A lower nose with faired-in headlamps gave the new MG a slightly more modern style, though it looked steadfastly traditional compared to the Triumph TR series, the Austin-Healeys, and the trend-setting Jaguars. By 1954 the TF's lack of straight-line speed compared to its new rivals had been addressed in part by the adoption of a 1466cc XPEG engine in place of the

1250cc XPAG unit of the TC and TD, but even so the MG had only 63bhp to play with – and unhelpful aerodynamics.

The EX175 shape was resurrected in 1954, and with the new 'corporate' BMC B-series engine under the hood it would go into production in 1955 as the MGA, after an early public debut in the ill-fated Le Mans 24-hours that year. Like the Jaguars and Porsches it was available in roadster and fixed-head form, giving it an extra string to its bow compared to the roadster-only Triumph and Austin-Healey. MG's enthusiasm for the concept proved to be well founded, because the MGA would sell more than 100,000 units – nearly 95 percent of them being exported, a record even the XK120 couldn't match.

By 1958 MG's Abingdon factory was also building another, smaller sports car, which ironically bore the name of the rival BMC sports car marque, Austin-Healey. Leonard Lord had identified the need for a small, cheap sports car and Donald Healey's team at Warwick had created the Sprite, based around the mechanical components of the Austin A35 sedan but using a new monocoque bodyshell – a modern enough idea for a fixed-head car, but quite something for a roadster. Cute, curvy styling by Gerry Coker originally included pop-up headlamps, but these proved too expensive: instead the lights were given fixed pods on top of the huge one-piece front end panel, earning the car its nicknames of 'Frogeye' (in the UK) and 'Bugeye' (in America). Power, just 43bhp, came from a twin-carb version of the A35's A-series engine, giving the diminutive Sprite a top speed of around 80mph (129km/h).

The 1950s had proved to be golden age for sports cars, with significant new marques and a host of new models appearing on the market from the affordable Sprite to the exotic engineering of Ferrari. The momentum would continue into the next decade, as the sports car developed and diversified still further – and produced some of the greatest road cars ever made.

Austin-Healey Sprite	
Manufacturer:	British Motor Corporation (Abingdon, England)
Production years:	1958-61
Engine location:	Front
Configuration:	In-line four-cylinder
Bore x stroke:	62.9x76.2mm
Capacity:	948cc
Valve operation:	Pushrod overhead valve
Fuel system:	Twin SU carburetors
Power:	43bhp at 5000rpm
Gearbox:	Four-speed manual
Driven wheels:	Rear wheel drive
Chassis/body:	Unitary steel body
Suspension:	Front: independent, wishbones and coil springs
	Rear: leaf-sprung beam axle
Brakes:	Hydraulically operated drums on all four wheels
Wheels/tires:	Pressed-steel disc wheels
Top speed:	80mph (129km/h)
Acceleration:	0-60mph (97km/h): approx. 20sec

Below: The MGA was a radical departure for MG, but proved immensely successful. Its export performance shaded even the XK120.

1960s: Sports Cars For All

Jaguar E-type	
Manufacturer:	Jaguar Cars (Coventry, England)
Production years:	1961-71 (V12 1971-75)
Engine location:	Front
Configuration:	In-line six-cylinder
Bore x stroke:	87x106mm
Capacity:	3781cc
Valve operation:	Twin overhead camshafts
Fuel system:	Triple SU carburetors
Power:	265bhp at 5500rpm
Gearbox:	Four-speed manual
Driven wheels:	Rear wheel drive
Chassis/body:	Unitary steel body
Suspension:	Front: independent, wishbones and torsion bars, anti-roll bar
	Rear: independent, wishbones and radius arms with coil springs, anti-roll bar
Brakes:	Hydraulically operated discs on all four wheels, servo assistance
Wheels/tires:	Center-lock wire wheels
Top speed:	145mph (233km/h)
Acceleration:	0-60mph (97km/h): 7.0sec

Jaguar had stunned the world with its XK120 in 1948, and over the next decade the XK had developed into the XK150S, a much heavier and more refined car powered by an enlarged 3.8-liter engine developing 265bhp. But already work was under way on a very different replacement model which would grab the headlines for Coventry all over again.

The first prototype of the new model, code-named E1A, had been built in 1957. Based around a central monocoque 'tub' and a tubular front subframe, like the D-type, it was fitted with a new independent rear suspension system which was being developed by William Heynes and Bob Knight. Malcolm Sayer penned the car's aerodynamic lines, and because of the low hood line that resulted E1A was given a short-block XK engine of just 2.4 liters. Christopher Jennings, respected editor of the British motoring weekly *The Motor*, was given unprecedented access to the prototype including a hush-hush weekend test drive and he returned with glowing praise.

A further prototype, E2A, followed in 1959, racing at Le Mans in 1960 in the hands of Briggs Cunningham where it recorded the fastest practice lap but failed to finish. Half a dozen prototypes of the roadgoing car, now being called the E-type, were built and tested throughout 1960 and in March 1961 the seventh prototype was shown to the world's press at Geneva. In fact, many of them had seen an E-type before as *The Motor*, *The Autocar*, and *Autosport*, among others, had already road-tested that fixed-head prototype, 9600HP, or a roadster press car registered 77RW. Top speeds of just on 150mph (241km/h) had been recorded, thanks largely to some diligent preparation by Jaguar; later production E-types weren't quite so quick.

Above: *Jaguar's E1A prototype.*

Right: *E2A was the second prototype for what became the Jaguar E-type. It raced at Le Mans in the hands of Briggs Cunningham in 1960, but retired.*

Previous page: *The Austin-Healey 3000 became softer in its final years, but the works rally versions, like this one, were as serious as ever.*

Jaguar's amazing E-type

It was just as well that 9600HP had been breathed on by the Experimental Department engineers at Jaguar, because there was a delay getting the car ready for the 'reveal' – the press launch – at Parc des Eaux Vives in Geneva. Jaguar's Bob Berry drove flat out for 17 hours to get 9600HP to the party on time. It was worth the effort, because the assembled journalists were awestruck – here was a production road car, from a British company, with space-age looks and the potential for 150mph (241km/h) but also the refinement and docility of a good sedan car. The E-type had rewritten the sports car rule book.

Better yet, the E-type – known as the XK-E in America – had an on-the-road price under £2200 ($3850) with the fixed-head coupé, curiously, costing slightly more than the roadster.

Above: *The E-type was launched to widespread acclaim at Geneva in 1961.*

Left: *Improvements led to the Series 2 E-type – note the lack of headlamp cowls.*

To get the same level of performance elsewhere you had to buy a hand-made supercar and spend considerably more: Aston Martin's DB4 cost another £1700 ($3000), the Mercedes-Benz 300SL was well over £4000 ($7000), and a Ferrari 250GT cost nearly £6000 ($10,500). It was much cheaper than its competitors, and while acquiring an E-type may have been only a dream for most motorists at least it was a dream that seemed like it might one day be fulfilled, which was more than most people could hope for in the case of a Ferrari. The E-type became an icon, the sports car that represented achievement without excess. The E-type was cool. Beatle George Harrison had one, and British TV star Simon Dee drove a white roadster during the opening credits of his show *Dee Time*. Such was the car's popularity that when ATV asked Jaguar to lend them a car for their new series *The Saint*, starring Roger Moore as Simon Templar, it's said that they declined the offer saying they didn't need the publicity. Instead Volvo stepped in and offered its P1800, turning the car into a star overnight. And Roger Moore liked it so much he bought one.

Right: BMC badge-engineering: Austin-Healey's MkII Sprite was also available with octagon badges as an MG Midget.

Below: The Daimler SP250 'Dart' was distinctive, but some thought it ugly. After the E-type appeared, it was always living on borrowed time.

Above: *With a six-cylinder engine and fastback roof, the Spitfire became the GT6, a credible pocket-sized E-type.*

Left: *The Triumph Spitfire was a popular 'Spridget' rival in the 1960s, and remains a well-loved classic today.*

The E-type quickly spelled the end for another promising sports car, from the normally staid Daimler company that Jaguar had taken over in 1960. The Daimler Dart was new from the ground up, introduced in 1959 as an attempt to cash in on the lucrative American export market. An Edward Turner-designed 2.5-liter V8 engine was the car's best feature, its 140bhp giving the lightweight Dart similar performance to the contemporary XK150. That light weight was a side effect of the glassfiber body, which Daimler had chosen principally because of the low tooling costs it involved. The styling was controversial, and so was the handling because the simple cruciform chassis was rather too flexible. Even the name was a problem because Dodge was already using 'Dart,' and so Daimler rapidly renamed the car the SP250. Improvements were made which ironed out some of the problems, and perhaps the Daimler's curious appearance meant it attracted more criticism than was justified. But the Jaguar/Daimler combine didn't really need two sports cars, and with the E-type program already well under way the Daimler's career was inevitably short.

Affordable sports cars

Good value though the Jaguar undoubtedly was, it still cost three times as much as a family sedan, and that hardly made it an 'affordable' sports car. Impecunious enthusiasts had to look elsewhere, but fortunately there were plenty of affordable options. Austin-Healey's Sprite was revised in 1961, adding a bolder front end and an opening trunk lid into a restyled tail. Much of the work had been done by MG at Abingdon, where the Sprite was built, and shortly after the new Sprite's announcement in May 1961 a new MG Midget joined the fold. Though Abingdon had put forward the idea of a modern sports car based on a BMC project called 'Sputnik,' which became the Mini, this wasn't it: instead it was a Sprite with some detail changes and MG badges. It was a result of BMC's policy of 'badge engineering,' where the same car was sold under the guise of several different marques with only minimal specification changes. The Midget was given slightly more luxurious equipment than the Sprite and commanded a higher price, and it proved popular.

Triumph Spitfire 4

Manufacturer:	Standard-Triumph (Coventry, England)
Production years:	1962-64 (other versions 1964-80)
Engine location:	Front
Configuration:	In-line four-cylinder
Bore x stroke:	69.3x76mm
Capacity:	1147cc
Valve operation:	Pushrod overhead valve
Fuel system:	Twin SU carburetors
Power:	63bhp at 5750rpm
Gearbox:	Four-speed manual
Driven wheels:	Rear wheel drive
Chassis/body:	Steel platform chassis, steel body
Suspension:	Front: independent, wishbones and coil springs, anti-roll bar
	Rear: independent, swing-axle with radius arms and transverse leaf spring
Brakes:	Hydraulic, disc front and drum rear
Wheels/tires:	Pressed-steel disc or center-lock wire
Top speed:	91mph (146km/h)
Acceleration:	0-60mph (97km/h): 15.5sec

Above: Attractive and practical, the MGB GT was well received by critics and customers alike.

Below: The MGB quickly became the world's most popular sports car.

The two tiny BMC sports cars soon had a new rival in the shape of the Triumph Spitfire, though the Triumph had very nearly been stillborn. In 1959 Standard-Triumph had introduced the new Herald sedan, and its chassis had been the starting point for a sports car, codenamed 'Bomb' and styled by Giovanni Michelotti. It was ready by the middle of 1960 but by then Standard-Triumph's financial situation was dire, and a new sports car was a long way down the order of priorities. The prototype Bomb sat in a corner under a dustsheet.

In 1961 Standard-Triumph was taken over by successful truck manufacturer Leyland, which installed Stanley Markland to run the Coventry car maker. Markland almost literally stumbled over the prototype Bomb, instantly recognized its potential, and approved it for production. It was slightly bigger than the 'Spridget,' as the Sprites and Midgets had been collectively termed, and offered more comfort and convenience. The Spitfire had wind-up windows in place of the Spridget's drafty side-screens, and overdrive was available for fuss-free cruising. The Spitfire's curvy good looks won it many friends too, though the cuteness of it also gave the Triumph the reputation of being a 'woman's car' rather than a roadster for red-blooded males. Such was the political incorrectness of the 1960s.

The Spridget and Spitfire were natural rivals, and would be at each other's throats until the end of the 1970s. In both cases, development brought in bigger engines and more power, with the addition of comfort features (such as wind-up windows and a better roof) on the Sprite/Midget and revisions to the sometimes wayward rear suspension on the Spitfire. Triumph also produced a hard-top coupé version of the Spitfire with a lusty six-cylinder engine, the GT6, which was a passable attempt at a pocket E-type but threw into sharp relief the inadequacies of the swing-axle rear suspension.

Triumph versus MG

Triumph and MG were also serious rivals in the next class up, where the TRs took on the MGA. MG had introduced a new high-performance MGA Twin Cam in 1958, the engine based on the overhead-valve B-series unit in the normal MGA. The engine had already proved its worth, breaking 16 international 1500c-class records in 1956 in EX179, a record-breaker built up from one of the prototype MGAs. The same year a supercharged version developing 280bhp was installed in the teardrop-shaped EX181, which Stirling Moss used to achieve 245mph (394km/h) on the salt flats at Utah – breaking MG's own 1500cc Class F record of 204.2mph (328.6km/h), which had stood since 1939. In 1959 EX181 returned to Utah with Phil Hill at the wheel, and recorded 254mph (409km/h).

MG MGB Mk1	
Manufacturer:	MG Car Company (Abingdon, England)
Production years:	1962-67 (other versions 1967-80)
Engine location:	Front
Configuration:	In-line four-cylinder
Bore x stroke:	80.26x88.9mm
Capacity:	1798cc
Valve operation:	Pushrod overhead valve
Fuel system:	Twin SU carburetors
Power:	95bhp at 5400rpm
Gearbox:	Four-speed manual
Driven wheels:	Rear wheel drive
Chassis/body:	Unitary steel body
Suspension:	Front: independent, wishbones and coil springs
	Rear: independent, leaf sprung live axle
Brakes:	Hydraulic, disc front and drum rear
Wheels/tires:	Pressed-steel disc wheels
Top speed:	108mph (174km/h)
Acceleration:	0-60mph (97km/h): 12sec

Left: MG's EX181 record-breaker achieved 254mph (409km/h) in 1959 with Phil Hill at the wheel.

Left: A fixed-roof MGB GT was added to the range in 1965.

Above: *Triumph rallied the TR4 – seen here on the 1964 Monte Carlo Rally – but it was unable to match the pace or strength of the Big Healeys.*

Below: *The TR5 was Britain's first fuel-injected production car.*

The twin-cam MGA was a formidable competition car in its class, and performed well at Le Mans in 1960 in low-drag, fixed-roof guise. But in production form the engine was too fragile: its high compression ratio meant that high-octane fuel was a necessity, and the ignition timing had to be spot on. Over-revving was easy because of the rapid acceleration and willing throttle-response. Quickly the MGA Twin Cam developed a reputation for unreliability, as one MG mechanic found out to his cost after a works MGA crashed on an Alpine rally. Dispatched to a local BMC dealer for parts, he was shown a workshop full of broken MGA Twin Cams, and thrown out...

By 1961 the MGA Twin Cam had been discontinued, and the MGA itself was replaced in 1962 by the MGB. Like the Spridget this used a modern monocoque bodyshell with no separate chassis. Though the BMC B-series engine was carried forward, its capacity was expanded from the 1622cc of the final MGAs to 1798cc, with a small improvement in power and a much larger increase in torque. Interior space and ride comfort improved considerably, and suddenly the sports car became accessible to everyone – no longer was it confined only to those enthusiasts prepared to put up with discomfort, high cost, unreliability, or inconvenience. MGB sales quickly reflected that, and it became the most popular sports car in the world. Perhaps the MGB was less involving than earlier sports cars, but that was what the market – and in particular the vital US market – wanted.

The MGB's popularity was further increased with the introduction in 1965 of a hard-top, fastback version called the GT. The initials stood for Grand Touring or *Gran Turismo*, which had become the term for fast fixed-head coupés that were often more about covering road miles than winning races. Because it was developed from the MGB roadster, the GT's strength came from the main part of the body, not the roof – so the roof and pillars could be relatively slender. That gave the MGB GT, like the fixed-head E-type, an attractive and elegant line. It weighed a little more but performance barely suffered and the top speed actually increased, thanks to the lower-drag fastback shape.

Triumph's rival to the MGB was the Michelotti-styled TR4. Mechanically it was much the same as the TR3A, with a wider version of the same chassis and the same engines – though now the larger 2138cc engine was standard and the 1991cc unit was an (unpopular) option. Better rack and pinion steering was fitted, along with an all-synchromesh gearbox with optional overdrive. It was a better car in many ways, but some American dealers didn't see it that way. Their customers preferred the traditional styling of the TR3, and a short run of 'TR3B' cars was built to satisfy demand.

By the mid-'60s the influence of sophisticated sports cars like the E-type was being felt across the board, and with its pushrod engine and cart-sprung live axle the TR4 was looking antiquated. The engine would continue in the TR4A of 1965, with slight tweaks for more power, but major improvements were made to the handling and ride. The TR adopted independent rear suspension, using the semi-trailing arm system that Triumph had introduced on its 2000 sedan in 1962. The TR now had a well-sorted chassis that cried out for more power.

That came in 1967 with the TR5 PI, which used a 2498cc in-line six derived from the unit in the 2000 sedan, developing around 150bhp. The letters 'PI' were significant, denoting the use of petrol (gas) injection. The TR5 was the first British car with a fuel-injected engine and, along with the Mercedes-Benz 300SL and Maserati 3500GTI, one of the pioneers of the technology. Sadly for American enthusiasts, emissions regulations were too tough for the fuel-injection system and they had to make do with a 104bhp carburetored version, the TR250.

Six-cylinder power

The new six-cylinder engine took the TR5 into Big Healey territory, though by that time the Austin-Healey 3000 had evolved into a very different machine. For 1964 a Mark III Healey was introduced, its plush interior trim, greater suspension travel, and tiny rear seats appealing to customers with more on their minds than rally victories. There was more power too, but the

Above: Regular revisions gave the Sprite and Midget more power and better weather equipment. This is the MkIV Sprite of 1966.

Left: The MGC was a six-cylinder MGB, intended to replace the Big Healey in BMC's sports car line-up.

Sunbeam Alpine

Manufacturer:	Rootes Group (Coventry, England)
Production years:	1966-68 (other models 1959-66)
Engine location:	Front
Configuration:	In-line four-cylinder
Bore x stroke:	81.5x82.5mm
Capacity:	1725cc
Valve operation:	Pushrod overhead valve
Fuel system:	Twin Stromberg carburetors
Power:	93bhp at 5500rpm
Gearbox:	Four-speed manual
Driven wheels:	Rear wheel drive
Chassis/body:	Steel cruciform chassis, steel body
Suspension:	Front: independent, wishbones and coil springs, anti-roll bar
	Rear: leaf-sprung live axle
Brakes:	Hydraulically operated, disc front, drum rear
Wheels/tires:	Pressed-steel disc wheels
Top speed:	100mph (161km/h)
Acceleration:	0-60mph (97km/h): approx. 13sec

Healey's character had become that of a fast tourer rather than a taut sports car, and by the late 1960s it was an old design. It didn't last long after the merger of BMC and Jaguar to form British Motor Holdings (BMH) in 1968. The TR5, meanwhile, evolved into the Karmann-styled TR6, which would take Triumph into the 1970s.

A six-cylinder version of the MGB, the MGC, effectively replaced the Healeys in 1967. It looked much the same as the MGB, except for bigger wheels and a noticeable hood bulge. Underneath the changes were more fundamental, because the bigger engine left no room for the MGB's coil spring suspension and a more compact torsion-bar layout had to be adopted. Coupled with nose-heavy weight distribution, the result was rather woolly handling, which meant that the MGC was, like the later Healeys, more of a tourer than a sports car. The MGC did, however, sire a pair of spectacular racing GTs, which ultimately developed over 200bhp and showed a great deal of promise. But by then BMH had merged with Leyland, and the Competitions Department closed.

The Leyland/BMH merger meant that Austin-Healey, MG, Jaguar, and Triumph were all now part of the same organization. Their biggest sports car competitor was The Rootes Group's Sunbeam Alpine, which had been introduced in 1959, reviving a name from earlier in the 1950s. The new Alpine used the cruciform chassis of the Hillman Husky estate car, with a pretty two-seat roadster body that incorporated stylish fins at the back – 1959 being the height of the fad for

fins in the United States. Power came from a four-cylinder engine displacing just 1494cc, so the Alpine had little chance of matching the performance of an MGB or TR4. Later cars employed 1592cc and then 1725cc engines, but even then Rootes preferred to avoid direct comparisons by calling the Alpine a 'sports tourer.'

More power was what was required, and it arrived in 1965 in the excitingly-named Sunbeam Tiger. American racing driver Carroll Shelby had already brokered a deal between Ford and AC to build the V8-engined Cobra (which we'll look at in the next chapter) and now Rootes turned to Shelby to do the same for the Alpine. A 4.2-liter Ford V8 was slotted into the engine bay, with some revisions required to the front suspension and steering to make it fit, and the result was a 115mph (185km/h) performance car which somehow seemed much greater than the sum of its parts. Even more power arrived with the 4.7-liter Mustang V8 in the 1967 Tiger II, but by then Chrysler had taken control of the Rootes Group and wouldn't countenance producing a car with a rival's engine – particularly such a high-profile model. Sadly Chrysler's own V8s wouldn't fit, so the Tiger died after just three years in production, just over 7000 having been made.

European sophistication

Despite their popularity, all the British sports cars (E-type apart) looked archaic compared to some of the continental competition. Alfa Romeo had got into its stride in the mid-1950s with the Giulietta Sprint, a stunning Bertone-built two-plus-two coupé based on the Giulietta sedan platform. In fact the Sprint arrived first, rushed into production in 1954 to reassure the public that the much-delayed Giulietta was really going to happen. The following year a Pininfarina-styled open roadster, the Giulietta Spider, was added to the range, using a slightly shorter wheelbase and with room for just two seats.

Mechanically the Alfas shared a specification which read more like a Porsche than an Austin-Healey. The engine was an all-alloy in-line four with twin chain-driven overhead camshafts, developing 65bhp in its original 1290cc form. Front suspension was independent, using wishbones and coil springs, while the rear used a well-located live axle with radius arms and an A-frame. The first cars had drum brakes and a four-speed gearbox but by 1962 disc brakes and five speeds were available, together with a 1.6-liter engine in the Giulia Sprint and Spider.

The new Alfas sold well, attracting many customers in the important American market but not so many in Britain, where high import duties made the Alfas very expensive. Even pricier were low-volume specials: Bertone built a striking coupé on the shorter Spider platform, called the Sprint Speciale or SS, while Zagato wrapped the smallest possible amount of metal over the Giulietta's mechanicals to produce the SZ. Though perhaps intended as a competition car, the SS was more of a stylish road machine, with hints of Mercedes 300SL in its styling. The SZ, on the other hand, was a true competition vehicle and proved it with wins in the Alpine Rally and the tough Liège-Rome-Liège 'Marathon de la Route.'

An even more specialized machine arrived in 1963 after a gestation period which had begun way back in 1959. The 'Tubolare Zagato' or TZ was supposedly derived from the recently-arrived new generation Giulia Sprint coupé, styled by the young Giorgetto Giugiaro, but in truth little more than the engine and gearbox were related to the production car. *Tubolare* signified that the TZ used a tubular spaceframe chassis, a rather haphazard affair by the standards of Mercedes or even Lotus but still resulting in a car 243lb (110kg) lighter than the SZ. With such light weight, and up to 170bhp from a highly-developed version of the 1.6-liter engine, the TZ was remarkably

Top: The Sunbeam Tiger combined the Alpine's good looks with Ford V8 power.

Center: The Giulietta Spider had a sophistication which left British sports cars far behind.

Above: Alfa Romeo's Giulietta Sprint spawned special-bodied versions from Bertone, as here, and Zagato.

Opposite: Rootes called its '60s Alpine a 'sports tourer' rather than an out-and-out sports car. It was never as quick as an MGB or TR.

Above: The Alfa 'Tubolare Zagato' or TZ was a successful tubular-framed racing machine.

Alfa Romeo Duetto

Manufacturer:	Alfa Romeo (Milan, Italy)
Production years:	1966-68 (other versions 1968-94)
Engine location:	Front
Configuration:	In-line four-cylinder
Bore x stroke:	78x82
Capacity:	1570cc
Valve operation:	Twin overhead camshaft
Fuel system:	Twin Weber carburetors
Power:	109bhp at 6000rpm
Gearbox:	Five-speed manual
Driven wheels:	Rear wheel drive
Chassis/body:	Unitary steel body
Suspension:	Front: independent, double wishbone and coil spring with anti-roll bar Rear: Coil-sprung live axle with radius arms
Brakes:	Hydraulically operated discs on all four wheels
Wheels/tires:	Pressed-steel disc wheels
Top speed:	111mph (179km/h)
Acceleration:	0-60mph (97km/h): approx. 11.2sec

Right: From 1966 Alfa Romeo's open sports car was the Duetto, which starred in the popular film The Graduate.

rapid and notched up numerous class wins in sports car racing, including third and fourth overall in the Targa Florio in 1964. A glassfiber-bodied TZ2 arrived in 1965, and continued the successes.

A new Spider followed the new generation Giulia coupé in 1966. Alfa Romeo invited ideas for what to call it, but after dismissing suggestions that the new machine should be named after such differing characters as Gina Lollobrigida, Joseph Stalin, and Adolf Hitler, the new Alfa was simply called the Duetto. The Giulia mechanicals were clothed in a sleek body, the last to be styled by Battista Pininfarina, who died in April 1966. It featured a long, rounded tail: in Italy the car's shape earned it the nickname of 'the cuttlefish.' In this form the car famously starred in the film *The Graduate*, where it was used and abused by the film's central character Benjamin Braddock, played by Dustin Hoffman.

The Duetto name was dropped in 1968. At the same time a 1779cc engine was introduced, and the car was known as the 1750 Spider Veloce, a name chosen to revive memories of the pre-war

6C 1750. In Europe the new engine was fed by a pair of twin-choke Webers, but for the emissions-conscious American market Alfa Romeo adopted Spica mechanical fuel injection – ironically, just as Triumph was replacing the Lucas mechanical injection of its TRs with carburetors for US markets because it couldn't make the injected engine clean enough. Equipment levels improved, and the package proved attractive to buyers across Europe and the United States (where half of the Spiders were exported).

Above: Fiat's alternative to the small British sports cars was this, the 850 Spider.

Fiat's sporting Spiders

Fiat, too, was producing sophisticated sports cars based on its more mundane sedan offerings. The 1100 'Trasformabile' of the 1950s had been more stylish than sporting, but the Bertone-built 850 Spider introduced in 1965 was a truly sporting machine. Based on the rear-engined 850 sedan it lacked outright straight-line performance, but it was fun to drive and a credible alternative to a Spridget or Spitfire. Its specification showed how far the British sports cars were lagging behind too, with disc brakes, independent suspension at both ends, and a punchy overhead-cam engine. Despite the fact that Fiat had their own 850 Coupé, Bertone marketed a fixed-roof version of the 850 Spider as the Bertone 850 Racer.

Below: Lancia's Fulvia enjoyed an illustrious career in rallying.

Another Fiat Spider, this time based on the more conventional mechanical components from the 124 sedan, followed in 1966. Announced at the Turin show, the 124 Spider was an Alfa Duetto rival, and like the Alfa it was styled by Pininfarina. Initially it was fitted with a 1438cc version of the long-running Fiat twin-cam engine, developing just 90bhp, and this survived into the 1970s. So in its initial form the 124 Spider was brisk rather than genuinely quick, but it had good road manners, pleasant styling, and a convenient design. Never officially imported into the UK, it was nevertheless a strong rival for the MGB in Europe and America, with none of the old-fashioned engine and suspension technology that had bedevilled the underdeveloped MG.

And that wasn't the end of Italy's sports car range. Lancia had already built the V6-engined Aurelia coupé, which with a 2.5-liter 118bhp engine and de Dion rear end was a swift and secure

The Sports Sedan Story

With their competition heritage, sports cars were the fastest cars around before World War II. But by the 1960s another group of sporting machines were rivalling sports cars in the minds of enthusiasts: the sports sedan had come of age.

Jaguar's compact monocoque sedans, which began in 1955 with what became known simply as the 'Mk1,' were the cars to beat in sedan car racing. The later 3.8 Mk2 was the fastest sedan in the world, and it had performance and handling to worry all but the greatest of the sports cars available – at a typically low Jaguar price.

By the mid-'60s there were more important sports sedans, with rapid machines from Alfa Romeo and BMW. But two cars stand out as important in the sports sedan story, both of them British and both what we would now call 'homologation specials.'

Alec Issigonis' revolutionary Mini offered exceptional roadholding and light weight, and when John Cooper slotted one of his Formula

Junior-spec A-series engines into a Mini a pocket performance car was born. The Mini Cooper, as it was called, would become the most successful rally car of the 1960s and prove to be a formidable circuit racer in the hands of John Rhodes.

The Lotus-Cortina used the Elan's Lotus twin-cam engine in the Ford Cortina body. Throughout the 1960s drivers like Jimmy Clark and Sir John Whitmore delighted crowds with the Lotus-Cortina's three-wheeling antics on the circuits. When the Mk2 Cortina took over in 1967 a new Cortina-

Lotus appeared, the reversal of the name being significant – the earlier car was assembled by Lotus, the later one by Ford. The Mk2 was probably a better car all round, but it didn't have quite the enthusiast appeal of the original.

All three of these cars showed that real performance was not just the preserve of the sports car, and gave enthusiastic drivers convenient, useful cars that were every bit as good to drive as noisy, drafty roadsters. The trend would continue, as the 1970s witnessed rivals to the sports car that seemed to threaten to replace it entirely.

Top: John Rhodes' Mini Cooper passes the wreckage of another Mini and a Sunbeam Rapier.

Above right: Jim Clark testing an early Lotus-Cortina: production models would be painted white and wear a famous green flash down the side.

GT car. The 1960s brought the Fulvia sedan, with front-wheel drive and a 1.1-liter narrow-angle V4 engine – so narrow, in fact, that a single cylinder head covered both banks of cylinders. The coupé that followed, with engines up to 1584cc and 115bhp, was tough and capable; it made a big name for itself in rallying in the 1960s and early '70s.

Porsche provided sophistication of a similar sort in its quicker and more expensive sports coupés. The final form of the 356 retained little of its Volkswagen ancestry, and with the biggest 2.0-liter engine was good for up to 125mph (201km/h). But by the early 1960s other sports cars and sporting sedans were exceeding the Porsche's performance. By then Porsche was concentrating on a new model using an air-cooled flat-six engine with a single overhead camshaft on each bank of cylinders, mounted at the rear as in the 356 and developing 130bhp. Strut suspension (with torsion bar springs) was adopted at the front in place of the 356's trailing links, and at the rear the 356's swing axles were replaced by a semi-trailing arm design, providing much better control of wheel movement than before. A longer body allowed less cramped accommodation; its distinctive shape was designed by Ferdinand Alexander Porsche. It was called the 901, until Peugeot objected: the French firm's models were always denoted by three-figure numbers with a zero in the middle, and as a result Porsche renamed their new model the 911.

Left: *Fiat's 124 Spider had a long and successful production run.*

Porsche 911	
Manufacturer:	Dr Ing hc F Porsche AG (Zuffenhausen, Germany)
Production years:	1964-67 (other models 1967-89)
Engine location:	Rear
Configuration:	Flat six-cylinder
Bore x stroke:	80x66mm
Capacity:	1991cc
Valve operation:	Single overhead cam per bank
Fuel system:	Triple Solex carburetors per bank
Power:	130bhp at 5600rpm
Gearbox:	Four-speed manual
Driven wheels:	Rear wheel drive
Chassis/body:	Unitary steel body
Suspension:	Front: independent, struts and torsion bars
	Rear: independent, semi-trailing arms and torsion bars
Brakes:	Hydraulic, discs on all four wheels
Wheels/tires:	Pressed-steel disc wheels
Top speed:	130mph (209km/h)
Acceleration:	0-60mph (97km/h): 8.5sec

Developing the 911

Despite Porsche's engineering reputation, the 911 which appeared in 1964 had its share of teething troubles. With its rearward weight bias caused by the rear-mounted engine the 911 was always going to exhibit some curious handling characteristics, but production cars proved to be much less predictable than the hand-built prototypes. The problem was that the suspension had to be built to very fine tolerances, which simply couldn't be matched on a production line, resulting in cars which had poor straight-line stability, strong initial understeer followed by violent lift-off oversteer, and which differed in their responses in left- and right-hand corners. Adding weight to the front of the car to change the weight distribution and polar moment (see Chapter 1) was the

Above: *Like earlier Porsches, the 911 was a natural competitor. This car is seen in rallying trim.*

Left: *Early 911s had unpredictable handling, but the design was refined and improved over time.*

Above: A cheaper alternative to the six-cylinder 911 was this, the four-cylinder 912. Some believed that the 912 handled better because its lighter engine improved the car's weight distribution.

initial fix, made by inserting a 24lb (11kg) cast-iron weight into each end of the front bumper. Another problem was carburation, the specially-designed triple Solexes on each bank of cylinders producing a marked flat spot in the middle of the rev range. A triple-choke Weber for each bank quickly solved the problem.

The 911 would survive in production until the end of the 1980s, and it would do so through consistent, diligent development that would slowly overcome the car's inherent shortcomings. A four-cylinder 912, with the 911 shell but a 356-derived four-cylinder engine, offered a lower price and better handling (thanks to more even weight distribution). More power was an early priority, and a 911S with bigger valves and higher compression appeared in 1967. Bigger engines and better handling would follow in the 1970s, gradually turning the 911 into a true supercar.

Alpine and Abarth

Specialist marques across Europe were now building sophisticated sports cars using production mechanical components. In France, Alpine used Renault engines and mechanical parts in its tiny rear-engined fastback coupés, whose traction and handling balance were ideal for the loose-surface, special-stage rallying that was now taking over from the old-style navigational events. For track use, Carlo Abarth built a succession of aerodynamic coupés and jewel-like roadsters using Fiat componentry, though by the end of the '60s the Abarth company was struggling financially, and would only just survive into the '70s as an independent car maker.

Some of the bigger car makers were also getting in on the act. Sports cars were emerging from Japan for the first time, and showing depth of engineering talent that was to become more and more important for the Japanese motor industry in the next two decades. Honda's tiny S800 owed much to motorcycle engine design, of which Honda became masters in the 1950s, with its roller-bearing crankshaft and high rev limit. Toyota's 2000GT was too rare to make a major impact on the world's sports car market and was compromised by being available only as a coupé – though a roadster version did appear in the James Bond film *You Only Live Twice*. More significant, perhaps, was Datsun's Fairlady Z – a close rival of the MGB, and a foretaste of what was to come. In Europe, GM's German arm Opel came up with a small two-seater called the Opel GT, inspired by some of the work on the Chevrolet Corvette's styling and displaying the kind of sensuous curves that few expected from a German marque. Chunkier, but no less attractive, was the 1963 Mercedes-Benz 230SL, which sought to replace both the supercar 300SL and the mainstream 190SL, and did so with much aplomb.

In Britain Colin Chapman's Lotus company had earned itself a reputation for designs which were clever and innovative, if not always absolutely reliable. Chapman's Elite sports car had proved its worth in sports car racing and had established Lotus as a road car manufacturer, but by the early 1960s Chapman felt a new car was needed. The Elite, with its glassfiber monocoque and racing-derived Coventry-Climax engine, was very expensive and time-consuming to build. What Chapman wanted was a sports car with all the Elite's performance and handling capabilities but without the cost and inconvenience – and, unlike the Elite, he wanted it to be available in roadster form.

Initial designs centered around a glassfiber monocoque, like the Elite. But the Elite had been designed with a fixed roof because that was the only way that the monocoque could be made stiff enough and at the same time light enough, and Chapman's stipulation that he wanted the new car to be a roadster gave the engineers headaches. One of them, Brian Luff, came up with a simple

Above: *In Italy Abarth was building Fiat-powered road and racing cars.*

Above: *Toyota's 2000GT marked the appearance of Japanese manufacturers in the sports car world.*

Opposite below: *The French concern Alpine built rear-engined, Renault-powered sports cars, like this A110 1600S, in small numbers.*

'backbone' chassis fabricated from sheet steel, forked at each end to carry the engine and suspension systems. It was only ever intended to be used in a 'mechanical prototype,' to help develop the suspension and drivetrain while work continued in parallel on the bodyshell, but the backbone chassis so elegantly solved all the new car's problems that another Lotus engineer, Ron Hickman, lobbied to retain it for production. Eventually Colin Chapman agreed. Hickman, by the way, later went on to greater fame as inventor of the folding workbench, the Workmate.

Sharing engines

Powering the new car, called the Elan, was a new engine derived from a production design. After the expensive Coventry-Climax engine, Chapman had realized that a production-based unit was essential for keeping the cost of the car down, so he looked around for the newest production engine with the most potential. Ford's new Cortina sedan of 1962 proved to be the answer, and Chapman engaged Harry Mundy – Technical Editor of *The Autocar* – to design a twin-overhead camshaft cylinder head to turn this unassuming family car engine into a powerful sports car unit. Chapman's plan went further: to reduce costs still further he envisaged using the engine not only in the Elan, but in a high-performance 'Lotus-Cortina.'

Those first Lotus twin-cam engines displaced just 1.5 liters, though the capacity was quickly upgraded to 1.6 liters. In this form the engine developed 105bhp, enough to give the lightweight Elan rapid acceleration and a top speed in excess of 110mph (177km/h). Thanks, also, to the car's light weight and to clever suspension design the Elan had spectacular roadholding, well-balanced handling, and also a smooth ride – unlike some of the more traditional live-axled sports cars, which generated smooth-road grip at the expense of ride comfort. The drawbacks were variable

Opposite above: *Mercedes-Benz replaced the 300SL and 190SL with this, the 230SL. The handsome styling hid real sports car agility and power.*

Left: *TVR's V8-powered Tuscan had shattering straight-line performance but could be a handful in corners.*

build quality – Lotus weren't renowned for screwing cars together consistently well, disgruntled owners claiming that 'Lotus' stood for Lots Of Trouble, Usually Serious – and a price approaching £1500 ($2625) in 1964, which was cheaper than an E-type but much pricier than most competitors.

Higher-spec engines soon followed, giving the Elan better straight-line performance and encouraging *The Motor* to describe it as the 'best all round sports car' available. It earned a reputation as the thinking man's sports car – and indeed the thinking woman's, as one of the best known Elan drivers of the 1960s was the black-clad Mrs Emma Peel in the television series *The Avengers*, played by Diana Rigg. The Elan took Lotus into the 1970s, by which time it was helping Colin Chapman in his aim to take Lotus upmarket, where profit margins were bigger. For the bottom end of its market Lotus introduced a cheaper car using a Renault engine rather than the Lotus-Ford twin cam, relying on light weight and innovative design to provide good performance. The result was the mid-engined Europa which, like previous Lotuses, was often supplied in a kit form to circumvent the taxes imposed on fully-built cars. The kits were often very easy to build, requiring the minimum of work necessary to qualify as kit cars.

Though Lotus had turned away from the pure glassfiber monocoque, in the north of England the tiny Rochdale company remained loyal to the idea. The highly-regarded Olympic sports car used a glassfiber tub fitted with tuned production engines, and was slowly developed throughout the 1960s and into the 1970s. Glassfiber bodies were also in evidence at TVR in Blackpool, which underpinned them with stout steel chassis: less sophisticated engineering, but still effective. TVR's output consisted of one basic fixed-head design, which by the late 1960s was powered by MGB's 1.8-liter engine. An alternative to this model, called the 1800S, was the Tuscan with a 4.7-liter Ford V8, which in the lightweight TVR provided shattering performance in a straight line.

The varied output of these specialist marques provided further evidence that Britain was still at the forefront of sports car design. But the most spectacular cars of the 1960s were cars much faster and more expensive than the Lotus, and were a whole new breed of sports car.

Lotus Elan	
Manufacturer:	Lotus Cars (Hethel, England)
Production years:	1964-71 (other models 1970-73)
Engine location:	Front
Configuration:	In-line four-cylinder
Bore x stroke:	82.6x72.8mm
Capacity:	1558cc
Valve operation:	Twin overhead camshaft
Fuel system:	Twin Weber carburetors
Power:	115bhp at 6000rpm
Gearbox:	Four-speed manual
Driven wheels:	Rear wheel drive
Chassis/body:	Steel backbone chassis, glassfiber body
Suspension:	Front: independent, wishbones and coil springs, anti-roll bar
	Rear: independent, Chapman strut, lower wishbones and coil springs
Brakes:	Hydraulically operated discs on all four wheels
Wheels/tires:	Center-lock pressed-steel disc wheels
Top speed:	118mph (190km/h)
Acceleration:	0-60mph (97km/h): approx. 7.6sec

Opposite below: *The Lotus twin-cam engine which powered the Lotus-Cortina also went into this, the Elan.*

1960-69:
The Age
of the
Supercar

Previous page: The Lamborghini Miura was
one of a new breed of mid-engined supercars.

Below: Never intended as a road car, the
Ferrari 250/275LM series won at Le Mans
in 1965.

Sports car racing was invented in the 1920s to provide a class of competition that was cheaper than the rarefied world of Grand Prix racing and at the same time more relevant to the average motorist. To start with, the cars racing in sports car events were roadgoing production models, or at least their close relations, but by the end of the 1950s sports car racing had developed into a highly specialized form of motor sport. In the mid-1950s cars racing at the premier international sports car event, the Le Mans 24-hour race, had often been driven to the circuit. By the mid-1960s few of the entries were strictly road legal.

The customer looking for the ultimate sports car for road use had a dilemma. The racing 'GT' cars were no longer appropriate for the road, and in any case were built in small numbers for racing teams, so even if you did want to run one on the road, you couldn't get hold of one to buy. The road cars that were available, good though some of them undoubtedly were, didn't have the ultimate performance and roadholding of the racing machines, nor their visual impact. There was a gap in the market for a whole new type of vehicle: the supercar.

Ferrari epitomized the sports-racing car manufacturers. The next step from its 250GT coupé had been the stunning 250GTO, built for the new World GT Championship of 1962. Beginning in 1960 engineer Giotto Bizzarrini had laid out the chassis – with old fashioned semi-elliptic springs at the back – and instead of entrusting it to Pininfarina to come up with a suitable body, as was normally the case, Bizzarrini had created a shape himself based on aerodynamic studies rather than mere styling. The 3.0-liter V12 engine was carried over from the Testa Rossa racing car, though the final three examples were fitted with a 4.0-liter engine based on the Superamerica unit.

Ferrari 250GTO

Manufacturer:	Ferrari (Maranello, Italy)
Production years:	1962-64
Engine location:	Front
Configuration:	V12
Bore x stroke:	73x58mm
Capacity:	2953cc
Valve operation:	Twin overhead cam per bank
Fuel system:	Six Weber carburetors
Power:	295bhp at 7400rpm
Gearbox:	Five-speed manual
Driven wheels:	Rear wheel drive
Chassis/body:	Tubular steel chassis, aluminum alloy body
Suspension:	Front: wishbones and coil springs Rear: Leaf springs, radius arms, Watt linkage
Brakes:	Hydraulically operated discs on all four wheels
Wheels/tires:	Center-lock wire wheels
Top speed:	185mph (298km/h)
Acceleration:	0-60mph (97km/h): 6.5sec

Right: Ferrari's stunning 250GTO was built
for GT racing.

Ferrari had embraced the mid-engined format with the 246 Formula 1 car, first seen at the Monaco GP in 1960. It retired with transmission failure – Monaco isn't the best track for the debut of a brand new transmission – but the subsequent 156 Grand Prix car with a 1.5-liter, 120-degree V6 took Phil Hill to the World Championship the following year, when both the 156 and 246 cars sported 'shark nose' front ends. Ferrari's racing sports cars went mid-engined in 1962 with the introduction of the 250P, followed by the 250/275LM series that would win at Le Mans in 1965. Even though a handful of these cars made it onto the road, they were intended only as competition machines: Maranello's road cars still retained front engines. From 1964 Ferrari's fastest roadgoing offering was the 275GTB, powered by a 3.3-liter V12 engine with 280bhp. A more luxury-orientated convertible, the 275GT Spyder, made do with 'only' 260bhp. In 1966 the GTB was upgraded with a four-cam engine producing 300bhp but the Ferraris retained their front-engined layout.

Above: Ferrari's fastest road cars were still front-engined: this is the 1965 275GTB.

Above: The 275GT Spyder was more comfortable and luxurious than the fastback 'berlinetta.'

Lamborghini takes on Ferrari

That four-cam engine was perhaps intended to keep Ferrari's road cars competitive with a new rival, Lamborghini, which had used four-cam V12s from its inception in 1963. Ferruccio Lamborghini had begun building agricultural tractors in 1949 and a decade later the company had done so well that Lamborghini was wealthy enough to purchase Italy's finest car – a Ferrari. But, the legend has it, Lamborghini decided that he could build a better car himself, the result being the 350GT, with a 3.5-liter four-cam V12 fed by no less than six Weber carburetors and generating around 360bhp.

For 1966 the engine was expanded to 3929cc in the 400GT, but the most significant news from Lamborghini that year was the announcement of the prototype for a new production model, the Miura. It was named after Don Eduardo Miura, a breeder of fighting bulls, as a result of Lamborghini's interest in bullfighting: he had been born under the sign of Taurus the bull, and had chosen a raging bull as the company's logo. Originally it had been conceived as a racing car, but the emphasis quickly switched to making the Miura an ultra-high-performance road car.

Above: *Lamborghini's Miura proved that the mid-engined layout was a successful formula for performance road cars.*

Lamborghini Miura P400

Manufacturer:	Lamborghini (Modena, Italy)
Production years:	1967-72
Engine location:	Mid-engined
Configuration:	V12
Bore x stroke:	82x62mm
Capacity:	3929cc
Valve operation:	Twin overhead cam per bank
Fuel system:	Four triple-choke Weber carburetors
Power:	350bhp at 7000rpm
Gearbox:	Five-speed manual
Driven wheels:	Rear wheel drive
Chassis/body:	Box-section steel chassis, aluminum panels
Suspension:	Front: wishbones and coil springs Rear: wishbones and coil springs
Brakes:	Hydraulically operated discs on all four wheels
Wheels/tires:	Center-lock alloy wheels
Top speed:	170mph (274km/h)
Acceleration:	0-60mph (97km/h): 6.3sec

It was designed by Gianpaolo Dallara, and carried its 3.9-liter V12 transversely, behind the driver, with the five-speed gearbox under the engine – a layout curiously similar to a Mini, though at the other end of the car. As if the technology wasn't enough, it was clothed in a dramatic coupé body from young Bertone designer Marcello Gandini. The Miura stood just over a meter tall, and within a simple overall shape Gandini had incorporated clever touches of individuality such as the skyward-facing headlamps (they swivelled forward for use) surrounded by 'eyelash' brake cooling ducts, the hidden door handles, and the 'venetian blind' let into the back of the car to cool the engine bay. As if its 350bhp was not enough, a 375bhp Miura S appeared in 1969 and a 385bhp Miura SV (with wider track, but no 'eyelash' air ducts) was built in 1971-72.

The Miura showed the way forward in two important respects. First, it was the final proof that the mid-engined layout was suited to high-performance road cars, following a few years after the pioneering mid-engined ATS of 1963 and before Ferrari's own mid-engined road car, the Dino 206GT that would be launched in 1967. The new Lamborghini highlighted that a new genre of road cars was emerging. Lamborghini did not race his products, and intended them only to be used as road cars even if they were faster than all but the fastest circuit racers – the Miura could hit 170mph (274km/h). The Miura and its ilk were the true progenitors of the roadgoing supercar, but the Lamborghini had been inspired by a car that was very much a racing machine.

In the mid-'50s Ford and Ferrari had been deep in negotiations which would have led to the formation of two new joint ventures, to be called Ford-Ferrari and Ferrari-Ford. Ford would control 90 percent of Ford-Ferrari, which would create fast, high-profile performance cars to improve Ford's image, while Ferrari-Ford would concentrate on motor racing and would be controlled by Enzo Ferrari. It took Ferrari quite a while to realize that the autonomy he demanded could never be achieved under the corporate umbrella of Ford, at which point he extricated

Above: Ferrari's first foray into mid-engined road cars was with the Dino 206 of 1965.

himself from the deal. He would later form an alliance with Italy's biggest car maker, Fiat. Ford, meanwhile, decided to play Ferrari at its own game – to compete at the top level of international motor sport. And win.

Ford and Le Mans

At the time, the American public's knowledge of motor sport was focused on the Indianapolis 500, and the NASCAR stock car series. International racing to Americans usually meant that curious street race round Monaco and the 24-hour affair at Le Mans. Early in the 1960s Ford chose to mount a challenge at the latter event. In Britain, Eric Broadley of racing car constructor Lola had just created a Ford-based mid-engined racing GT and Ford started by acquiring the rights to the car and Broadley's services to help develop it.

The Lola GT of 1963 became the Ford GT40 of 1964, so-called because it stood just 40 inches (1016mm) tall – so low that works racing cars later sported a 'Gurney bulge' in the roof to accommodate the helmet of lanky drivers, such as Dan Gurney. The car was developed and built at the new Ford Advanced Vehicles Operations factory in Slough, in the south of England, managed by former Aston Martin racing team boss (and later General Manager) John Wyer. The new sports car used the 4.2-liter Ford V8 engine that had been developed for Ford's 1963 Indy 500 program, based on the 289cu in Fairlane production engine and retaining the prosaic pushrod valve operation – though the racing version did benefit from a light-alloy cylinder block and heads. Tuned for long-distance racing on normal pump fuel, it produced about 350bhp. The unit was mounted longitudinally in front of a combined gearbox/final drive 'transaxle' between the rear wheels, with the V8's complex tubular exhaust pipes passing over the transaxle and rear suspension to exit in the center of the tail.

Above: The ATS 2500 of 1963 had pioneered the mid-engined layout for road cars, but it was not successful.

Below: When the Ford/Ferrari deal went sour, Ford determined to beat Ferrari in international motor sport. The GT40 was the car that did the job.

The car's early performances were not encouraging. The GT40 had been designed to achieve 210mph (338km/h) but at Le Mans practice in 1964 it could manage only 192mph (309km/h) on the Mulsanne straightaway. The problem was the elaborate ducting which routed air to cool the cockpit and engine: tests had suggested the drag caused by the ducting would absorb about 30bhp, but the real figure turned out to be over 70bhp. As if that wasn't bad enough, development drivers Roy Salvadori and Bruce McLaren complained of instability at high speed. Bodywork changes helped, but then unreliability intervened and both cars retired from the race with mechanical maladies.

Le Mans victory

Development of the car was moved to America, where a 7.0-liter MkII version was built, using the 427cu in engine that had been developed for the NASCAR Galaxies. More mechanical failures caused all four 1965 Le Mans entries to retire, but finally in 1966 Ford got what it wanted – victory in the Le Mans 24-hour race, the MkIIs finishing first, second, and third. In 1967 a very different MkIV Ford GT won the race, and then changing regulations made the original GT40 competitive again: John Wyer's JW Automotive team added another two Le Mans wins in 1968 and 1969.

The Slough factory's 'production' GT40s included cars for road use and, as such, the GT40 was probably the last true racing sports car to be usable on the road – at least until the revival of the GT class in sports car racing in the 1990s. About 130 GT40s were built, 35 of them supplied as road cars and seven more in 'MkIII' specification – an attempt to produce a more usable roadgoing GT40, with more luggage space, a central gearshift and the availability of left-hand drive. One of the MkIIIs went to the famous German conductor, Herbert von Karajan.

Ford GT40 MkIII

Manufacturer:	Ford Advanced Vehicle Operations (Slough, England)
Production years:	1966-68
Engine location:	Mid-engined
Configuration:	V8
Bore x stroke:	101.6x72.9mm
Capacity:	4736cc
Valve operation:	Pushrod overhead valve
Fuel system:	Holley four-choke carburetor
Power:	306bhp at 6000rpm
Gearbox:	Colotti four-speed manual
Driven wheels:	Rear wheel drive
Chassis/body:	Steel body tub with glassfiber panels
Suspension:	Front: wishbones, coil springs and anti-roll bar
	Rear: trailing arms, lower wishbones, transverse top link, coil springs and anti-roll bar
Brakes:	Hydraulically operated discs on all four wheels
Wheels/tires:	Center-lock wire wheels
Top speed:	160mph (258km/h)
Acceleration:	0-60mph (97km/h): 5.5sec

Above left: *A GT40 run by Alan Mann Racing stops for fuel and tires. The deep cut-outs at the front of the car are exit ducts for air from the front-mounted radiator.*

Left: *Early GT40s were beset by performance and reliability worries. The driver, standing to the right of the car, is Chris Amon.*

Ferrari 365GTB/4 Daytona

Manufacturer:	Ferrari (Maranello, Italy)
Production years:	1968-73
Engine location:	Front
Configuration:	V12
Bore x stroke:	81x71mm
Capacity:	4390cc
Valve operation:	Twin overhead cam per bank
Fuel system:	Six Weber carburetors
Power:	352bhp at 7500rpm
Gearbox:	Five-speed manual
Driven wheels:	Rear wheel drive
Chassis/body:	Tubular steel chassis, aluminum alloy body
Suspension:	Front: wishbones and coil springs
	Rear: wishbones and coil springs
Brakes:	Hydraulically operated discs on all four wheels
Wheels/tires:	Center-lock alloy wheels
Top speed:	174mph (280km/h)
Acceleration:	0-60mph (97km/h): 5.4sec

By the end of the decade the demands of racing at the highest levels were such that Ferrari, too, was drawing distinctions between its racing cars – which were all now mid-engined – and its ultra-fast road cars, which continued to follow a more conventional front-engined path. The fastest of these was the 365GTB/4, known by everyone except Ferrari themselves as the Daytona, which made its debut at the Paris Salon in 1968. Again it used a four-cam V12 engine mounted at the front and developing 352bhp from its 4.4-liters – enough to give the Daytona a top speed of 174mph (280km/h). Pininfarina's styling gave the Daytona a simplicity and elegance of line which contrasted with the more aggressive character of the Miura. To preserve this simplicity the headlamps were faired in behind plastic covers, but by the time the production version of the Daytona appeared the following year, concerns about the legality of the lights in some markets – particularly some American states – had seen them replaced by pop-up units.

The following year a 'Daytona spider' convertible was introduced, around 150 being made in a production run which lasted only until 1973. Most Daytonas were coupés, around 1200 being made, but in the classic car value boom of the 1980s the rare open versions commanded such a premium that several coupés were converted by coachbuilders.

The conventional front engine and rear-wheel-drive package that Ferrari continued to offer for its road cars was also the preferred layout for most other 1960s supercars. In Britain, Aston Martin had developed its DB4 of the late 1950s into the short-wheelbase DB4GT and lightweight DB4GT Zagato, which took on Ferrari's 250GT in sports car racing. On the road the DB4 evolved into the DB5, which was famously used by James Bond in the film *Goldfinger*, and then the DB6 models which had aerodynamic tweaks proven on Aston Martin's racing cars. The DBS revealed in 1967 was bigger, heavier, and as it was fitted with the same 3995cc twin-cam six as the DB6, it was inevitably slower. But Aston Martin had an answer.

Opposite above: *The ultimate front-engined Ferrari was the 365GTB/4, popularly known as the Daytona.*

Opposite below: *The open-top 365GTS/4 became so valuable in the 1980s that several GTBs were converted.*

Below: *Aston Martin's DB4GT Zagato: a shape that still influences modern Aston Martin styling.*

The Changing Face of Sports Car Racing

Sports car racing had been conceived as a cheaper alternative to Grands Prix, and one that could use cars which were more familiar to the everyday motorist. Post-war, sports car racing changed out of all recognition, practically severing any direct connection between roadgoing sports cars and motor sport.

The racing sports cars of the 1950s had started off as thinly disguised road cars, but became more and more specialized as the decade wore on. Jaguar used lightweight versions of its XK120 on the track, then the tubular-frame C-type, then the stressed-skin D-type. Though all these cars were built in a production form and available for sale, they

were clearly becoming less and less like the kind of car that could be usable on the road.

By the 1960s sports car racing had split into classes. 'GT racing' was for sports cars which were in low-volume production – like the Ferrari 250GT and Aston Martin DB4GT. 'Sports prototypes' were further removed from road cars, and by the mid-'60s they were mid-engined cars like the Ferrari 250LM, Ford GT40, and the stillborn Jaguar XJ13.

This was the last era of racing sports cars which could be used on the road. The next generation of racing sports cars – led by Porsche's 917 – were for track use only, and sports car racing would stay that way until

the revival of interest in GT racing in the 1990s, when cars like the McLaren F1, Jaguar XJ220, and Chrysler Viper would be battling for honors at Le Mans.

Above right: The stillborn Jaguar XJ13.

Aston Martin DBS V8

Manufacturer:	Aston Martin (Newport Pagnell, England)
Production years:	1969-72 (V8 1972-89)
Engine location:	Front
Configuration:	V8
Bore x stroke:	100x85mm
Capacity:	5340cc
Valve operation:	Twin overhead cam per bank
Fuel system:	Bosch mechanical fuel injection
Power:	Approximately 345bhp at 5000rpm
Gearbox:	Five-speed manual
Driven wheels:	Rear wheel drive
Chassis/body:	Steel platform, box-section body frame with aluminum alloy body
Suspension:	Front: wishbones, coil springs and anti-roll bar
	Rear: de Dion with coil springs and Watt linkage
Brakes:	Hydraulically operated discs on all four wheels
Wheels/tires:	Alloy wheels
Top speed:	160mph (257km/h)
Acceleration:	0-60mph (97km/h): 6.0sec

The DBS had been designed for a new V8 engine being developed by Polish engineer Tadek Marek. Early versions of the engine had been run at Le Mans in a pair of Lola GT cars and had failed early on, showing up significant weaknesses in the V8's design. A major rework was necessary, and that meant the DBS had to be introduced with its original six-cylinder engine, as work continued on the V8. The all-alloy 5.3-liter V8, with twin overhead camshafts per cylinder bank and fuel injection, was ready the following year and with it the Aston was good for 160mph (257km/h) or more with the right rear-axle ratio, and 100mph (161km/h) was achievable from rest in less than 14 seconds. This was Ferrari-style performance and the Aston had the important advantages of two rear seats and a much lower price, though the hand-made car from Newport Pagnell could hardly be considered cheap.

American V8s in Europe

British rivals to the Aston came from Jensen and Bristol. Jensen had used a 4.0-liter Austin engine in a bespoke chassis with an innovative glassfiber body to create the 541, and had then switched to American V8 power from Chrysler for the aggressive-looking CV8. The metal-bodied Interceptor followed in 1966. Bristol had already switched to Chrysler V8 power for the 407 of 1961, and in France the Facel Vega was another to use Chrysler's V8. Chevrolet power was used for the rare Gordon-Keeble. All these cars were luxury sedans with high performance rather than real sports cars.

The revival in popularity of the 'hybrid' European car with a big American engine had come about because of the horsepower race developing in the US. With more and more high-performance engines becoming available at moderate prices, it seemed sensible to use them in accomplished European chassis to create instant supercars. In Italy, Renzo Rivolta did just that, following up his first attempt at car manufacture – the 1950s' Isetta bubble car – with the Iso Rivolta of 1962, a

Above: Aston Martin's DB4, DB5, and DB6 models were available in closed and open form. This is a DB5.

Left: The Jensen Interceptor blended English quality and Italian style with robust American V8 power. A four-wheel-drive FF model was also available.

Above: Aston Martin road cars stepped up a gear with the introduction of the DBS V8.

Bertone-styled GT car with a 300bhp Chevrolet V8 in a chassis designed by Giotto Bizzarrini, who had designed the 250GTO for Ferrari. The following year a shortened Rivolta chassis was used to create the much more sporting Grifo. As more and more powerful V8s became available throughout the 1960s, the Grifo became quicker and quicker, ultimately being capable of 180mph (290km/h) or more when powered by a monster 7.4-liter Corvette engine.

Above: Another Euro-American hybrid, the Iso Rivolta.

Iso Grifo	
Manufacturer:	Iso (Italy)
Production years:	1963-74
Engine location:	Front
Configuration:	V8
Bore x stroke:	108x95mm
Capacity:	6998cc
Valve operation:	Pushrod overhead valve
Fuel system:	Four-barrel carburetor
Power:	390bhp at 5200rpm
Gearbox:	Five-speed manual
Driven wheels:	Rear wheel drive
Chassis/body:	Steel platform chassis, alloy body
Suspension:	Front: wishbones and coil springs
	Rear: de Dion, radius arms and coil springs
Brakes:	Hydraulically operated discs on all four wheels
Wheels/tires:	Center-lock wire wheels
Top speed:	171mph (275km/h)
Acceleration:	0-60mph (97km/h): 7.1sec

Above: AC's Ace was available with AC, Bristol, or tuned Ford engines – but a great deal more power was on the way. This example used a Ford Zephyr 6-cylinder tuned by Ruddspeed.

Shelby's Cobra

Of all the 1960s 'hybrids,' though, the most famous must be the AC Cobra, which had a convoluted development which began early in the 1950s with a sports-racing car constructed around a simple twin-tube chassis by John Tojeiro, with independent suspension at both ends using transverse leaf springs. One car was fitted with a Bristol engine by its owner, Cliff Davis, and it proved successful in club motor sport. It was acquired by Charles Hurlock of AC, to form the basis of AC's Ace sports car, which was announced in 1953. AC's own venerable straight-six was used in the first cars, but the Ace later became available with the Bristol 100D2 six or a tuned Ford Zephyr engine.

The man behind the Cobra was American racing driver Carroll Shelby, who suggested to AC that the Ace could make a good competition car with the addition of more power – and that the extra power required could come from one of Ford's compact V8s. Production began in 1962, AC building the chassis and bodies and shipping them to Shelby's California factory for the fitment of engines. The chassis was essentially carried over from the Ace, with its transverse leaf suspension and disc front brakes, and the body was very similar to the earlier car but incorporated widened wheel arches front and rear to cover fatter tires. The engine used was initially a 260cu in (4.2-liter) Fairlane V8, offering twice the output of the Ace's sixes. After the first 75 cars had been made, a 'Mark II' model was introduced with an even more powerful 289cu in (4.7-liter) engine. The simple chassis and light weight meant that acceleration was phenomenal for the day, and despite the open top and its poor aerodynamics the Cobra was good for 138mph (222km/h).

An even bigger engine was fitted to the Cobra in 1965 – the high-performance Ford 427cu in (7.0-liter) V8, developing about 400bhp. Major changes were needed to handle the power, and the Mark III Cobra was given a stiffer chassis with 4in (100mm) diameter main tubes, and independent suspension using coil springs and wishbones at both ends. Even wider arches covered Halibrand alloy wheels, replacing the traditional wire wheels on the earlier cars. AC, meanwhile, made their own derivatives using the better-behaved MkIII chassis and the milder 289 engine and called, simply, the AC 289. That was followed up by a more elegant machine using a longer version of the same chassis (designed with aid from the Ford computer in Dearborn) with Ford's 428cu in production engine and called, predictably, the AC 428. The 428, available in handsome drophead and fixed-head coupé forms, wanted to be an Aston Martin rival but couldn't really match the Newport Pagnell cars' handling: only 80 were made.

As Shelby had predicted, the Cobra was almost unbeatable in its class in sports car racing, though you had to be a hardy soul to take on a long-distance race in that drafty cockpit. For Le Mans a sleek coupé derivative was designed, by eye rather than through wind-tunnel testing, and this car took the GT Championship away from Ferrari in 1965 – much to the Italians' disgust. Shelby had managed to get the coupé approved for racing as a mere derivative of the Cobra, rather than the much-changed vehicle that, in reality, it was. Ferrari had pulled the same stunt with the GTO…

Faster Mustangs

Despite having his hands full with the Cobra, and overseeing the American end of the Ford GT40's development, Shelby still found time to get involved with the Sunbeam Tiger and create a high-performance version of the Ford Mustang, the GT-350. The 350bhp GT-350R was the racing version, but there was also a slightly more manageable GT-350S street machine. Early cars were

AC Shelby Cobra 289

Manufacturer:	AC (Thames Ditton, England)/Shelby American (Los Angeles, USA)
Production years:	1963-65 (other models 1962-68; 1983 on)
Engine location:	Front
Configuration:	V8
Bore x stroke:	101x72mm
Capacity:	4735cc
Valve operation:	Pushrod overhead valve
Fuel system:	Four-barrel carburetor
Power:	300bhp at 5700rpm
Gearbox:	Four-speed manual
Driven wheels:	Rear wheel drive
Chassis/body:	Tubular steel chassis, aluminum body
Suspension:	Front: wishbones and transverse leaf spring
	Rear: wishbones and transverse leaf spring
Brakes:	Hydraulically operated discs on all four wheels
Wheels/tires:	Center-lock wire wheels
Top speed:	138mph (222km/h)
Acceleration:	0-60mph (97km/h): 5.6sec

Above left: The Cobra had Ford V8 power and this later 427 model also had a redesigned chassis.

Above: Racing driver and engineer Carroll Shelby in one of the first Cobras.

Left: The Cobra was very effective in 1960s sports car racing. Dan Gurney is the driver.

only available in white, with twin blue stripes over the hood and roof, but by 1966 the range of colors had broadened slightly, and the cars had gained air ducts in front of the rear wheels and small quarter windows in place of the vents in the rear pillars. That year almost 1000 GT-350s were available to hire through Hertz: more than one came back after a weekend on hire with the remains of racing numbers visible on the doors, and it is reputed that one car was returned with a 'cooking' straight-six under the hood after a Mustang owner tried a late-night engine swap.

The GT-350 had been conceived as a rival to the Corvette in Sports Car Club of America (SCCA) races. By now the Corvette had entered its third generation, a completely new car having been introduced in 1962. A ladder chassis had replaced the old cruciform frame and the Corvette now sported independent suspension at the back, with a transverse leaf spring and fixed-length driveshafts. But it wasn't all good news: to keep a lid on developments costs, the front suspension and steering was carried over, as were the all-round drum brakes. Commonly the Corvette came with a 327cu in (5.3 liter) engine with a claimed 300bhp, though tuned versions were said to pump out 360bhp. For most people, though, the biggest news was the Corvette's new styling, by Larry Shinoda and Chevrolet design chief Bill Mitchell and based on Mitchell's 'Sting Ray' racing car of a couple of years earlier. The production Corvette Sting Ray had pop-up headlamps, and there was a fixed-head coupé version with a distinctive split rear window.

Below: *For Le Mans Shelby created this 'Cobra coupé' which was in reality a very different car.*

American Muscle

Chrysler started it all in 1955 with the 300, a 140mph (225km/h) leviathan with a claimed 300bhp. A decade later Ford was selling the Mustang 'pony cars' as fast as it could make them, with engines ranging from docile sixes to a 4.7-liter V8 which offered 120mph (193km/h) performance – and at prices competitive with MGs and Triumphs. At the same time, the big manufacturers were vying for supremacy in the NASCAR stock car championship, leading to the development of production-based engines with well over 500bhp.

The result was the 'muscle car,' using street versions of the big racing V8s. By the

end of the 1960s those V8s were claiming to develop more than 400bhp – though the SAE testing standards in use gave plenty of scope for exaggeration and the car makers took full advantage. Marques like Aston Martin, unwilling to lie about their thoroughbred engines in order to compete, eventually decided to keep their power outputs to themselves.

Power outputs reached their peak around 1968, when Ford introduced its famous racing 427cu in V8 to the Mustang, and Dodge announced its new Charger, with the option of 426cu in (6981cc) Hemi power. In this form it was good for a 0-60mph (97km/h) time of 4.8 seconds, with the standing quarter mile despatched in 13.5 seconds at a terminal speed of 105mph (169km/h). Handling wasn't a strong suit, but in a straight line these cars were quick...

In 1969 Dodge revealed a Charger Daytona, with droop snoot front end and enormous rear wing which improved the Charger's aerodynamic efficiency. Dodge

made 500 to ensure eligibility for NASCAR racing, where the improvement in aerodynamic drag and reduction of rear-end lift were vital on the fast oval circuits.

But the writing was on the wall for the muscle car. In 1968 insurance premiums for young drivers in fast cars had hit $1000, and they would double by 1970 – the same year that the Clean Air Bill would be passed by Congress, forcing American manufacturers to reduce their cars' harmful exhaust emissions. Public opinion was turning against the muscle cars, and as oil prices rose into the early 1970s the big V8s would start to be viewed as profligate and anti-social.

Above left: American manufacturers battled it out in the NASCAR series in the 1960s.

Top right: One of the 'muscle cars' that emerged from the 1960s horsepower race was the Dodge Charger.

The horsepower race

On the road the Corvette's handling benefited enormously from the independent rear suspension, as did traction: now it was much harder to get the car to squander its power away from a standing start or in a tight corner by spinning a driving wheel. On the track the better chassis helped, but now in some events the Corvettes were up against Shelby's lightweight Cobras, and struggled to compete. Fuel injection was introduced to improve power, the 'fuelie' 327 supposedly delivering 375bhp. Disc front brakes followed in 1965, the same year that a 396cu in (6489cc) engine option, the L78, was made available. But with the advent of the 427 Cobra, Zora Arkus-Duntov and his Corvette engineers were in danger of being left behind.

Fortunately, Chevrolet had its own big-block 427cu in (6997cc) engine, which had first been seen at the Daytona 500 stock car race in January 1963. Internally it was known as the L72, but early on it acquired the nickname of 'porcupine head,' because of the odd angles of the valve stems that were revealed when the rocker covers were removed. With the L72 engine the Corvette could record phenomenal standing start acceleration times: 60mph (97km/h) came up in under five seconds, and 100mph (161km/h) in a little over 10. And that was just the start.

As the 'muscle car' phenomenon (see 'American Muscle' above) gathered speed, the Corvette kept pace. Numerous options were available, from heavy-duty close-ratio gearboxes and

Above: Not content with the Cobra and Tiger, Carroll Shelby also reworked the Mustang as a racing car and fast road car.

Chevrolet Corvette L71

Manufacturer:	General Motors (St Louis, USA)
Production years:	1967 (other Corvette models 1953–today)
Engine location:	Front
Configuration:	V8
Bore x stroke:	108x97.8mm
Capacity:	6997cc
Valve operation:	Pushrod overhead valve
Fuel system:	Three two-barrel carburetors
Power:	435bhp at 6400rpm
Gearbox:	Five-speed manual
Driven wheels:	Rear wheel drive
Chassis/body:	Steel chassis, glassfiber body
Suspension:	Front: wishbones and coil springs
	Rear: transverse leaf spring
Brakes:	Hydraulically operated discs on all four wheels
Wheels/tires:	Center-lock alloy wheels
Top speed:	150mph (241km/h)
Acceleration:	0-60mph (97km/h): 5.5sec

Positraction limited-slip differentials to racing exhausts and deletion of the heater to save weight. The L71 engine, a 427cu in (6997cc) V8 with three two-barrel carbs, offered a claimed 435bhp, while option L89 gave the buyer aluminum cylinder heads. At the top of the tree for 1967 was the L88, a high-compression 427 which, in a bizarre twist to the 1960s horsepower race, was touted at just 430bhp when in reality it had a gross output nearer 560bhp. The deliberate deception – coupled with a near-$1000 price premium – meant it attracted only a handful of customers, who got near enough a roadgoing racing car.

Bill Mitchell had unveiled a show car called Mako Shark II in 1965 which demonstrated the future styling for the Corvette. That replacement model had been intended for the 1966 season, and then for 1967, and it would finally appear in time for 1968. Under the sleek new skin the engineering was much as before, though a new ZL1 aluminum alloy version of the 427 was cataloged. Rumors told of a gross output as high as 585bhp, but to keep it away from uninformed drivers it was claimed to deliver just 430bhp, and given an option price of $3000. Later a longer-stroke 454cu in (7440cc) engine was cataloged, an all-aluminum LS7 version being conservatively rated at 460bhp – but none was seriously offered for sale.

By then the horsepower race was all but over. The 1960s had seen the emergence of the supercar as an ultra-fast road car in its own right, and the last of the roadgoing versions of racing machinery. American power had arrived with its domestic 'muscle cars,' but worries over insurance premiums, emissions, and fuel economy were forcing the big US car makers to tone down their products. The days of the Euro-American hybrids utilizing those big V8s would inevitably be numbered too. The sports cars of the 1970s would have to be safer, quieter, cleaner, and more fuel-efficient than any that had gone before them. But could they be as much fun?

Above: Corvettes were available as closed coupés or open roadsters. This is a 1963 Stingray 'small block' 5.3 liter V8.

Left: The split-window Corvette was one of the most distinctive shapes of the 1960s.

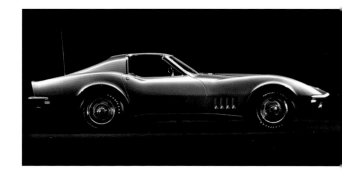

Above: The 'Mako Shark' shape Corvette took over in 1968.

1970s: Safe at Any Speed

Previous page: Maserati's V8-engined Bora was one of the fastest cars of the 1970s.

Above: Porsche's 911 Targa retained a fixed roll-over bar for added safety.

Below right: The VW-Porsche 914 was intended to be a cheaper route to Porsche ownership.

VW-Porsche 914/6	
Manufacturer:	Volkswagen/Porsche (Germany)
Production years:	1969-72 (914/4 1969-76)
Engine location:	Mid-engined
Configuration:	Flat six-cylinder
Bore x stroke:	80x66mm
Capacity:	1991cc
Valve operation:	Single overhead cam per bank
Fuel system:	Two Weber triple-choke carburetors
Power:	110bhp at 5800rpm
Gearbox:	Five-speed manual
Driven wheels:	Rear wheel drive
Chassis/body:	Unitary steel body
Suspension:	Front: struts and torsion bars Rear: semi-trailing arms, coil and rubber springs
Brakes:	Hydraulically operated discs on all four wheels, ventilated at front
Wheels/tires:	Alloy wheels
Top speed:	126mph (202km/h)
Acceleration:	0-60mph (97km/h): 8.8sec

Sports car manufacturers had enjoyed boom years in the 1960s. Not since the 1930s had there been so many sports cars from so many different manufacturers, exhibiting such a variety of type, price, engineering, and style. From the fastest Ferrari and iconic E-type Jaguar down to the MG Midget and Fiat 850 Spider, there was a sports car to suit everyone. But the optimism of the 1960s would become the harsh reality of the 1970s, and the sports car would have to fight for its survival.

Air quality was beginning to be taken seriously by the environmental lobby, and from the mid-1960s emissions regulations were progressively tightened, strangling performance engines and giving manufacturers headaches as they sought to comply with rules that differed from state to state. Rising insurance costs dealt another blow to performance cars of all sorts, and the Yom Kippur war of 1973 in the Middle East strangled supplies of oil to the western world, resulting in gas shortages and high prices.

Safety first

America had always been a major market for sports car manufacturers, and the good weather enjoyed by some of the more affluent states – notably California – made them an ideal market for roadsters. But in the USA the mood was changing, and the same nation that had applauded the excess of the muscle cars now questioned the pursuit of performance. Ralph Nader's book *Unsafe at Any Speed* railed against what he saw as the designed-in inadequacies of American cars, and suddenly public opinion was more in favor of safety than straight-line speed. The National Highway Safety Administration decreed that cars sold in America would soon have to be equipped with a 'passive restraint' to avoid occupants being thrown forward during a collision, and would have to pass stringent roll-over tests. By the early 1970s it seemed almost certain that these new American rules would ban open cars altogether on the grounds that they performed poorly in roll-over accidents. They were tough times for sports car makers.

Sports car buyers were also a changing breed. Racing cars had become so specialized that there was now little connection between the racing machines and the roadgoing sports cars. Sporting road cars weren't bought for competition, they were bought for their style and the fun of driving a responsive car. While performance and handling were still vitally important, sports car buyers now needed more comfort and convenience, and were less inclined to put up with the inevitable hardships of running a race-spec car on the road. Roadsters were declining in popularity – a trend that had begun in the 1950s and gathered momentum in the 1960s, with the popularity of the fixed-head E-type, Alfas, Porsches, and Lotuses, not to mention the MGA coupé and MGB GT. Compromises were sought.

When Porsche added an open 911 to the range in 1965 to fill the gap left when 356 production ended, the car was not a 356-style 'Speedster,' but instead featured a substantial fixed roll-over hoop with a removable roof section. Originally this 'Targa' top (named after the Targa Florio road race) also had a drop-down rear window, but this was quickly changed to a fixed, wrap-around rear screen. The effect was similar to the 'Surrey top' Triumphs, which were said to have inspired the Targa, though the Porsche offered much better roll-over protection.

A similar roof arrangement found its way onto another Porsche destined for the American market, which was designed as a joint venture between Porsche and Volkswagen. The VW-Porsche 914 was intended to be a lower-cost alternative to the 911, with a mid-mounted engine inside a cleanly-styled sports car for two. Two versions were available when the car was introduced in 1969: the 914/4, with a Volkswagen 411E engine (a fuel-injected, air-cooled flat four) and the 914/6 with a 2.0-liter 911 engine.

Porsche had hoped that the economies of scale created by production of the high-volume Volkswagen-engined car would allow their Porsche-engined car to be priced lower, giving Volkswagen a sporty up-range model and Porsche a sub-911 entry level car. In the event the bodies (built by Karmann for Volkswagen) turned out to cost even more than the 911 bodies, which made the 914/6 uncomfortably close to the 911 in price. It was dropped after just three years, while the Volkswagen version soldiered on until 1976 – latterly with Volkswagen's own

Above: Porsche intended to replace the 911 with water-cooled cars like the front-engined 928.

Right: *Carrera RS – the ultimate 911.*

Below: *Porsche turned to turbocharging with the 930, better known as the 911 Turbo.*

Porsche 911 Turbo 3.3	
Manufacturer:	Porsche (Germany)
Production years:	1978-88
Engine location:	Rear
Configuration:	Flat six-cylinder
Bore x stroke:	97x74.4mm
Capacity:	3299cc
Valve operation:	Single overhead cam per bank
Fuel system:	Bosch K-Jetronic fuel injection
Power:	300bhp at 5500rpm
Gearbox:	Four-speed manual (five-speed from 1989)
Driven wheels:	Rear wheel drive
Chassis/body:	Unitary steel body
Suspension:	Front: independent, struts, torsion bars and anti-roll bar
	Rear: independent, semi-trailing arms, torsion bars and anti-roll bar
Brakes:	Hydraulically operated ventilated discs on all four wheels
Wheels/tires:	Alloy wheels 7x16in front, 8x16in rear. 205/55x16 front, 225/50x15 rear tires
Top speed:	160mph (257km/h)
Acceleration:	0-60mph (97km/h): 5.3sec

2.0-liter engine. Porsche had built 11 prototypes of a 916 version, with a fixed roof and the 190bhp flat-six engine out of the 911S, and these demonstrated the potential of the mid-engined chassis. But the 916 never reached production – customers would have been few and far between, as it would have cost more than a 911 – and none of the derivatives of the 914 ever achieved the success that, in some ways, the car deserved.

It was effectively replaced in 1976 by another new Porsche, and another a joint venture with Volkswagen. Built at the old NSU factory at Neckarsulm, the 924 had been commissioned by Volkswagen but ended up in production under the Porsche name, using a water-cooled overhead-cam engine of Audi origin, mounted well back in the nose of the car and canted over to the left. The driveline was unusual, with a transaxle layout where the gearbox sat at the back of the car in unit with the final drive. This helped to balance out the mass of the engine to improve the handling balance, but the bulky transmission at the back of the car resulted in a relatively shallow luggage area. A wrap-around rear window lifted for access. Two tiny rear seats were just about suitable for accommodating children.

The 924's Volkswagen ancestry made it less of a thoroughbred than many expected of Porsche, and there were grumblings about the van engine under the hood, as the 924 unit was closely related to the 2.0-liter slogger in the VW LT series. In Porsche form, however, it generated 125bhp and made the 924 decently quick as well as pleasantly frugal, qualities which combined with typical Porsche build quality to generate a sizable following for the new sports car.

Porsche goes V8

A year after the 924's debut Porsche introduced another front-engined coupé with a water-cooled engine and transaxle drivetrain, but unlike the joint-venture 924, the 928 was all Porsche. A brand new V8 engine sat under the hood and the 928 had a uniquely distinctive, curvaceous body with its bumpers hidden behind deformable plastic nose and tail sections. Inside, the cocooning interior was distinctive too, with standard upholstery in an 'op art' checkerboard pattern that polarized opinion. There was no argument about performance, however: the 4474cc V8 delivered 240bhp and propelled the 928 to more than 140mph (225km/h), the optional automatic transmission doing little to blunt the performance.

Quick as it was, the 928 was not Porsche's fastest offering of the 1970s. The 911 was still in production, and had been continually developed. In 1971 the stroke of the flat-six engine had been increased from 66mm to 70.4mm, the resulting 2341cc engine being described as a '2.4-liter,' perhaps to make the additional 146cc seem more significant. No such subterfuge was necessary in 1973 for the introduction of the Carrera RS, with a big-bore 2687cc engine and 210bhp. Performance was further aided by a lightweight body combining thinner metal with plastic and alloy components, thinner glass, and the deletion of the rear seats, and the combination of power and lightness made the Carrera RS one of the fastest 911s of the 1970s. Not quite *the* fastest, though.

Above *Morgan used Rover's V8 engine in its rapid Plus 8.*

Below left: *Another car to employ the Rover V8 was MG's MGB GT V8.*

Morgan Plus 8	
Manufacturer:	Morgan (Malvern, England)
Production years:	1968-2003
Engine location:	Front
Configuration:	V8
Bore x stroke:	88.9x71.1mm
Capacity:	3528cc
Valve operation:	Pushrod overhead valve
Fuel system:	Twin SU carburetors
Power:	168bhp at 5200rpm
Gearbox:	Four-speed manual (later five-speed)
Driven wheels:	Rear wheel drive
Chassis/body:	Steel ladder chassis, wood-frame body with aluminum body panels
Suspension:	Front: sliding pillar
	Rear: leaf-sprung live rear axle
Brakes:	Hydraulically operated discs on all four wheels, servo assisted
Wheels/tires:	5.5x15in alloy wheels, 185x15 tires
Top speed:	125mph (201km/h)
Acceleration:	0-60mph (97km/h): 6.7sec

Right: By 1978 when this car was made, MGs wore ugly black bumpers in response to new American legislation.

MGB GT V8

Manufacturer:	MG (Abingdon, England)
Production years:	1973-76
Engine location:	Front
Configuration:	V8
Bore x stroke:	88.9x71.1mm
Capacity:	3528cc
Valve operation:	Pushrod overhead valve
Fuel system:	Twin Stromberg carburetors
Power:	137bhp at 5000rpm
Gearbox:	Four-speed manual
Driven wheels:	Rear wheel drive
Chassis/body:	Unitary steel body
Suspension:	Front: wishbones and coil springs
	Rear: leaf-sprung live axle
Brakes:	Hydraulically operated, disc front, drum rear, servo assisted
Wheels/tires:	Steel/alloy wheels
Top speed:	125mph (201km/h)
Acceleration:	0-60mph (97km/h): 8.0sec

Below: The final incarnation of the E-type was fitted with a new V12 engine, but performance was no better than the first E-types of 1961.

Porsche had been developing turbochargers since 1969, and had used them with success in the fearsome 1000bhp racing cars for the Can-Am series. The basic principle was similar to the superchargers used by Bentley and others in the 1920s: rather than allow the engine to suck in as much air and fuel as it could, a pump was provided to blow air/fuel mixture into the cylinders under pressure. The supercharger was directly driven from the engine by belt or geartrain; by contrast the turbocharger had a turbine wheel powered by the exhaust gases, which was connected to a compressor to pressurize the intake charge. The experience Porsche gained with turbochargers led them to believe that a turbo engine could combine a high power output with a good emissions performance, and at the same time use less fuel when driven gently. The turbo engine generated little boost at low revs and closed throttle, but a great deal at wide throttle openings and high engine speeds, giving high performance when needed and good economy at part-throttle.

Turbos on the road

In 1974 an experimental racing 911 Carrera had used a 2.1-liter turbo engine, the odd capacity a result of the displacement multiplier of 1.4 introduced by the regulators – a turbo engine was treated as having a capacity 1.4 times its true displacement, so 2.1-liter turbo was about the largest eligible for a nominal '3.0-liter' class. For road use Porsche used the 3.0-liter capacity of the latest Carrera as a basis, to produce a turbo engine developing around 260bhp and give the 911 true supercar performance. With the bore widened out to 97mm in 1978 for a capacity of 3299cc and an intercooler to lower the intake charge temperatures and improve volumetric efficiency, Porsche created the definitive 3.3-liter Turbo with upward of 300bhp.

The 911 would continue into the 1980s with yet more development, even though the front-engined, water-cooled 928 series had been mooted as a replacement for the ageing rear-engined car. What Porsche had not yet understood was that the 911 was the embodiment of what Porsche customers wanted, even with its obvious limitations in handling, packaging, and convenience factors. Nothing else – however well engineered – could take its place.

One sports car company that did understand that philosophy was the tiny firm of Morgan, which had been producing much the same car since the 1930s, with 911-like regular development. Though Morgan's Plus 4 and 4/4 models looked old fashioned, they continued to keep abreast of modern technology where, Morgan felt, it was most required – so the separate chassis, wood-frame body, and 1930s body style might have been retained but the cars sported such refinements as modern engines and disc brakes.

Above: *The last E-types were built in 1975.*

Below: *Jaguar replaced the E-type with the XJ-S, more of a luxurious GT than a true sports car.*

Above: Like the MGB, the Midget lost its chrome bumpers in the 1970s. This picture shows a 1969 model.

Below: The TR6 was a classic old-school roadster, but its TR7 replacement was very different.

Rover V8 power

Morgan entered a whole new performance zone with the Plus 8 in 1968. Essentially this 'new' car was the old Morgan body and chassis with a new engine – the light-alloy 3.5-liter Rover V8 that had recently made its debut in Rover's P5 and P6 sedans. Developed from a General Motors design, the all-alloy V8 was light in weight, and delivered a reliable 150bhp or more, depending on its state of tune. In the 17cwt (864kg) Morgan that translated into a 0-60mph (97km/h) time well under 7.0 seconds, and despite vintage-style aerodynamics the Morgan was capable of well over 120mph (193km/h). Only the vintage-style flexible chassis and lively rear axle marred the Morgan's roadability, though this was all part of what the road testers at *Motor* called the car's 'vintage individuality.'

MG made a more convincing modern sports car using the same engine, both MG and Rover now being part of the same British Leyland combine. The idea of a V8-powered MGB had originally come from Ken Costello, whose private conversions were popular and highly regarded despite a conversion cost that added 60 percent to the price of a new MGB. Though Costello happily converted both MGB roadsters and GTs, the 'official' V8 car that followed in 1973 was only ever a GT because Leyland argued that the roadster shell wasn't stiff enough to handle the power of the V8 engine. The V8 'B also used the detuned Range Rover version with just 137bhp rather than the Rover passenger car unit rated at 160bhp, possibly due to some political maneuvering within British Leyland. Certainly Abingdon struggled to get a good supply of engines – which were used for several other Leyland products – and MGB GT V8 production only reached 2591 cars in four years. It was a missed opportunity for MG and Leyland, because the MGB GT V8 was a characterful package with effortless performance.

By the time the final MGB GT V8 models were built in 1976, all the MGBs and Midgets had acquired ugly black polyurethane-faced bumpers, MG's response to new American legislation

Datsun 240Z	
Manufacturer:	Nissan (Japan)
Production years:	1969-74
Engine location:	Front
Configuration:	In-line four-cylinder
Bore x stroke:	83x73.7mm
Capacity:	2393cc
Valve operation:	Single overhead cam
Fuel system:	Twin SU carburetors
Power:	150bhp at 5600rpm
Gearbox:	Five-speed manual
Driven wheels:	Rear wheel drive
Chassis/body:	Unitary steel body
Suspension:	Front: MacPherson struts
	Rear: MacPherson struts
Brakes:	Hydraulically operated, disc front, drum rear, servo assisted
Wheels/tires:	4.5x14in steel wheels, 175x14 tires
Top speed:	125mph (201km/h)
Acceleration:	0-60mph (97km/h): 8.3sec

prompted by the insurance industry. This decreed that all cars had to be able to sustain a 5mph (8km/h) impact without permanent damage to the car's bodywork or lights, and it spelled the end for the traditional chrome-plated steel bumpers that practically all cars had carried up to that point. On the MGB the first step had been to fit huge black rubber over-riders, known as the 'Sabrina' type because it reminded Abingdon of a well-endowed British show-biz star of the 1950s. The regulations for 1974 were more stringent, and MG responded with massive steel bumpers with polyurethane covers, with the car's ride height raised to bring the bumpers up to the statutory minimum level. The fact that raising the ride height and thus the center of gravity ruined the MG sports cars' handling – and thus made them less safe rather than more – seems not to have given the rule makers any cause for concern…

Changing safety regulations also had an impact on Jaguar, which was now part of the British Leyland empire alongside MG. The E-type had been developed and improved with a torquier 4.2-liter engine and the option of a longer 2+2 body, but it was getting old. A replacement, known at the time as the 'XK-F' was being designed, but as the safety goalposts kept moving the car's gestation took longer and longer – not helped by the extra red-tape associated with the labyrinthine British Leyland management structure. While work continued on the XK-F, Jaguar revised the E-type – a much easier and quicker process since it would only need to survive for a few years, whereas XK-F had to be capable of a long life in order to recoup its development costs. A stillborn mid-engined racer, the XJ13, had carried a four-cam V12 which was essentially two XK sixes mounted at 60 degrees to each other with a common crankshaft; now a road-car V12 with a single overhead camshaft on each bank of cylinders was being readied for production, and it would boost the E-type's final years.

The 5343cc V12 was designed by Walter Hassan, who had been responsible for the successful Coventry-Climax Grand Prix engines in the 1960s, and Harry Mundy who had penned the light-alloy cylinder head for Lotus' Twin Cam engine. Fuel injection was planned but in E-type form the engine carried Zenith-Stromberg carburetors, and thanks to its all-alloy construction it

Above left: Datsun's 240Z was Japan's answer to the Austin-Healey 3000 – but it was only available in coupé form.

Below: By the 1980s the Datsun Z cars had grown heavier and more comfortable – they were no longer true sports cars. This example is a Datsun 280 ZX.

Right: The TR7 was designed as a fixed-roof coupé because of worries that convertibles would be outlawed by new US safety rules.

Triumph TR7

Manufacturer:	Triumph (Coventry, England)
Production years:	1975-82
Engine location:	Front
Configuration:	In-line four-cylinder
Bore x stroke:	90.3x78mm
Capacity:	1998cc
Valve operation:	Single overhead cam
Fuel system:	Twin SU carburetors
Power:	105bhp at 5500rpm
Gearbox:	Four-speed manual (later five-speed)
Driven wheels:	Rear wheel drive
Chassis/body:	Unitary steel body
Suspension:	Front: MacPherson struts and anti-roll bar
	Rear: coil-sprung live-axle with trailing arms and anti-roll bar
Brakes:	Hydraulically operated, disc front, drum rear, servo assisted
Wheels/tires:	5.5x13in steel or alloy wheels, 175/70x13 tires
Top speed:	110mph (177km/h)
Acceleration:	0-60mph (97km/h): 9.5sec

weighed only 80lb (36.3kg) more than the XK six. The benefits were turbine-like smoothness, remarkable flexibility and prodigious mid-range torque. But the V12 E-type was no quicker than the Series 1 six-cylinder car had been way back in 1961, and in some quarters the E-type was now seen as middle-aged, overweight, and past its best. Consequently Jaguar's new car couldn't come soon enough.

It came in 1975, the XK-F project having spawned the XJ-S production car using the platform from the XJ sedan in modified form. Again the V12 engine was employed, now with Bosch fuel injection releasing the full 285bhp, and there was a choice of manual and automatic gearboxes – most customers opting for the latter. A refined and luxurious GT car rather than a true sports car, the XJ-S was a fixed-head with 2+2 seating and controversial looks; Sir William Lyons no longer had the final word on styling at Leyland-owned Jaguar. One observer unkindly suggested that the XJ-S looked as if the front, middle, and rear had been designed by three different people – who had never met. Though the XJ-S sold steadily throughout the latter half of the '70s there was always the feeling that it should have been doing better. Certainly when the producers of the eagerly-awaited TV program *The Return of the Saint* asked for the loan of a white XJ-S, Jaguar responded rather more positively than it had in the 1960s.

Right: Leyland attempted to improve the TR7's image by rallying V8-powered cars, which would eventually reach production as the TR8.

New cars and old

Leyland's other sports car brand, Triumph, mixed new products and old favorites throughout the 1970s. The Spitfire soldiered on with some styling updates and a 1493cc engine, which MG enthusiasts were horrified to discover under the hood of the revised 'rubber bumper' MG Midget in 1974. US emissions regulations forced British Leyland to clean up the Midget and Spitfire engines if they wanted to keep selling the cars in the United States, and it was much cheaper to re-engineer one engine for both cars than to work on two different engines. But both small sports cars, that seemed so right and so clever in the early 1960s, were outclassed a decade later. They still sold, though, as there were few new roadsters around to challenge them and they still had plenty of appeal.

In the next class up Triumph had the fuel-injected TR6, which had assumed the mantle of the traditional British sports car after the demise of the big Austin-Healey in 1967 and the failure of the MGC to capture the public's imagination. Like the Spitfire, the TR6 was looking increasingly old-fashioned and, more importantly, the lusty straight-six no longer gave it a performance advantage over its competitors. There were new competitors, too, the most significant of which was Datsun's 240Z coupé – itself powered by a lusty straight six, and with eye-catching styling

Above: The Jensen-Healey and this, the Jensen GT developed from it, failed to save Jensen from receivership.

Jensen-Healey	
Manufacturer:	Jensen (West Bromwich, England)
Production years:	1972-75
Engine location:	Front
Configuration:	In-line four-cylinder
Bore x stroke:	95.2x62.9mm
Capacity:	1973cc
Valve operation:	Twin overhead cam, 16 valves
Fuel system:	Twin Dellorto carburetors
Power:	140bhp at 6500rpm
Gearbox:	Four-speed manual
Driven wheels:	Rear wheel drive
Chassis/body:	Unitary steel body
Suspension:	Front: wishbones and coil springs
	Rear: coil-sprung live axle with
	four links
Brakes:	Hydraulically operated, disc front,
	drum rear, servo assisted
Wheels/tires:	5.5x13in alloy wheels, 185/70x13
	tires
Top speed:	121mph (195km/h)
Acceleration:	0-60mph (97km/h): 7.8sec

Left: The wedge-shaped Lotus Elite offered the handling and performance of a sports car with accommodation for four people.

Right: This modified Lotus Esprit featured in the James Bond film The Spy Who Loved Me.

Lotus Esprit	
Manufacturer:	Lotus (Hethel, England)
Production years:	1975-99
Engine location:	Mid-engined
Configuration:	In-line four-cylinder
Bore x stroke:	95.2x62.9mm
Capacity:	1973cc
Valve operation:	Twin overhead cam, 16 valves
Fuel system:	Twin Dellorto carburetors
Power:	160bhp at 6200rpm
Gearbox:	Five-speed manual
Driven wheels:	Rear wheel drive
Chassis/body:	Steel backbone chassis, glassfiber body
Suspension:	Front: wishbones, coil springs and anti-roll bar
	Rear: Semi-trailing arms, transverse links and coil springs
Brakes:	Hydraulically operated discs on all four wheels
Wheels/tires:	6x14 in front, 7x14in rear alloy wheels. 205/70x14in front, 205/60x14 rear tires
Top speed:	135mph (217km/h)
Acceleration:	0-60mph (97km/h): 7.5sec

from Count Albrecht von Goertz, who had penned BMW's 507 a decade earlier. Fortunately for Datsun the 'Z car' was far more successful than the BMW, offering an attractive blend of qualities. There was TR6-style performance and a proper sports car soundtrack, but unlike the sometimes slapdash fit and finish of the British sports cars, the Datsun gave buyers Japanese reliability and efficiency. It was only available in fixed-head form, once again demonstrating that sports car makers and buyers were turning away from traditional roadsters.

The 260Z followed in 1974, bringing a new 2+2 option for sports car buyers with young families and cementing the Z cars' place as the world's favorite sports car. The 280ZX of 1978 offered still more convenience and comfort, but in a package which had grown and softened to the point where its status as a sports car started to be questioned. Triumph now had an opportunity to reassert itself as a major player in the budget sports car market.

But the car that British Leyland came up with to carry the flame for Triumph was a curious and controversial machine. The TR7 of 1975 owed nothing to the long line of previous TR sports cars. Gone was the broad-shouldered shove of the straight-six engine, the well-balanced but sometimes wayward chassis and the traditional roadster shape. In came a fashionable wedge-shaped hard-top, with pop-up headlamps, and a snug two-seater cabin. Power came from a fairly

Right: The Lotus Eclat was a fastback variation on the Elite theme.

Britain's sports car specialists

Britain has always had dozens of tiny specialist sports car makers alongside its varied range of racing car manufacturers. For these tiny companies the 1970s were a tricky time, because of the increasing cost and complication of safety and emissions regulations, the oil crisis of 1973 and its effect on European economies. In Britain, Value Added Tax (VAT) was imposed upon kit cars in April 1973, and this hit the specialists hard as many of their cars were sold in kit form.

Biggest of the specialists was Lotus, which stopped building kit cars as part of its inexorable move upmarket. Another part of

that move was to hive off production of the Seven to the biggest and most enthusiastic Seven dealer, Caterham Cars, which has continually developed the car. It remains in production to this day.

TVR met the imposition of VAT and the subsequent downturn in its UK sales by concentrating on exports of its Triumph-engined 2500M and Ford-engined 3000M.

But TVR never seemed to have a firm business footing, until current owner Peter Wheeler took over.

Interesting sports cars from Ginetta, Gilbern, Clan, and Trident all struggled to make money during the 1970s, while the extrovert Panther grabbed the headlines on account of its bizarre six-wheeler rather than its outstanding sales perfomance.

tame four-cylinder engine which had already seen service in the Dolomite sedan. Traditionalists were disappointed with the TR7's odd looks and lukewarm performance, while buyers were dismayed at the Triumph's appalling build quality. Industrial unrest in the British car industry hit the TR7 perhaps more than any other car, and production was switched from Speke near Liverpool to Canley near Coventry and finally to Solihull, in an attempt to streamline the process and raise build standards.

Above left: Caterham Cars took over manufacture of the Lotus Seven, and still makes the cars today. The picture shows a 1969 Lotus Seven Series 3 Twin cam SS with a 125bhp Lotus Holbay engine.

Top right: TVR concentrated on exporting its 2500M and, here, 3000M cars.

Left: Lamborghini replaced the Miura with the Marcello Gandini-styled Countach. This example is a 1981 Countach LP400S.

Right: Mid-engined cars were all the rage in the mid-1970s: this is Maserati's 1979 V6-engined Merak Turbo prototype.

By the time the TR7 appeared in production, initially for the US market only, a series of court actions had clarified American safety rules and the result was that roadsters were back on the agenda. Suddenly everyone wanted one, giving old stagers like the MGB and Triumph Spitfire a new lease of life, but leaving the TR7 – designed from the start as a fixed-head coupé – in a difficult position. Triumph sent a TR7 to its favorite stylist, Michelotti in Italy, to turn it into a drophead, but when the open car was finally brought on stream in 1979, it was too late. Neither could the installation of a Rover V8 engine, first in a high-profile rally car and then in the production TR8, help to prevent the inevitable: British Leyland had more important things to worry about than mere sports cars, and by 1982 all Leyland's roadsters – MG's Midget and MGB, Triumph's TR7, Spitfire, and Stag – had bitten the dust.

Below: De Tomaso's Pantera supercar used a relatively humble Ford V8 engine.

Healey returns

Though Donald Healey's Austin-based sports car had seen the end of the road late in the 1960s, the Healey name would soon be associated with sports cars again. The Jensen-Healey project gave the fine old English marque of Jensen, which had built the bodies for the big Healey in the 1960s, the lifeline of a small, relatively inexpensive sports car. It seemed ideal to tide them over during the uncertain days of the '70s, when their big, expensive machines powered by huge American V8 engines looked increasingly unsustainable. The car itself was an attractive-looking two-seater roadster with a comfortable, modern cockpit and a new Vauxhall-based Lotus engine under the hood. Sadly the Lotus engine was underdeveloped, and the Jensen-Healey was let down by a multitude of minor problems which customers were left to cope with themselves. Cash-strapped Jensen – on its knees thanks to the oil crisis of the early '70s – didn't have the resources to sort out the problems quickly, and the Jensen-Healey died along with the estate-like Jensen GT that it had sired and the other Jensen models, in 1975. The name lived on, but only as a parts operation. As established names like Jensen and Aston-Martin struggled in the harsh conditions the oil crisis had created, British government money was being spent to set up a brand new sports car project in Northern Ireland, under the leadership of John Zachary DeLorean…

Lotus did survive, however, moving upmarket by selling off the Seven to Caterham Cars and replacing the Europa and Elan with a series of new models powered by the Vauxhall-based engine that had been supplied for the Jensen-Healey. The Elite and Eclat were close-coupled four seaters with fashionable wedge profiles, while the Esprit was an out-and-out sports car with the same engine mid-mounted. Again the styling was a sharp-edged wedge, based on a show car from Giugiaro in the early 1970s. Lotus struggled with quality, and by now the genius of Colin Chapman was being spread between such diverse products as road cars, Grand Prix cars, boats, and even microlights. But the new Lotuses received critical acclaim, and the Esprit earned welcome early exposure in 1976 in the James Bond film *The Spy Who Loved Me*. Not since the Aston Martin DB5 in *Goldfinger* had a film role done so much for a car: everyone remembered the Esprit diving off a jetty in the Bahamas and turning into a submarine at the push of a button.

Mid-engined cars became something of a fad in the mid-'70s. In addition to the Lotus Esprit, which was certainly quick and had fine handling, but didn't quite make it into the supercar bracket on account of its small engine, there was also clutch of true supercars all using the mid-

Ferrari 512BB	
Manufacturer:	Ferrari (Maranello, Italy)
Production years:	1976-81 (512i 1981-84)
Engine location:	Mid-engined
Configuration:	Flat 12-cylinder
Bore x stroke:	82x78mm
Capacity:	4942cc
Valve operation:	Twin overhead cam per bank
Fuel system:	Electronic fuel injection
Power:	340bhp at 6800rpm
Gearbox:	Five-speed manual
Driven wheels:	Rear wheel drive
Chassis/body:	Tubular steel chassis, aluminum body panels
Suspension:	Front: wishbones and coil springs
	Rear: wishbones and coil springs
Brakes:	Hydraulically operated discs on all four wheels
Wheels/tires:	Alloy wheels
Top speed:	180mph (290km/h)
Acceleration:	0-60mph (97km/h): 5.5sec

Above: The replacement for the Daytona, the 365 GT4 'Berlinetta Boxer,' had its flat-12 engine mid-mounted.

Left: BMW's M1 supercar was used in a short-lived Procar racing series.

Right: The crisp Pininfarina shape of the Berlinetta Boxer or 'BB' still had a little in common with the earlier, front-engined Ferraris.

engined layout. Lamborghini replaced the Miura with the Marcello Gandini-styled Countach and introduced the smaller Urracco, while up the road in Modena, Maserati concocted the V6-engined Merak and very fast V8 Bora. The Bora was undoubtedly blisteringly quick in a straight line, but it lacked the cornering precision to go with it: the very experienced sedan car racer David Brodie was asked to give high-speed rides to journalists at a Silverstone press day in the UK, and found the Maserati quite a handful in the Northamptonshire track's fast, sweeping corners. Brodie went as fast as he dared, only to be overtaken round the outside with some ease by a Mercedes sedan full of journalists…

The mid-engined layout had also attracted Alessandro de Tomaso for his impressive Pantera supercar, which used a Ford V8 engine inside an Italian body – a combination which gave both style and reliability, and proved remarkably popular. Another mid-engined arrival was the BMW M1, which gave birth to the short-lived 'Procar' series in which Grand Prix drivers were invited to compete.

Below: Bertone designed the Dino 308GT4, an unusual mid-engined four-seater.

Ferrari's 'Boxer'

Ferrari, too, went down the mid-engined route. The replacement for the Daytona in 1973 was the 365GT Berlinetta Boxer (usually abbreviated to 'BB'), 'Boxer' indicating that the new mid-engined car used a horizontally-opposed engine reflecting Ferrari's recent Grand Prix and endurance race designs. In 1976 Ferrari introduced a revised version with a slightly larger engine, called the 512 – though the number now represented a nominal 5.0-liter capacity and 12 cylinders, rather than being the capacity of a single cylinder as had previously been the case. Capable of around 180mph (290km/h), the BB was one of the fastest cars on the market.

Lower down the range Ferrari employed the mid-engine design again on its new models. The popular Dino 206 had been replaced by a larger-engined 246, which itself had made way for the Dino 308GT4 in 1973. The 308GT4 was unusual in two main respects: first, it offered 2+2 accommodation in a mid-engined car, and second it was a Ferrari designed by Bertone, which presented its favorite angular wedge style. Suspension followed 246 lines with double wishbones at both ends, but the engine was a new transverse 2927cc V8 with twin camshafts per cylinder bank and a maximum output of 250bhp at a lofty 7700rpm. In 1975 the same engine went into a pretty two-seater, the 308GTB, this time designed by Leonardo Fiovoranti at Pininfarina. The GTB's voluptuous curves – in glassfiber for the first couple of years of production, then in steel and alloy – led some observers to call the latest mid-engined Ferrari the most beautiful car in the world.

If you drove a Ferrari in your dreams but couldn't quite stretch to the real thing, there were a variety of alternatives. Almost there was the Fiat Dino which had been introduced in 1966 and died along with Ferrari's Dino 246 in 1973. The Fiat's V6 engine had much in common with the Ferrari's, and in Spyder form the Pininfarina styling was every bit as sensational. For the more sober there was a subtler Bertone-styled coupé on the same running gear, which made fine transport for the Mafia in the film *The Italian Job*.

Bertone was again involved with another Italian coupé with Ferrari power, this time intended for a very different task. Optimum traction seemed to be the way to win rallies early in the 1970s, with the rear-engined Porsche 911 and Alpine-Renault showing the way, and Ford working on the

Above: Fiat's Dino Spider offered near-Ferrari thrills.

Lancia Stratos	
Manufacturer:	Lancia (Turin, Italy)
Production years:	1974-75
Engine location:	Mid-engined
Configuration:	V6
Bore x stroke:	92x60mm
Capacity:	2418cc
Valve operation:	Twin overhead cam per bank
Fuel system:	Triple, twin-choke Weber carburetors
Power:	190bhp at 7000rpm
Gearbox:	Five-speed manual
Driven wheels:	Rear wheel drive
Chassis/body:	Steel monocoque, glassfiber panels
Suspension:	Front: wishbones and coil springs Rear: MacPherson struts
Brakes:	Hydraulically operated discs on all four wheels
Wheels/tires:	14in alloy wheels, 205/70x14in tires
Top speed:	140mph (225km/h)
Acceleration:	0-60mph (97km/h): 5.9sec

Left: Lancia Stratos was built for rallying.

Above: The Lancia Beta Montecarlo suffered from early handling and braking worries which were later resolved.

Fiat X1/9 1500

Manufacturer:	Fiat (Turin, Italy)
Production years:	1978-88 (1300 1972-78)
Engine location:	Mid-engined
Configuration:	In-line four-cylinder
Bore x stroke:	86.4x63.9mm
Capacity:	1498cc
Valve operation:	Single overhead cam
Fuel system:	Twin-choke Weber carburetor
Power:	85bhp at 6500rpm
Gearbox:	Five-speed manual
Driven wheels:	Rear wheel drive
Chassis/body:	Unitary steel body
Suspension:	Front: MacPherson struts
	Rear: MacPherson struts
Brakes:	Hydraulically operated discs on all four wheels
Wheels/tires:	5x13in alloy wheels, 165/70x13 tires
Top speed:	110mph (177km/h)
Acceleration:	0-60mph (97km/h): 9.9sec

mid-engined GT70. Lancia, under Cesare Fiorio, conceived a mid-engined rally car which could be built in just enough volume (400 cars) to qualify as a production car. The result was the Dino-powered Stratos, which was first seen in prototype form in 1971. Fast, short, and nervous to drive, it proved to be a World Championship rally winner from 1974 to 1979, including a Monte Carlo Rally triple in 1975-77 in the hands of Sandro Munari.

The baby Ferrari

It was Bertone's idea to offer a mid-engined baby Ferrari. In 1969 they had unveiled the Runabout show car, a striking mid-engined wedge that was refined into the Fiat X1/9 production car of 1972. It was a small and neat package, with a Porsche-style fixed roll-over bar and removable roof panel, and storage space under the front hood and in the tail behind the engine. The Fiat 128 sedan provided the engine, but with just 1290cc and 75bhp performance was hardly in the Ferrari class – though roadholding was impressive and the Fiat was a well-balanced handler. A bigger, 1498cc engine with another 10bhp arrived in 1978, but in America emissions regulations took their toll and X1/9s were delivered in the US with as little as 67bhp. A bigger sister car with more power was mooted, but this 'X1/20' ended up in production not as a Fiat, but as a Lancia – the Montecarlo, a car which would be dogged by handling worries during its early period of production.

Apart from the Montecarlo, Lancia concentrated on sedans and sports tourers such as the elegant Beta Coupé and Spyder. Alfa Romeo, too, was answering a growing demand for more sophisticated sporting cars, replacing the Giulia coupés with a fastback Alfetta GT that was a swifter and more refined road car. But it had also introduced the wild Montreal – a show car that

became a production reality, carrying a V8 engine that was all but a racing unit – and would continue producing the Alfa Spider with ever larger engines. Like the British roadsters, the Spider would see out the decade but unlike the British cars it would last all through the next, as the open-topped sports car bounced back into fashion.

Above: *The fine-handling Fiat X1/9 always cried out for more power.*

Left: *Alfa Romeo's Montreal combined show-car looks and a detuned racing engine.*

1980-89: The Roadster Reborn

Previous page: The curvy TVRs of the 1970s gave way to a new wedge-shaped family of cars. The 350i featured Rover V8 power.

Above: *Later X1/9s had Bertone badges.*

Below: *Alfa Romeo revised the Spider with better trim and a rather unsightly bodykit.*

By the end of the 1970s there were few real sports cars left on the market. Enthusiasts who wanted a performance car chose a hot hatch or a sports sedan, and got the same performance as a roadster – perhaps better – without having to put up with a drafty and leaky roof. They could also enjoy the convenience of hatchbacks and four seats. Though the mid-'70s safety legislation that had been expected to make roadsters a thing of the past had never come to fruition, the car buyers of the 1980s were telling the manufacturers that the sports car was dead anyway.

Classic cars were a different matter, and during the early 1980s speculators moved into the market and boosted values of classic cars to levels never before seen. Suddenly people who had never considered themselves classic car enthusiasts got involved – some because they saw the chance to make money, but others who had initially been attracted by the hype and publicity found there was something to enjoy about classic cars regardless of their monetary value. Classic cars were cool, and the coolest of all were classic roadsters, not least because they were completely different to almost everything else on the roads. If you wanted to drive a roadster, it had to be a classic – or one of the few cars still in production from that earlier era.

Alfa Romeo, for instance, simply facelifted the venerable Spider in 1983 with new bumpers and a soft rubber spoiler at the back to bring the car a little more up to date – though the modifications rather spoiled its clean lines. More welcome were interior improvements and, later, a new version of the 2.0-liter engine with fuel injection and variable valve timing. Falling sales had led Alfa Romeo to drop the right-hand-drive version of the Spider in 1978, but the steady trickle of British customers that remained was still catered for thanks to a conversion by Alfa dealer Bell and Colvill. The Alfa Spider's great rival, Fiat's 124 Spider, was also still in production, though now it was being built by Pininfarina and sold in America as the Pininfarina Azzura (in Europe it was the Spidereuropa) which would remain available until 1987. Meanwhile, Bertone had taken over assembly of the Fiat X1/9, instead of just making the bodyshells as had previously been the case. In revised form the characterful mid-engined X1/9 remained on sale until 1988, finishing with a 'Gran Finale' special edition.

Left: In 1971 the 'Pagoda roof' Mercedes SL was replaced by a handsome new car which was designed very much with safety in mind. Production continued right through the 1980s.

Below: TVR went back to its curvier styling with the Ford-powered S.

Long live the SL

Mercedes-Benz had replaced its 'Pagoda roof' SL as far back as 1971 with the R107 SL, a car so tough it became popularly known as the 'Panzerwagen.' Throughout the 1970s three versions of the R107 were available, customers being offered a choice of a 2.8-liter straight six and a pair of V8 engines, the strongest a 4.5-liter unit developing 225bhp. Revised engines appeared in 1982, by which time it looked as if that would be the last round of changes for the 11-year-old dinosaur before production ended. But the SL continued to sell, and sell well, and development went on.

Right: Toyota's mid-engined MR2 updated the X1/9 theme.

Toyota MR2

Manufacturer:	Toyota (Japan)
Production years:	1984-89
Engine location:	Mid-engined
Configuration:	In-line four-cylinder
Bore x stroke:	81x77mm
Capacity:	1587cc
Valve operation:	Twin overhead cam
Fuel system:	Electronic fuel injection
Power:	122bhp at 6600rpm
Gearbox:	Five-speed manual
Driven wheels:	Rear wheel drive
Chassis/body:	Unitary steel body
Suspension:	Front: MacPherson struts with anti-roll bar
	Rear: MacPherson struts with anti-roll bar
Brakes:	Hydraulically operated discs on all four wheels
Wheels/tires:	5.5x14in alloy wheels, 185/60x14 tires
Top speed:	122mph (196km/h)
Acceleration:	0-60mph (97km/h): 8.0sec

Below: The Pontiac Fiero was another attempt at a mid-engined sports car, but an inefficient engine and poor aerodynamics gave it insipid performance.

A comprehensive update in 1986 improved the SL's aerodynamics, fuel economy, and power. The R107 would last until 1989, giving it the longest production life of any Mercedes. By the end US buyers would have a 5.6-liter V8 at their disposal, though thanks to increasingly tough emissions rules its 227bhp output was little better than the European 4.5-liter V8 had been in the 1970s. Meanwhile 'dirty' Europe got a 5.0-liter V8 with 240bhp.

British specialists like Panther, Morgan, and TVR continued to produce conventionally-engineered roadsters in small numbers, the latter refining its tough, simple sports cars and gaining in confidence and respect with each new model. The '70s-style sharp-edged looks of TVR's cars were softened, and tuned Rover V8 engines replaced the Ford Essex V6s that had powered the earlier cars. TVR also introduced a new version of the old 1970s Taimar body, called the TVR S, powered by a fuel-injected Ford Cologne V6.

But if you were looking for a truly modern sports car in the early 1980s, then your options were limited. In America, there was the Pontiac Fiero, a brave attempt by General Motors to offer an X1/9-like mid-engined car which had unstressed glassfiber outer panels so the styling could be easily updated. Though the Fiero's 'Iron Duke' engine displaced a considerable 2457cc it

produced only 92bhp, and the Fiero was both heavy and aerodynamically inefficient – all of which gave it a rather pedestrian top speed of less than 100mph (161km/h). A 140bhp V6 engine and a fastback restyle helped, but a recall following a series of engine fires was a blow, and rising insurance rates for sports cars didn't help either. The Fiero's disappointing run ended in 1988.

Above: Nissan's 200SX evolved into a credible mid-range sporting coupé.

Toyota's MR2

Toyota provided a more effective mass-market mid-engined sports car in 1984, with the introduction of the MR2 (standing for 'Midship Runabout Two-seater'). Though there were automatics and 1.5-liter single-cam 'cooking' models, the best known MR2 used a 1587cc '4A-GE' engine, a classic twin-cam in-line four with four valves per cylinder, which had already been seen in the rear-wheel-drive Corolla GT Coupé and front-drive Corolla GT hot hatch. The MR2

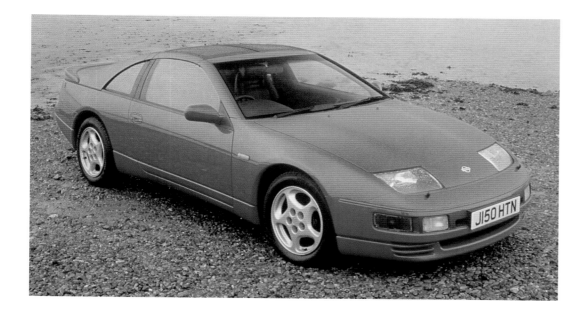

Left: The 300ZX was altogether more technologically advanced, with a turbocharged V6 engine and four-wheel steering.

Right: The rotary-engined Mazda RX-7 survived through several generations.

Below: Toyota's Supra was available with removable roof panels and a strong turbocharged 3.0-liter engine.

Above: The 944, here in Turbo form, was Porsche's best-balanced car.

also shared the front-drive Corolla's end-on transmission and transverse engine location, though of course the engine was at the opposite end of the car. With 130bhp (at a heady 7600rpm) the MR2 could hit 120mph (193km/h), and later there was a supercharged version with 146bhp which was, naturally, even quicker. Handling was good and roadholding secure in the dry, though the MR2 was a little less forgiving in the wet. Being slightly taller and wider than the old X1/9, it offered a roomier cabin – though the dominating black plastic trim, typical of the era, wasn't to everyone's taste even if it was well constructed. Combined with the usual faultless Japanese reliability, the MR2 was an attractive package that sold well throughout the decade, until a new and larger model took its place.

The Japanese marques had also made inroads into the market for sporting coupés, which had long been the preserve of European cars such as Alfa Romeo's GTV6 and Ford's Capri. Nissan's Silvia and 200SX were aimed at the lower end of this market, and above them sat the technology-

Above: *Porsche refined the 928 with styling tweaks and larger engines.*

packed 300ZX with a turbocharged V6 engine and four-wheel steering. Somewhere between the two was Mitsubishi's turbocharged Starion, a successful rally car, and the rotary-engined Mazda RX-7. The Mazda had been introduced in 1978 and was replaced by a new model in 1985 after nearly half a million had been made.

Celica and Supra develop

Into this market Toyota pitched a succession of Celica models, and a high performance Celica Supra. In 1985 a new Celica appeared, sporting styling which had been inspired by the Panhards of the 1960s and available with Toyota's efficient 16-valve engines. A turbocharged, four-wheel-drive Celica GT-Four arrived soon after, and was used as the basis of a successful rally car. Meanwhile, the Supra became a model in its own right with a lusty 3.0-liter straight-six engine, available in normally-aspirated and turbocharged forms – the latter good for 235bhp and nearly 140mph (225km/h).

The Japanese coupés were all aimed at a market headed by Porsche's water-cooled models. The 924's image had been improved by a 924 Turbo and a short run of blisteringly quick Carrera GTs intended to homologate the model for motor sport use. In 1984 it was joined by a 944 using the same body but fitted with a 'proper' Porsche engine – a 2479cc in-line four with twin contra-rotating balancer shafts to improve smoothness, an underlying vibration being the Achilles' heel of a big-straight four. In its most muscular form, with a KKK turbocharger but only two valves per cylinder, this developed 220bhp and gave the Porsche a top speed approaching 160mph (257km/h). So convincing a package was the 944 Turbo – particularly in comparison to the rather lukewarm 924 that sired it – that *Motor* was moved to call it 'the runt that became a prince.'

If the 944 wasn't fast enough or grand enough for you Porsche still offered the V8-engined 928, heavily revised in 1982 S2 form and given a more powerful 32-valve engine for its 1986 S4 incarnation, featuring refinements including anti-lock brakes and a multi-mode Mercedes-Benz

Porsche 944 Turbo

Manufacturer:	Dr Ing hc F Porsche AG (Zuffenhausen, Germany)
Production years:	1984-
Engine location:	Front
Configuration:	In-line four-cylinder with twin balancer shafts
Bore x stroke:	100x78.9mm
Capacity:	2479cc
Valve operation:	Single overhead cam
Fuel system:	Electronic fuel injection
Power:	220bhp at 5800rpm
Gearbox:	Five-speed manual
Driven wheels:	Rear wheel drive
Chassis/body:	Unitary steel body
Suspension	Front: MacPherson struts with anti-roll bar
	Rear: semi-trailing arms and torsion bars with anti-roll bar
Brakes:	Hydraulically operated discs on all four wheels
Wheels/tires:	7x16in front and 8x16in rear alloy wheels. 205/55x16 front, 225/50x16 rear tires
Top speed:	158mph (254km/h)
Acceleration:	0-60mph (97km/h): 6.0sec

Below: The Porsche 959 was a technological tour-de-force, with computer-controlled four-wheel drive and a twin-turbo flat-six engine.

Below: It took Porsche 25 years to make the 911 available in stripped-down Speedster form.

automatic transmission. The 911, too, soldiered on with regular revisions, including the addition of a 231bhp 3.2-liter engine – still an air-cooled flat six, of course – and a full cabriolet option for the first time. A fearsome twin-turbocharged four-wheel-drive derivative, the 959, proved to be one of the fastest supercars ever – rivaling Ferrari's limited-edition 288GTO and F40. With the front-engined, water-cooled models and the venerable rear-engined 911, Porsche seemed to have cornered the market in quality sports coupés, though the Japanese marques steadily made inroads – and Porsche had competitors in Europe, too.

Lotus abandoned its slow-selling Elite early in the 1980s, and concentrated on redeveloping the fastback Eclat to produce the Excel, probably the best-handling front-engined car of the time. The two-seater Esprit was given a turbocharger, boosting the 16-valve four-cylinder engine to 210bhp and giving the mid-engined Lotus the straight-line performance that its crisp, forgiving handling and prodigious roadholding had always demanded. The supple ride was a surprising bonus. Though the Esprit's hollow engine note couldn't compete with the musicality of multi-cylinder exotics like Ferrari's 328GTB and Testarossa, it didn't carry a Ferrari-esque price tag either. If there was a drawback to the Esprit package it was, perhaps, the 1970s styling: the sharp-edged Giugiaro design had dated quickly. A Peter Stevens restyle in 1987 updated the Esprit astonishingly well, given that no part of the body was altered by more than 2in (50mm) from the original design, and gave Norfolk's fastest road car a new beginning. Development of the turbo engine continued, and a later Esprit SE version with 264bhp had genuine supercar pace.

The DeLorean Debacle

In 1978 John DeLorean, former GM vice-president, announced plans to build a sports car in a new factory at Dunmurry, near Belfast in Northern Ireland. The DeLorean DMC12 was a curious design, with a steel backbone chassis, glassfiber body, and unpainted stainless steel outer panels, gullwing doors, and a rear-mounted Douvrin V6 engine. The British government, keen to boost an economically depressed area, backed the project with more than £50 million ($88 million) of public money.

Even Lotus engineering expertise couldn't make the DeLorean go and corner the way it needed to, because the basic rear-engined design was inadequate. Shortly after the car went on sale in 1981 – nearly a year late – complaints started pouring in about creaking bodywork, stainless steel panels which showed finger marks and were difficult to clean, and failing door electrics which trapped occupants inside. Meanwhile, the cost of getting the car into production and certifying it for sale in the US had been underestimated. The British government made an additional loan of £14 million ($25 million) and then agreed to guarantee £10 million ($17.5 million) of bank loans.

But DeLorean finally ran out of money, and the British government put DeLorean Motor Cars – the manufacturing subsidiary, which it jointly owned with John DeLorean – into receivership in 1982. The advanced DeLorean plant had been set up to build up to 150,000 cars a year, but only about 4000 DeLoreans were built. Plans had already been under way for a DeLorean sedan styled, like the DMC12, by Giugiaro, and a turbocharged version of the DMC12 was under development. A convertible was expected to follow.

Desperate to secure the money to keep his dream car in production, DeLorean got involved in financial deals which were part of a money laundering and drug trafficking operation, which happened to be the subject of an FBI sting aimed at someone else. DeLorean was charged with drug offenses, but his defense claimed he had been the subject of illegal entrapment, and he was acquitted in 1984. In another court case in 1985 it was claimed that DeLorean had siphoned funds out of the car company, but again he was not convicted. More recently he has been linked with a high-end watchmaking project – and it's said that DeLorean, now nearly 80, wants to build another sports car. The greatest fame achieved by his first effort was as the time machine that featured in the movie *Back to the Future*.

Above: *DeLorean's stainless steel-clad sports car lost millions.*

Left: *The Ferrari 288GTO was descended from the 308GTB.*

Right: Four seats and a prancing horse badge were combined in the Mondial.

Lotus and the Corvette

After the death of Colin Chapman at the end of 1982, Toyota had become a major stakeholder in Lotus, but in 1985 the company was taken over by General Motors. One result was that the renowned engineers at Lotus were set to work on America's favorite sports car, the evergreen Chevrolet Corvette, which had been completely restyled in 1983 with crisp, modern lines (but still no convertible option, which had been discontinued due to falling demand in 1975). Though still powered by a V8 engine of 5.7-liters capacity the output was just 205bhp – 5bhp less than the Lotus Esprit's turbo engine which had less than half the displacement. GM wanted a performance engine for the Corvette; what they got was the LT5, still a 5.7-liter V8 but with a wider bore and shorter stroke than the original engine, twin overhead camshafts on each bank of cylinders, and

Below: The limited-edition Ferrari F40 was one of the fastest supercars of all.

four valves per cylinder. Careful engineering sent power soaring from the 230bhp that GM had squeezed out of the original V8 to a colossal 385bhp, propelling what was called the Corvette ZR1 to 180mph (290km/h). To help the ZR1 through emissions and fuel consumption regulations, its six-speed manual gearbox was fitted with a computer control unit that automatically changed up from first gear to fourth unless the driver was using more than three-quarters of the available throttle travel.

Meanwhile, Lotus had been working on a completely new car to take them back into the lower-priced sports car market. For a long time the company had wanted to build a relatively affordable sports car, and design studies began in the early 1980s. After the GM takeover the project was reborn, the intention being to keep costs down by using production engines and other components from within the GM empire – stretching from Vauxhall in the UK to Holden in Australia to Cadillac, Chevrolet, and several other marques in the US. Lotus found that GM's Japanese arm Isuzu was working on a new small-capacity engine, and a deal was done where

Above: Peter Stevens restyled the Lotus Esprit very successfully in 1987.

Lotus Esprit Turbo

Manufacturer:	Lotus (Hethel, England)
Production years:	1981-98
Engine location:	Mid-engined
Configuration:	In-line four-cylinder
Bore x stroke:	95.3x76.2mm
Capacity:	2174cc
Valve operation:	Twin overhead cam, 16 valves
Fuel system:	Electronic fuel injection, turbocharger
Power:	210bhp at 6000rpm
Gearbox:	Five-speed manual
Driven wheels:	Rear wheel drive
Chassis/body:	Steel backbone chassis, glassfiber body
Suspension:	Front: wishbones, coil springs and anti-roll bar
	Rear: transverse links, radius arms, coil springs
Brakes:	Hydraulically operated discs on all four wheels, inboard at rear
Wheels/tires:	15in alloy wheels. 195/60x15 front, 205/60x15 rear tires
Top speed:	150mph (241km/h)
Acceleration:	0-60mph (97km/h): 5.5sec

Left: The Lotus Eclat was developed into this, the Excel – one of the best-handling sports coupés on sale anywhere.

Lotus would help develop the engine in twin-cam performance form and would then use it in their new sports car, codenamed M100.

When M100 was revealed it was called the Elan, reviving a great name from the 1960s and '70s. But the new Elan was very much a modern machine because that Isuzu-based engine was mounted across the nose of the car driving the front wheels, just like a hot hatchback. High-performance front-wheel-drive cars generally suffer from understeer under power, as the front wheels fight to transmit both steering input and tractive effort. The Lotus answer was to mount the front suspension wishbones using a subframe (Lotus called it a 'raft'), which was allowed to move relative to the car in a controlled way using carefully tuned bushes. They were almost too successful: the Elan generated spectacular grip, but some journalists muttered that it was uninvolving to drive. Sales were disappointing, the Elan's detail finish letting it down and its styling probably not helping – from some angles it looked fantastic, but from others it seemed overweight and ungainly. In the image-conscious decade of the designer label, a roadster's looks were perhaps even more important than the quality of its engineering.

Style is king

BMW's Z1 was another roadster that polarized opinion with its appearance. Its construction was unusual, with a steel frame and a composite floor, clothed in unstressed glassfiber panels which could be swapped for a complete new set in about half an hour. The Z1's doors, too, were controversial, as they dropped down into the sills rather than opening normally, and you could drive the car with them open. The driveline was normal enough, though, with the very smooth fuel-injected in-line six-cylinder engine from the 325i sedan, driving the rear wheels through the obligatory five-speed manual gearbox. The Z1 was an interesting machine with excellent handling and roadholding, though it was no lightweight and perhaps deserved more power.

Below left: The Panther Six made headlines, but could not save the company.

Below right: The Kallista was introduced by Panther's new Korean owners.

Panther's Rise and Fall

Robert Jankel's Panther concern made a name building 1930s-styled sports cars, starting with the Jaguar-powered J72 in 1972. Jankel followed up this SS100-inspired car with Ferrari-powered, Ferrari-inspired designs and a retro limo, the DeVille, before venturing into a more modern idiom with the Panther Six.

The Six was a huge convertible with six wheels, four of them at the front – like the contemporary Tyrrell P34 Formula 1 car. Power came from a Cadillac V8 between the rear wheels and rumors circulated that the thing would do 200mph (322km/h). But Panther had over-reached themselves, and even the much cheaper Vauxhall-based Lima couldn't save them.

Rescue came in the form of the Korean Kim family, who relaunched the Lima under the name Kallista, and began work on the Solo, a modern mid-engined sports car. Originally intended to be a cheap, mass-market car, the Solo was re-engineered after the Toyota MR2 appeared, Panther realizing it

could not compete with the Toyota's low price. The much quicker Solo II used Sierra Cosworth power and four-wheel drive. It was a good package, but at its high price buyers expected more than humble Ford mechanicals: perhaps 30 or so were built.

Left: Lotus developed the Corvette ZR-1.

Unhappy styling hampered Reliant's SS1 roadster. There was little innovation under the glassfiber skin, but the Ford-powered SS1 (later a turbocharged Nissan engine was an option) was competent and fun to drive. But the styling, by Michelotti, was a curious jumble of sharp edges and squared-off curves.

Sub-contract work kept Reliant afloat, notably building the roadgoing versions of the RS200 rally car for Ford: the 'Group B' rules now allowed purpose-built supercars to be used in international rallying, with only 200 examples having to be sold to make the car eligible. Peugeot made a mid-engined 205, the T16; Lancia followed up its Montecarlo-based 038 with the Delta S4, which boasted both a turbocharger and a supercharger. MG, now restricted to badge-engineered hot hatches rather than true sports cars, built the outrageous Metro 6R4, with a bespoke 90-degree V6 engine and input from the Williams Formula 1 team.

But these were expensive, low-volume cars built expressly with the aim of winning rallies, and the roadgoing versions often didn't make the best road cars because there was no incentive

Lotus Elan	
Manufacturer:	Lotus (Hethel, England)
Production years:	1989-92 (S2 1994-95)
Engine location:	Mid-engined
Configuration:	In-line four-cylinder
Bore x stroke:	80x79mm
Capacity:	1558cc
Valve operation:	Twin overhead cam, 16 valves
Fuel system:	Electronic fuel injection, turbocharger
Power:	165bhp at 6600rpm
Gearbox:	Five-speed manual
Driven wheels:	Front wheel drive
Chassis/body:	Steel backbone chassis, glassfiber body
Suspension:	Front: raft-mounted wishbones, coil springs and anti-roll bar
	Rear: wishbone, transverse link, coil springs and anti-roll bar
Brakes:	Hydraulically operated discs on all four wheels
Wheels/tires:	7x16in alloy wheels, 205/45x16 tires
Top speed:	135mph (217km/h)
Acceleration:	0-60mph (97km/h): 7.0sec

Left: The front-wheel-drive Lotus Elan failed to capture the public's imagination.

Above: BMW's Z1 featured novel drop-down doors. It could be driven with the doors open.

BMW Z1

Manufacturer:	BMW (Munich, Germany)
Production years:	1988-91
Engine location:	Front
Configuration:	In-line six-cylinder
Bore x stroke:	84x75mm
Capacity:	2494cc
Valve operation:	Single overhead cam
Fuel system:	Electronic fuel injection
Power:	170bhp at 5800rpm
Gearbox:	Five-speed manual
Driven wheels:	Rear wheel drive
Chassis/body:	Steel monocoque with glassfiber outer panels
Suspension:	Front: MacPherson struts Rear: semi-trailing arms with coil springs
Brakes:	Hydraulically operated ventilated discs on all four wheels
Wheels/tires:	Alloy wheels
Top speed:	140mph (225km/h)
Acceleration:	0-60mph (97km/h): 8.0sec

for the manufacturers to develop them properly. At the other end of the scale there were few affordable sports cars left – the Triumph Spitfire and the MG Midget and MGB, starved of significant development for so long, had all finally ended their production runs and had not been replaced. But there was still a demand for affordable sports cars, and in particular for an affordable roadster. It was Mazda who would fill that niche, with the MX-5 – a product of its new California design studio.

Rebirth of the roadster

Mazda had previously restricted itself to family sedans, the odd hot hatch, and the rotary-engined RX-7 sports coupé but the MX-5, known as the Miata in the US and the Eunos Roadster in Japan, was a real roadster. The aim had been to produce a modern car with all the appeal of a classic roadster, and it was clear that one particular classic roadster – the 1960s Lotus Elan – had been in the Mazda engineers' minds when the car was designed. The body bore a striking resemblance to the Lotus from some angles, though the Mazda was all steel rather than glassfiber, and the characteristic shape of the cam cover on the Lotus-Ford engine was repeated on the Mazda's twin-cam unit. The alloy wheels fitted to most versions were another '60s throwback, looking like a reinterpretation of classic Minilite magnesium alloy rims. But the Miata was far more than just a pastiche of previous designs.

Where the Mazda scored was that it offered the appeal and the driving experience of a proper roadster, without many of the shortcomings. There's little to touch the handling of an Elan, but the Mazda's road manners were safe, tidy, and entertaining, like the Lotus. Its straight-line speed couldn't match the best of the Elans, either, the 1.6-liter twin-cam engine (from the 323 hatchback) delivering a very smooth 116bhp and giving the Miata a top speed of 121mph (195km/h). But the Miata was far roomier than an Elan, much better built, far safer in an accident and met all the new regulations about emissions performance. It was also packed with convenience features that the American market, in particular, demanded – electric windows, air conditioning, cruise control, and power steering were all available. It was as easy to drive as a

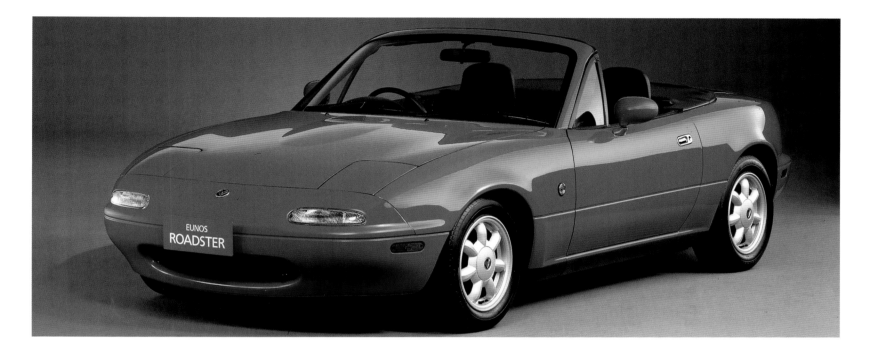

modern Japanese hatchback, but rewarding for a press-on driver. It offered much of the convenience, comfort, and performance of a hot hatch, but with an extra dose of style.

The Miata was immensely popular. In Britain, tuners Brodie Brittain Racing sought to exploit the Mazda's fine chassis with extra power by grafting on a turbocharger and intercooler, boosting power to 200bhp; the conversion was sold through Mazda dealers. One-model racing championships using Miatas kept the car in the public eye, while numerous special editions kept the car fresh.

Meanwhile other car makers were seeing a new market segment opening up. By the end of the 1980s the roadster had recovered from its near extinction at the hands of the American safety lobby to become a growing, vibrant market. But more was to come. Sports cars of all sorts would appear from the established names and newcomers – and one of the greatest sports car names of old would be resurrected from the dead.

Above: The Mazda Miata is the world's best-selling lightweight open two-seater sports car. It has continued to create a stir since its launch in 1989.

Mazda Miata (MX-5)

Manufacturer:	Mazda (Japan)
Production years:	1989-98 (new MX-5 1998 on)
Engine location:	Front
Configuration:	In-line four-cylinder
Bore x stroke:	78x83.6mm
Capacity:	1597cc
Valve operation:	Twin overhead cam
Fuel system:	Electronic fuel injection
Power:	116bhp at 6500rpm
Gearbox:	Five-speed manual
Driven wheels:	Rear wheel drive
Chassis/body:	Unitary steel body
Suspension:	Front: wishbones, coil springs, anti roll bar
	Rear: wishbones, coil springs, anti roll bar
Brakes:	Hydraulically operated discs on all four wheels, servo assisted
Wheels/tires:	Alloy wheels
Top speed:	121mph (195km/h)
Acceleration:	0-60mph (97km/h): 8.8sec

Left Reliant's Scimitar suffered because of its unhappy styling.

1990s: Widening the Choice

Previous page: The Marcos was constantly developed, with new engines and a convertible body style. This Mantis dates from 1997.

Above: The Targa roof continued on Porsche's new 911.

Below right: Superficially similar to the old 911, the new car (known internally as the 964) was very different under the skin. This is a 1990 Carrera 4.

Porsche 911 Turbo (993)

Manufacturer:	Porsche (Stuttgart, Germany)
Production years:	1997
Engine location:	Rear-engined
Configuration:	Flat six-cylinder
Bore x stroke:	100x76.4mm
Capacity:	3600cc
Valve operation:	Twin overhead cam per bank
Fuel system:	Electronic fuel injection, twin turbochargers
Power:	408bhp at 5750rpm
Gearbox:	Five-speed manual
Driven wheels:	Rear wheel drive
Chassis/body:	Unitary steel body
Suspension:	Front: MacPherson struts with anti-roll bar
	Rear: multi-link with coil springs and anti-roll bar
Brakes:	Hydraulically operated discs on all four wheels
Wheels/tires:	8x18in front, 11x18in rear alloy wheels. 225/40x18 front, 295/30x18 rear tires
Top speed:	181mph (291km/h)
Acceleration:	0-60mph (100km/h): 4.3sec

Porsche entered the 1990s with a new interpretation of the evergreen 911, known internally as the 964 and in public as the Carrera 4. Though the shape was familiar and the Carrera 4 still had an air-cooled flat-six engine mounted in the tail, there had been sweeping changes in the new 911's design.

The engine, known at Porsche as the M64, was heavily revised with a wider bore (at 100mm) and longer stroke (76.4mm) giving a displacement of 3600cc. Twin ignition was used, and the engine management system which ran it used input from a pair of knock sensors to retard the ignition momentarily in any cylinder suffering from pre-ignition, allowing the M64 to use a higher compression ratio without danger of damage. Multi-valve engines were now the fashion, but the M64 heads were of conventional two-valve configuration, the exhaust ports being fitted with ceramic liners to reduce cylinder head temperatures. A variable geometry intake system was provided, with a plenum chamber for each bank of cylinders and an auxiliary throttle valve under control of the engine management system which could be opened at high engine speeds to optimize engine breathing. M64 developed 250bhp at 6100rpm, a worthwhile improvement over its 3.2-liter predecessor, and also met noise and emissions regulations worldwide.

The old 911's basic suspension layout was retained, with MacPherson struts at the front and trailing arms at the rear, but the execution was entirely different. Coil springs replaced the old 911's torsion bars, allowing Porsche to introduce compliant bushes which could improve ride comfort and refinement, as well as optimizing wheel movement for better handling. But the biggest news was the introduction of four-wheel drive, using a system based on 911s built for the Paris-Dakar rally. Normally a central differential split torque 31 percent front, 69 percent rear but the differential could lock automatically when wheelspin was detected to push torque to the axle with more grip. A similar electrically-controlled differential at the rear provided limited-slip

characteristics and also operated if the throttle was closed mid-corner, to reduce the lift-off oversteer to which the 911 had always been prone.

Above: A 408bhp 911 Turbo was introduced for 1996.

More new 911s

A two-wheel-drive Carrera 2 followed, many commentators claiming its handling was at least the equal of the four-wheel-drive car and it was more involving to drive. Traction, of course, was rarely an issue with any 911, so some wondered if the Carrera 4 was too much of a good thing. Inevitably, faster versions of the 964 followed: a hurriedly-developed 320bhp turbo powered by

Left: Chevrolet's Corvette evolved into a new generation in 1997.

Above: *The Panoz AIV was nothing if not distinctive.*

Right: *Carroll Shelby returned to the sports car scene with the Shelby Series 1.*

Opposite below: *The Viper GTS coupé was more powerful and even quicker than the original Viper roadster.*

the old 3.3 engine in 1991, and then in 1993 came a proper M64-based turbo with 360bhp and a normally-aspirated '3.8-liter' (actually 3746cc, or 3.7-liters) Carrera RS with 300bhp. For 1994 the 964 was heavily revised to become the 993, with yet more power (now at least 270bhp), a six-speed gearbox, and new multi-link rear suspension. For 1996 the engine gained a 'Varioram' variable-length intake system, and Porsche announced a new 911 Turbo with twin turbochargers and a colossal output of 408bhp.

A year later a new version of another established automotive name was announced. The 1997 Chevrolet Corvette still had a glassfiber body, available in first in coupé and convertible forms and later joined by a hardtop version with removable roof panels, and boasting a drag coefficient as low as 0.29. Underneath there was a tubular chassis carrying double-wishbone suspension at each end with transverse composite leaf springs, and the Corvette's handling was assisted by an automatic system that controlled engine output and brake pressure to avoid trouble. Power came from a new all-alloy V8 engine developing 345bhp from its 5.7-liters, and by the end of the decade there was a Z06 version with a 385bhp V8.

Above: Chrysler's Viper used an enormous 8.0-liter V10 engine.

Dodge Viper RT/10	
Manufacturer:	Chrysler (Detroit, US)
Production years:	1992-2002
Engine location:	Front
Configuration:	V10
Bore x stroke:	101.6x98.5mm
Capacity:	7990cc
Valve operation:	Pushrod overhead valve
Fuel system:	Electronic fuel injection
Power:	400bhp at 4600rpm
Gearbox:	Six-speed manual
Driven wheels:	Rear wheel drive
Chassis/body:	Tubular frame with composite panels
Suspension:	Front: double wishbones with coil springs and anti-roll bar
	Rear: double wishbones with coil springs and anti-roll bar
Brakes:	Hydraulically operated discs on all four wheels
Wheels/tires:	17in three-spoke alloy wheels, 275/40x17 front tires, 335/35x17 rear
Top speed:	166mph (267km/h)
Acceleration:	0-60mph (97km/h): 4.7sec

Right: *MG returned with a redeveloped MGB V8, the MG RV8.*

TVR Griffith 4.3	
Manufacturer:	TVR (Blackpool, England)
Production years:	1992-2001
Engine location:	Front
Configuration:	V8
Bore x stroke:	94.04x77mm
Capacity:	4280cc
Valve operation:	Pushrod overhead valve
Fuel system:	Electronic fuel injection
Power:	280bhp at 5500rpm
Gearbox:	Five-speed manual
Driven wheels:	Rear wheel drive
Chassis/body:	Tubular steel chassis, glassfiber body
Suspension:	Front: double wishbones, coil springs and anti-roll bar
	Rear: double wishbones, coil springs and anti-roll bar
Brakes:	Hydraulically operated discs on all four wheels, ventilated at front
Wheels/tires:	7x15in front, 7.5x16in rear alloy wheels. 215/50x15 front, 225/50x16 rear tires
Top speed:	155mph (249km/h)
Acceleration:	0-60mph (97km/h): 4.8sec

Below: *TVR moved into a new era with the desirable Griffith.*

Roadsters in America

But no longer was the Corvette America's only sports car. Donald Panoz had been building his Panoz AIV – Aluminum Intensive Vehicle – in small numbers since 1996, with Ford V8 power and distinctive, if quirky, styling. The AIV evolved into Esperante, with more mainstream styling, in 2000. Meanwhile Panoz ran front-engined sports cars at Le Mans, earning some success and a lot of respect.

Carroll Shelby, who had created the Cobra, Mustang GT-350, and Sunbeam Tiger in the 1960s, was back on the sports car scene. Shelby would eventually produce cars under his own name, but first he was involved in the creation of a big, new sports car for Chrysler, egging on Chrysler's bullish new chairman, Bob Lutz. It was known as the Viper, a hint that it applied a similar philosophy to the Cobra: outrageous styling, lots of power, and don't worry too much about sophistication. First seen in concept form at the Detroit Motor Show in 1989, the Viper carried in its nose an 8.0-liter V10 engine based on a new pushrod unit that would be used in Chrysler trucks and 'sports ute' vehicles. Lamborghini, now part of the Chrysler empire, had replaced the cast-iron cylinder block of the truck version with a light-alloy block. Simple two-valve cylinder heads were retained, but tuning and tweaking lifted the power output by a third to 400bhp, with a torque maximum of 450lb ft at 3600rpm. These vast torque reserves meant the Viper could cope with a 'skip shift' Borg-Warner gearbox which, like that in the Corvette ZR-1, would miss out intermediate gears during gentle driving to improve fuel economy and reduce noise. Not that the intermediate gears were all that relevant to the Viper's impressive performance anyway, as almost all traffic could be left behind by accelerating in fourth gear, at any speed from 20mph (32km/h) upward.

Rudimentary weather protection meant that driving a Viper was a rare dry-day event in northern Europe, but Chrysler displayed a solution to that problem at the Los Angeles show in 1993. It was no surprise that the GTS coupé was more aerodynamically efficient than the Viper roadster, but it was also lighter and had been given an engine with 450bhp, making it significantly quicker. It went into production in 1996, by which time Chrysler was working on more powerful versions of the Viper, culminating in the 635bhp Venom 600 of 1997. The same year, Carroll Shelby's GM V8-powered Series 1 and the new-shape Chevrolet Corvette both made their debut, showing that America's sports cars were experiencing something of a revival.

Another revival was happening in England. MG, one of the greatest sports car marques of all, had stopped making the MGB and Midget in the early 1980s and since then had concentrated on rebadged versions of the Metro and Maestro hatchbacks and the Montego sedan – plus the rally

Above: TVR went from strength to strength in the 1990s. The Cerbera coupé widened the company's range still further.

Below: The Chimaera was intended to be a more practical TVR.

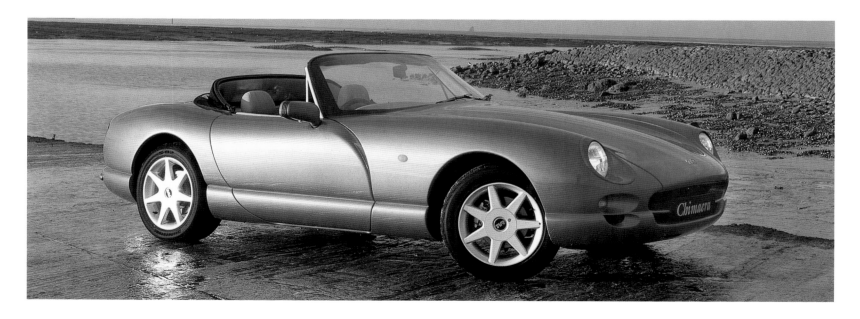

special Metro 6R4. Meanwhile interest in the classic MGs remained strong, and a boom in classic car values saw more and more MG sports cars being restored. The British Motor Industry Heritage Trust had been set up to preserve the history of the British motor industry, and its commercial arm British Motor Heritage now saw the opportunity to collect together the original tooling for MG bodies and start manufacturing panels to help restorers. From there it was a short step to building complete bodyshells for restoring cars which were too rust-riddled to save. Production began in 1988, the shells being welded together in a new factory on an industrial estate at Faringdon, just a few miles up the road from the old MG factory.

Above: The Mitsubishi 3000GT was packed with technology.

Right: Jaguar's supercharged XKR combined supercharged power with head-turning style.

Below: The XKR was developed from the highly successful XK8 coupé.

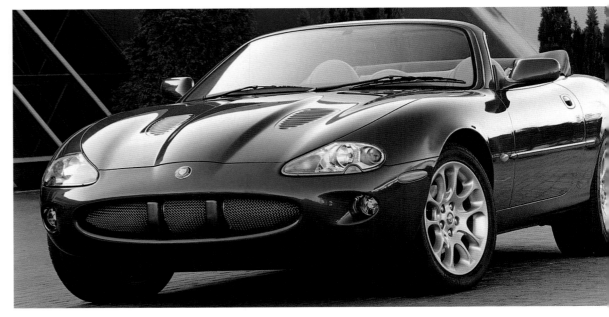

Return of the MGB

The idea of bringing the MGB back as a production car was then mooted, but that would have stretched British Motor Heritage's resources too thin. Instead a 'special projects' team at Rover Group, as MG's parent company was now called, was brought in to mastermind the operation. Project Adder – perhaps an ironic reference to the '60s Cobra – was to be a new MGB roadster with Rover V8 power, the long-running ex-Buick V8 now in 3950cc fuel-injected form with 190bhp rather than the previous MGB V8's 3528cc and 137bhp from a pair of SU carbs. Leyland's claims back in 1973 that the roadster shell wasn't up to the V8's output had obviously been quietly forgotten in the intervening two decades. The original MGB structure was retained, but constructed with more modern attention to sealing and painting to ward off corrosion, while

Above: *Honda's NSX was a genuine supercar.*

Audi TT quattro

Manufacturer:	Audi (Ingolstadt, Germany and Györ, Hungary)
Production years:	1999 onward
Engine location:	Front
Configuration:	In-line four-cylinder
Bore x stroke:	81x87mm
Capacity:	1781cc
Valve operation:	Twin overhead cam
Fuel system:	Electronic fuel injection, turbocharger
Power:	225bhp at 5900rpm
Gearbox:	Six-speed manual
Driven wheels:	Four wheel drive
Chassis/body:	Unitary steel body
Suspension:	Front: MacPherson struts with anti-roll bar
	Rear: trailing arms and transverse links with anti-roll bar
Brakes:	Hydraulically operated discs on all four wheels
Wheels/tires:	17in alloy wheels, 225/45x17 tires
Top speed:	147mph (237km/h)
Acceleration:	0-62mph (100km/h): 6.7sec

Left: *The car to be seen in at the turn of the century: Audi's Bauhaus-influenced TT.*

Above: The Audi TT's styling was just as successful in roadster form.

Below: Awesome styling and a twin-turbo rotary engine made the 1990s Mazda RX-7 an instant hit.

the outer panels were beefed up to give the car a fresher and more aggressive appearance. All four fenders bulged out to cover fatter tires, and there were new integrated bumpers at the front and rear which were far more attractive than the black polyurethane efforts of the 1970s. A wood-and-leather interior completed the package, which was called the MG RV8.

The result, as some said, was what the MGB might have become had it remained in production and been continually developed. It was still, in essence, a 30-year-old car and had a distinctly old-fashioned feel, retaining such unsophisticated engineering as a leaf-sprung live axle and drum brakes at the rear. Grip was in short supply for a '90s sports car, but it appealed to those who fancied the idea of a traditional British roadster yet couldn't face the unreliable realities of driving a classic. Sales were slow in the UK but many went to Japan, and around 2000 were built.

Blackpool rocks

A more modern interpretation of the same theme was already in production, though not by MG. TVR in Blackpool had been quietly honing their glassfiber-bodied sports cars, also powered by Rover V8 engines. The 1980s wedge shapes had been softened and the S-series had reintroduced the classic TVR curves of the 1960s and '70s, and then in 1990 a brand new body appeared. Clean, taut, and with little external decoration, it was an instant hit and reached the showrooms a couple of years later as the TVR Griffith. The show car had been based on a TVR V8S chassis but the new Griffith had a new chassis based on the company's successful Tuscan racing car with double-wishbone suspension at both ends, delivering grip and handling that was well up to the strong performance of the V8 engines, tuned by TVR's Coventry-based engine subsidiary TVR Power. Three different engine specifications were available: a 4.0-liter (actually the same 3950cc as the MG RV8, which Land Rover called a '3.9-liter') with either 240bhp or 250bhp, and a 280bhp 4.3-liter.

Left: The MGF was a skillful blend of existing and new components.

MGF 1.8 VVC

Manufacturer:	Rover Group (Longbridge, England)
Production years:	1995-2002
Engine location:	Mid-engined
Configuration:	In-line four-cylinder
Bore x stroke:	80x89.3mm
Capacity:	1796cc
Valve operation:	Twin overhead cam, variable valve timing
Fuel system:	Electronic fuel injection
Power:	145bhp at 7000rpm
Gearbox:	Five-speed manual
Driven wheels:	Rear wheel drive
Chassis/body:	Unitary steel body
Suspension:	Hydragas gas springs, interconnected front to rear
Brakes:	Hydraulically operated discs on all four wheels
Wheels/tires:	16in alloy wheels, 215/40x16 tires
Top speed:	130mph (209km/h)
Acceleration:	0-60mph (97km/h): 7.0sec

The Griffith quickly stole customers away from much more expensive machinery, and TVR responded by taking the car upmarket with a more powerful V8 engine – first a 5.0-liter Rover-based V8 and then its own in-house AJP V8, delivering 325bhp. The lower end of the market was served by another new car, the Chimaera, based on the Griffith chassis but offering more of a grand-tourer feel with slightly softer suspension, slightly less exhaust noise and the option of power steering. Otherwise the recipe was much the same: Rover V8 engines up to 4.3-liters and 280bhp, wrapped in a fabulously curvy glassfiber body styled by TVR themselves, every line being OK'd by TVR boss Peter Wheeler. Even Wheeler's dog Ned had his say: TVR shapes are concocted by carving a full-size mock-up from a lump of foam, and at one point Ned bit a lump out of the front corner of the nascent Chimaera. The canine bite mark added something, the team thought, and in the final car its location became an air vent which also carried a direction indicator lamp. Like the Griffith, the Chimaera was warmly received and throughout the 1990s TVR went from strength to strength. Its range of in-house AJP engines was expanded to include straight sixes and a V12, and a further model, the fixed-head coupé Cerbera, was added to the range.

Left: BMW's Z3 had a starring role in the James Bond film GoldenEye.

Above: The back-to-basics Lotus Elise put driver involvement at the top of its priorities.

Above: Westfield employed a variety of engines in its own stark sports cars.

Below: Caterham's rebodied Seven, called the 21, simply couldn't compete with the Elise on price.

For sophisticated technology, though, buyers had to look elsewhere. Jaguar offered it in the new XK8 grand tourer, with a five-speed ZF automatic gearbox and a silky new V8 engine, followed up by a searingly quick supercharged XKR. Mitsubishi offered four-wheel drive, four-wheel steering, electronically adjustable suspension and turbocharged V6 power in the 3000GT, while Toyota revealed a new twin-turbo Supra with more than 300bhp. Honda's NSX went a step further with a classic mid-engined supercar layout, and a normally-aspirated 3.0-liter V6 engine which developed 270bhp thanks to VTEC variable valve timing and a variable-length intake manifold. In a lower price band, Audi's TT offered a turbocharged engine with five valves per cylinder and the company's trademark four-wheel-drive transmission, all crammed inside an arresting bodyshape by stylist Freeman Thomas that drew inspiration from the functional elegance of 1930s Bauhaus design. Both coupé and roadster versions were available, and the TT quickly became *the* sports car to be seen in.

Not that there was a lack of competition. Mazda had introduced a new RX-7 with striking looks and a turbocharged rotary engine. BMW employed its well-respected engines in a new roadster, the Z3, which appeared as James Bond's transport in the film *GoldenEye*. Alfa Romeo returned to the sports car arena with a new GTV and Spider which may have shared much of their componentry with other cars from Alfa's parent company, Fiat, but which still had real character.

Mid-engined MGs

Nor had MG stood still, the RV8 being merely a starting point. A new MG sports car was announced in 1995, and this time it really was a new car rather than a reincarnation of a classic design. The MGF was the first mass-market mid-engined MG, the rally-special 6R4 being built in very limited numbers, though it followed a stillborn mid-'70s study called ADO21 and a mid-'80s supercar concept called EX-E. The engine for the new production car was Rover's acclaimed K-series unit, also used in the Metro and Rover 200 hatchbacks, though for the MGF the capacity was increased to 1796cc. Two versions were available, the more powerful unit developing 143bhp thanks to an electro-hydraulic variable valve timing system. Modified Metro subframes were used and the MGF retained the Metro's Hydragas suspension system with gas-filled chambers in place of conventional steel springs and fluid interconnection between front and rear wheels. At launch

Above: *The 1950s styling of Gordon Murray's Rocket hid a modern superbike engine.*

both versions of the MGF were fitted with conventional five-speed manual gearboxes, but a CVT automatic that Rover called Steptronic was added to the range in 1999. Normally the system provided continuously-variable gearing, but it could also be used as a sequential manual transmission with six fixed ratios, the driver selecting between them using buttons mounted on the steering wheel in the manner of the latest Formula 1 cars.

The MGF had plenty going for it. Trendy 'organic' looks were supplemented by clever detailing like the MGB-inspired nose and the Allen-bolt surround to the fuel filler cap. Easy to drive, comfortable and well packaged, the new MG stole customers both from other small sports cars like the Mazda Miata and hot hatches in the mold of the Volkswagen Golf GTI. But some drivers felt that the MG didn't feel as special as a good sports car should: convenient and refined it may have been, but it lacked the raw driving appeal that is an essential part of a good sports car's character. For that, buyers had to look elsewhere.

Fortunately there was plenty of choice. Lotus had failed to capture the public's imagination with the front-wheel-drive Elan sports car, and had now passed into the control of Romano Artioli of Bugatti. Now the company's hopes were pinned on a new small sports car, named Elise after Artioli's granddaughter and powered by the same 1.8-liter Rover K-series engine that sat in the back of the MGF. But the Lotus was a very different car, with a clever new structure and the accent firmly on driver appeal rather than everyday practicality. The Elise chassis was made from aluminum extrusions, bonded together using Epoxy adhesives to form an incredibly light structure, weighing just 154lb (70kg). It was also very stiff, and the stiffness was important: a flexible chassis allows the whole car to act like a giant spring, reacting to the loads transferred by the suspension. With a stiff structure the suspension can be fine-tuned more precisely and wheel movements controlled more accurately, delivering fine roadholding and deft handling. If ever a car proved the point, the Elise was it.

Rocket	
Manufacturer:	Light Car Company (Cambridge, England)
Production years:	1992 onward
Engine location:	Mid-engined
Configuration:	In-line four-cylinder
Bore x stroke:	75.5x56mm
Capacity:	1002cc
Valve operation:	Twin overhead cam, 20 valves
Fuel system:	Electronic fuel injection
Power:	143bhp at 10,500rpm
Gearbox:	Five-speed manual (with two-speed final drive)
Driven wheels:	Rear wheel drive
Chassis/body:	Tubular space frame, glassfiber body panels
Suspension:	Front: double wishbones and coil springs
	Rear: double wishbones and coil springs
Brakes:	Hydraulically operated ventilated discs on all four wheels
Wheels/tires:	6x15in alloy wheels, 195/50x15 tires
Top speed:	140mph (225km/h)
Acceleration:	0-60mph (97km/h): 4.5sec

Above: By the end of the 1990s Lamborghini's front-line supercar was the Diablo, seen here in SV form.

Below: The short-lived Bugatti revival produced the EB110 supercar. This is car number 25, owned by Bugatti's head at the time, Romano Artioli.

The Elise excites

The little Lotus proved to have remarkable on-the-limit handling coupled with high limits of adhesion. So what if there was plenty of engine noise, and merely rudimentary weather protection; the Elise was intended to provide driving thrills rather than practical transport, and it succeeded brilliantly, becoming a favorite machine for track days. Lotus had finally built a spiritual successor to the Lotus Seven, a car which was itself still in production in a much modified form and offering an equally raw driving experience.

Caterham Cars, makers of the Seven since the early 1970s, had been quietly developing the product beyond Colin Chapman's original ideas. The rear suspension had been upgraded to a de Dion system, and Caterham had taken advantage of modern engine technology, making the Seven available with the 150bhp, 16-valve Vauxhall engine that Cosworth had developed for the Astra GTE and Cavalier GSi 2000. A tuned version of the same engine went into the Seven JPE, which was shatteringly fast through the gears – though its top-end pace was limited by its aerodynamically inefficient separate fenders and freestanding headlights. Such was the Seven's pace with these modern engines that Caterham offered a driver-training course to buyers so they could learn how to use all that performance safely. Later in the decade Caterham and Lotus both employed tuned Rover K-series engines, including a 190bhp motor destined for a Rover 200 racing series that never happened. An evolution of the Seven with full-width bodywork, the Caterham 21, was well-received by the press but did not sell well: it trod much the same path as the Elise, but couldn't compete with the Lotus on price. Instead, Caterham concentrated on the Seven.

Westfield built an equally raw machine, also inspired by the Lotus Seven, but had their own ideas about power units. While Caterham opted for tuned versions of the Vauxhall engine – eventually pushing power up to a phenomenal 250bhp – Westfield turned to turbocharging and bigger capacities. The turbocharged four-cylinder unit from the Ford Sierra Cosworth delivered over 220bhp, giving the Westfield scorching acceleration up to a relatively low maximum speed. As an alternative Westfield built the SEiGHT, powered by 3.5-liters of Rover V8 engine and delivering wheelspin almost on demand. At another extreme they then started to use superbike engines, delivering respectable power outputs in cars of much lower overall weight.

A similar idea had already been tried by the Light Car Company's Rocket which, though a very different machine, had also been inspired by Colin Chapman's Lotus Seven. Designed by

Supercar Shoot-Out

Competition for the title of fastest production car in the world reached new heights in the 1990s. Back in the 1950s the fastest car you could buy was the gullwing Mercedes-Benz 300SL, essentially a racing car adapted for road use but a proper production car all the same. Then Ferrari's road cars took over in the 1960s, with the 365GTB/4 Daytona just a fraction quicker than Lamborghini's mid-engined Miura. The Miura's replacement, the Countach, could reach 175mph (282km/h) but Ferrari claimed well over 180mph (290km/h) for the Berlinetta Boxer.

Porsche entered the fray in 1987 with the turbocharged 959, capable of 197mph (317km/h), and Ferrari replied the following year with the 201mph (323km/h) F40. Lamborghini crept ahead with its new Diablo in 1990, only to be comprehensively overtaken a few months later by the Jaguar XJ220, capable of an astounding 213mph (343km/h).

Bugatti's EB110 was a fraction slower but the Italian marque revealed a revised version, the SS, in 1993 which bettered the Jaguar's top speed by 4mph (6km/h). But the Bugatti's reign was short-lived: in 1994 Gordon Murray's McLaren F1 appeared. The McLaren easily beat the Bugatti's 217mph (349km/h) and an example was timed at 240mph (386km/h) in 1998 – by which time production had ended. In terms of top speed, and much else, the McLaren is still the benchmark for supercar manufacturers.

Gordon Murray, who had made his name designing Formula 1 cars for Brabham and then McLaren, the Rocket achieved prodigious performance through extreme light weight. A purpose-built spaceframe chassis, bespoke suspension and transmission components, light glassfiber and carbonfiber bodywork, and a Yamaha superbike engine kept overall weight down to just 775lb (352kg), though in part that was because the Rocket was never intended to be practical, so there was no roof and just a low aero-screen protecting the driver. Though the Rocket looked like a single-seater (the body design reflected open-wheeled racers of the 1950s) there was a second seat behind the driver's. Murray's work on this tandem-seat design later went into McLaren's 'Adrenaline' project which built a two-seater version of its Formula 1 car.

Above: *Jaguar's fastest car was the XJ220S.*

Below: *The wild Cizeta Moroder was powered by a transverse V16 engine.*

Above: Peter Stevens made his name with work for Jaguar and a successful restyle of the Lotus Esprit in 1987.

McLaren F1

Manufacturer:	McLaren Cars (Woking, England)
Production years:	1993-97
Engine location:	Mid-engined
Configuration:	V12
Bore x stroke:	86x87mm
Capacity:	6064cc
Valve operation:	Twin overhead cam per bank, VANOS variable valve timing, four valves per cylinder
Fuel system:	Electronic fuel injection
Power:	627bhp at 7400rpm
Gearbox:	Six-speed manual
Driven wheels:	Rear wheel drive
Chassis/body:	Carbonfiber composite monocoque
Suspension:	Front: double wishbones, coil springs, anti-roll bar Rear: double wishbones, coil springs, anti-roll bar
Brakes:	Hydraulically operated discs on all four wheels
Wheels/tires:	Magnesium alloy, 9x17in front with 235/45ZR17 tires, 11.5x17in rear with 315/45ZR17 tires
Top speed:	240mph (386km/h)
Acceleration:	0-60mph (97km/h): 3.2sec

Right: Another Stevens design was the no-compromise McLaren F1.

The Rocket was a car Murray had wanted to build for a long time, and the world would soon see another. McLaren had built a handful of M6 road cars in the late 1960s, but these were based on its contemporary sports-racing machines: the M6 GT, as the roadgoing car was called, was hardly a practical production car. Now McLaren had decided to build a proper, roadgoing supercar – and at a time when new supercars seemed to be appearing daily. Lamborghini was replacing the Countach with the Diablo, while Jaguar's XJ220 was metamorphosing from a 6.2-liter V12-engined show car into a twin-turbo 3.5-liter V6 production machine. Bugatti had been revived with a four-wheel-drive, twin-turbocharged supercar. Strong demand had seen Ferrari continue production of its F40 well beyond the planned run of 450 cars. Nearby, Claudio Zampolli had set up shop to produce the Cizeta, a wild new supercar, with financial help from music producer Giorgio Moroder – and the talk was of a 200mph (327km/h) car, powered by a transversely-mounted V16 engine. And all of them – except for the sadly stillborn Cizeta – would be vying for the title of the fastest supercar on the planet (see 'Supercar Shoot-Out').

McLaren's supercar, first mooted in 1988, would be quite simply the best car the company could make, regardless of cost. On March 12, 1990 Murray gathered together his small team to brief them about the car they would build. The 10-hour meeting saw Murray explain that the McLaren – to be called the F1 – would be a three-seater, with the driver in the center, powered by a normally-aspirated engine. Light weight and careful management of the aerodynamics would make it both fast and stable. The car's styling would be in the capable hands of Peter Stevens, who had won considerable acclaim for the Lotus Elan and the restyled Esprit, and then for the Jaguar XJR-15 racing car. He had worked with Murray back in his Brabham days.

Power for McLaren

At that stage no decision had been reached about the source of the engine. Honda engines were then powering the McLaren Formula 1 cars that were dominating Grand Prix racing in the hands of Ayrton Senna and Alain Prost, and Murray had identified Honda as one of only three companies already building large, normally-aspirated engines with a 'specific output' (power per liter) of more than 100bhp; the other two were BMW and Ferrari. Though Honda seemed a likely partner, in the end it was BMW who supplied a 6064cc, 60 degree V12 engine which was just 24in (600mm) long and, at 586lb (266kg) with all its ancillaries, just a fraction over Murray's

Left: *McLaren's previous road car had been the M6 GT, a mildly modified racing car.*

target weight. Though some components, such as the VANOS variable valve-timing system, were essentially carried over from other BMW engines, this was a bespoke unit with twin overhead camshafts on each bank of cylinders and dry-sump lubrication to help keep the center of gravity low. Behind it sat a clever transverse gearbox from Traction Products that helped to keep the overall length of the powertrain to a minimum, while still offering the driver six forward ratios to choose from. Modern driver aids – traction control, anti-lock brakes, even power steering, and a brake servo – were eschewed to save weight and provide maximum driver involvement.

To meet Murray's demanding weight and stiffness targets the F1's structure had to be created the same way as a Grand Prix car's, based around a carbonfiber composite shell that was laid up by hand and then cured under heat and pressure in an autoclave oven. McLaren took over the former Ferrari Grand Prix team facility at Shalford in Surrey to build the F1's bodies, each one the result of around 3500 man hours of work. Assembly of the first cars at McLaren Cars' Woking factory took a further 2500 hours.

Two mechanical prototypes based on Ultima kit cars had been used to prove the running gear and drivetrain during 1991/92, and the first F1 prototype (chassis XP1) ran in December 1992. XP1's career was short, as it was destroyed in a crash during testing in March 1993, the driver emerging unhurt even after XP1 had rolled several times. XP2, completed just a couple of days after XP1's demise, was also crashed – but this time deliberately, to prove the car passed the necessary 30mph (48km/h) impact regulations. The F1 proved so strong that it was still drivable after the crash test...

It was, without doubt, the fastest and most uncompromising supercar ever created – and also one of the most expensive, at $900,000. A lighter competition version, the GTR, won at Le Mans in 1995 and went on to claim the new FIA GT Championship in 1995 and 1996. To celebrate, five 'F1 LM' cars were built, finished in McLaren's orange racing livery of the 1960s and replete with 41bhp more than the standard car. Just eight examples of a GT version with longer and wider bodywork followed in 1997, the year that McLaren ended production of the F1. Though they had talked of building up to 300 cars, just 100 had been made.

During testing at Nardo in southern Italy, XP3 had managed 231mph (372km/h) – with former Grand Prix driver Dr Jonathan Palmer at the wheel. An independent test in 1998 saw an F1 reach 240mph (386km/h), sealing its claim as the fastest production car ever made – a title it still holds.

Above: *The last F1 derivative was the longer and wider F1 GT.*

Today's Sports Cars

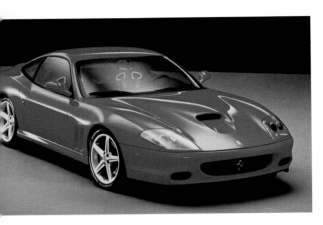

Above: *Currently the fastest front-engined Ferrari, the 575M.*

Previous page: *The revised MG revived the 'TF' badge.*

Below: *Just 349 Ferrari Enzos will be built.*

Recent motor shows have been crammed with debutant sports cars. Just about every car maker now seems to be adding roadsters and sports coupés to its range – and that's great news for sports car fans. Even better is the news that new sports cars are appearing throughout the market, from the exotic supercars down to roadsters that are truly affordable.

At the top end of the market, Ferrari continues to offer a range of supercars – a mid-engined two-seater, a front-engined two-seater, and a front-engined 2+2. The mid-engined car is the F360 Modena latest in a line of mid-engined 'mainstream' Ferraris that started with the Dino in the 1960s, and has more recently generated the 348 (unloved in retrospect, if not at the time) and the F355. In 2003 Ferrari introduced a stripped-out pseudo-race version, the Challenge Stradale, for those who feel that the latest Ferrari road cars are just a little too civilized. Fastest of the front-engined cars is now the 575M, a larger-engined derivative of the 550 Maranello that debuted in 2000 – marking the end of an era where Ferrari's fastest was a mid-engined car (latterly the Testarossa and 512TR). In 2003 the 575M was given a high-profile role in the Will Smith/Martin Lawrence film *Bad Boys II*, where it avoids all sorts of mayhem in a spectacular chase sequence. Back in the real world, for Ferrari drivers with friends the 456 replaced the 400 series, and then became the 456M (M for *modificato*) in 1998.

For the fortunate few there is one more Ferrari, the Enzo, planned for a production run of just 349 cars – just like the previous ultimate Ferrari, the F50. Powered by a 6.0-liter, 65-degree V12 developing 660bhp the Enzo is capable of 218mph (351km/h), but unlike the even faster McLaren F1 – which relied on simplicity and light weight to provide shattering performance and a high level of driver involvement – the Enzo is packed with technical solutions to a supercar's problems. Active aerodynamic systems manage the airflow around the car to provide grip-

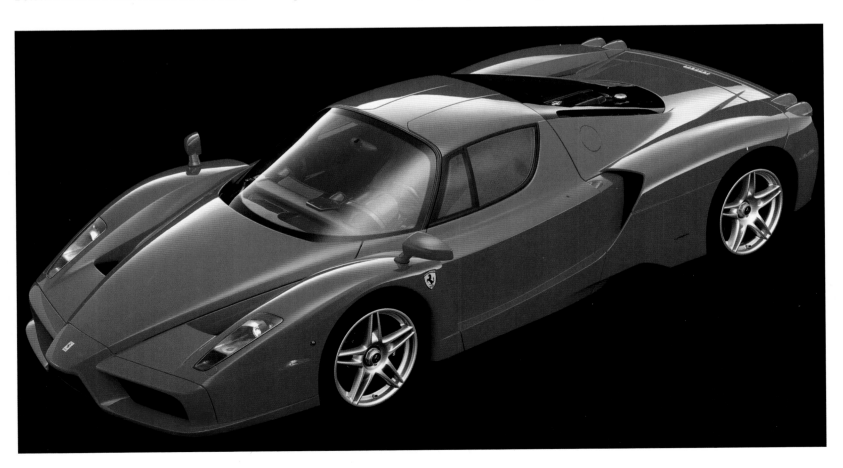

Left: First product of Audi's stewardship of Lamborghini, the Murciélago.

Lamborghini Gallardo

Manufacturer:	Automobili Lamborghini (Modena, Italy)
Production years:	2003 onward
Engine location:	Mid-engined
Configuration:	V10
Bore x stroke:	82.5x92.8mm
Capacity:	4961cc
Valve operation:	Twin overhead camshafts per banks, variable valve timing
Fuel system:	Electronic fuel injection
Power:	500bhp at 7800rpm
Gearbox:	Six-speed paddle-shift manual
Driven wheels:	Four wheel drive
Chassis/body:	Aluminum spaceframe with composite panels, steel doors
Suspension:	Front: double wishbones with coil springs and anti-roll bar
	Rear: double wishbones with coil springs and anti-roll bar
Brakes:	Hydraulically operated discs on all four wheels
Wheels/tires:	19in alloy wheels, 235/35x19 front tires, 295/30x19 rear
Top speed:	192mph (267km/h)
Acceleration:	0-60mph (97km/h): 4.7sec

enhancing downforce as the car's speed rises, the ride height and suspension damping constantly readjust to suit, there's a drive-by-wire throttle and a paddle-shift semi-automatic gearbox, and computerized traction control. Well-heeled Ferrari enthusiasts couldn't wait to sign on the dotted line, despite a price tag of around £420,000 ($735,000).

The latest Lamborghinis

Ferrari rival Lamborghini is now part of the Volkswagen Group, and operates under the control of Audi. Improved quality control was one of the first noticeable changes, while the new cars that have appeared from Sant'Agata in recent years have been more convenient and more efficient,

Below: The Gallardo is Lamborghini's new challenger in the junior supercar market.

Right: Ford's cute Streetka is the modern interpretation of the Sprite and Spitfire.

Above: Fiat has not replaced the charming Barchetta, which ended its production run in 2004.

Below: At the other end of the scale Ford-owned Aston Martin produces exclusive supercars like the Vanquish.

though no less extravagant or exciting. A 6.0-liter version of the Diablo paved the way for a replacement car, the Canto, on which Lamborghini had begun work in 1995. Zagato produced the original Canto shape, complete with enormous scoops on the rear pillars to direct cooling air to the engine, but after the Volkswagen acquisition in 1998 three more styling houses were asked to contribute ideas. The final shape for the new model, to be called the Murciélago after a famous fighting bull, was drawn in-house by Volkswagen stylist Luc Donckerwolke. The scoops were replaced by movable flaps which opened to provide cooling air to the engine, a long-stroke, 6.2-liter version of the Diablo V12. A dry-sump lubrication system allowed the engine to be mounted lower, lowering the car's center of gravity and improving its handling.

Lamborghini quickly followed up the Murciélago with a smaller, cheaper car to rival Ferrari's F360 Modena. The Gallardo offers clean, crisp styling – typical of Audi-era Lamborghini since the 6.0 Diablo of 2000 – together with the usual strong performance, and a new level of grip and security. It's powered by a new 4961cc V10 engine, fitted with variable valve timing and variable-length intake systems so that it generates 500bhp and a smooth, flat torque curve. The two banks of cylinders have been opened out from a V10's usual 72 degrees to a wider 90 degrees to reduce overall height while dry-sump lubrication and a tiny twin-plate clutch also help to reduce the height of the powertrain, keeping the masses low and aiding the Gallardo's handling thanks to a low center of gravity. That unusual V-angle also fuels speculation that the Gallardo V10 is related to Audi's Le Mans-winning R8 engine, another 90-degree V10. Another Audi-style feature is four-wheel drive, the system pushing most of the drive torque to the rear wheels except in unfavorable conditions, thus retaining a handling balance similar to a rear-drive car. While a manual gearbox is one option, Lamborghini expects most Gallardos to be fitted with its sequential semi-automatic 'E-gear' transmission.

Aston advances

Equally exclusive are the latest products from Aston Martin, topped by the V12 Vanquish. Seen in concept form in 1998 the Vanquish entered production in 2001 after the most exhaustive development process an Aston had ever seen, much of it centered on the new car's innovative structure. Unlike the previous V8 models, with their steel platform chassis and hand-rolled aluminum alloy bodywork, the Vanquish was based around a high-tech structure built from

Smart Roadster	
Manufacturer:	MCC Smart (Hamblach, France)
Production years:	2003 onward
Engine location:	Rear-engined
Configuration:	In-line three cylinder
Bore x stroke:	66.5x67mm
Capacity:	698cc
Valve operation:	Single overhead cam
Fuel system:	Electronic fuel injection
Power:	81bhp at 5250rpm
Gearbox:	Six-speed semi-automatic
Driven wheels:	Rear wheel drive
Chassis/body:	Unitary steel body
Suspension:	Front: MacPherson struts
	Rear: de Dion with coil springs
Brakes:	Hydraulically operated disc front, drum rear
Wheels/tires:	5x15in front, 6x15in rear alloy wheels. 185/55x15 tires
Top speed:	109mph (175km/h)
Acceleration:	0-62mph (100km/h): 10.9sec

Below: The Smart Roadster is fun to drive even at low speeds.

Above: Mazda's Miata continues with a new face and revised engines.

Above right: Caterham's R500 is one of the fastest-accelerating cars on the planet.

Lotus Elise	
Manufacturer:	Lotus (Hethel, England)
Production years:	1996 onward
Engine location:	Mid-engined
Configuration:	In-line four-cylinder
Bore x stroke:	80x89.3mm
Capacity:	1796cc
Valve operation:	Twin overhead cam
Fuel system:	Electronic fuel injection
Power:	118bhp at 6600rpm
Gearbox:	Five-speed manual
Driven wheels:	Rear wheel drive
Chassis/body:	Extruded aluminum frame, composite body panels
Suspension:	Front: double wishbones and coil springs
	Rear: double wishbones and coil springs
Brakes:	Hydraulically operated discs on all four wheels
Wheels/tires:	5.5x15in front, 7x16in rear alloy wheels. 185x55x15in front, 205/50x16in rear tires
Top speed:	126mph (203km/h)
Acceleration:	0-60mph (97km/h): 5.9sec

carbonfiber and extruded aluminum, with a carbon/steel/aluminum subframe carrying the engine and front suspension. Aluminum panels were still used, though they were now shaped by a new process called 'Superforming' before being fettled and fitted by Newport Pagnell's craftsmen. Powering the car was a development of the V12 engine already seen in the DB7 Vantage, a 5.9-liter, 460bhp unit coupled to a semi-automatic transmission which the driver controlled using paddles behind the steering wheel. James Bond was an early customer, the Vanquish appearing in the hands of Piers Brosnan in the film *Die Another Day*.

Aston Martin's parent company, Ford, also offers sports cars at the opposite end of the price range. A sporting coupé, the Puma, was followed by Ford's first pocket-sized roadster, the Streetka – based on the Ka hatchback and inspired, so Ford said, by the Frogeye Sprite and MG Midget. Designed by Ford's in-house styling company, Ghia, the original Streetka concept won considerable acclaim when it first appeared at the Turin show in 2000. Italian coachbuilder Pininfarina helped in the transformation from show car to production machine which took just two years, the nose styling being revised along the way and the Streetka gaining a rear spoiler to improve high-speed stability. The finished Streetka was then introduced to the public with 'teaser' appearances during singer Kylie Minogue's European tour in 2002. Like the Spridgets of old, the production version of the Streetka offers performance which is reasonable rather than rapid, the four-cylinder Duratec 8V engine delivering just 95bhp, but makes up for it in sheer affordable fun.

Smart Roadster

There's little competition in the 'submini' sports car class at the moment, but the Streetka has been joined by a new arrival from Smart. The first Smart was a city car combining the talents of the Swatch watch combine and DaimlerChrysler, makers of Mercedes-Benz cars. Now there's a Smart Roadster, using the same rear-mounted turbocharged, three-cylinder gasoline engine and sequential semi-automatic gearbox as its more pedestrian stablemate in a lower, more stylish body. It's a compact package that provides driving thrills at less than license-losing speeds, and

Above: *Lotus has restyled the Elise, giving it mini-Ferrari looks.*

Left: *Also built by Lotus, the Vauxhall VX220.*

Vauxhall VX220 Turbo	
Manufacturer:	Vauxhall (Luton, England)
Production years:	2003 onward
Engine location:	Mid-engined
Configuration:	In-line four-cylinder
Bore x stroke:	86x86mm
Capacity:	1998cc
Valve operation:	Twin overhead cam, 16 valves
Fuel system:	Electronic fuel injection, turbocharger
Power:	200bhp at 5500rpm
Gearbox:	Five-speed manual
Driven wheels:	Rear
Chassis/body:	Extruded aluminum frame, composite body panels
Suspension:	Front: double wishbones and coil springs
	Rear: double wishbones and coil springs
Brakes:	Hydraulically operated ventilated discs on all four wheels
Wheels/tires:	17in alloy wheels. 175/55x17 front, 225/45x17 rear tires
Top speed:	151mph (243km/h)
Acceleration:	0-60mph (97km/h): 4.7sec

should prove popular. A high performance version was built in 2003 using two Smart three-cylinder engines on a common crankshaft to produce a twin-turbo V6 of 1796cc, delivering 170bhp – but it's unlikely to reach production. Those searching for more performance can, however, expect a tuned Smart Roadster from Brabus in due course. The only other rival to compete with these two is Daihatsu's new Copen, with an attractive teardrop shape and a 660cc turbocharged engine. The Copen's party-piece is its Mercedes SLK-style folding hard top.

Above: Alfa Romeo's GTV and Spider are as stylish as ever.

Fiat's charming Punto-based Barchetta, introduced in the mid-1990s, has finally reached the end. Despite its undoubted appeal some British drivers were still put off by the lack of a right-hand-drive version. The Barchetta bridged the gap to the next class up where competition is hotter, with Toyota's new third-generation MR2 facing up against Mazda's revised Miata (now with a choice of 1.6-liter and 1.8-liter engines) and MG-Rover's revised MGF, now known as the TF. Mazda has maintained the interest in the Miata with numerous special-edition models offering special paint and extra equipment, but its wonderfully well-balanced chassis cries out for more power. Meanwhile the MG has been given new, more conventional coil-spring suspension and a wider range of K-series engines, the strongest delivering 158bhp (15bhp more than the Mazda). Early in 2003 the TF was judged the 'World's Most Beautiful Cabriolet' by a panel of 13 international judges chosen from design experts from outside the automotive industry. It was praised for 'blending great originality and typical elements of MG tradition, with a strong casual and dynamic character.'

Sheer performance

Spend more and you can choose whether you want your sports car to offer comfort and convenience alongside driver appeal, or whether you're prepared to sacrifice everything for the last word in driver involvement. If it's sheer performance and handling that you're interested in, for road or track use, Westfield can offer stark sports cars with engines ranging from superbike motors to Rover's venerable V8. Caterham, too, still offers the Seven in a variety of guises, ranging from the 105bhp Classic to the top-of-the-range R500, a 230bhp projectile which despatches the 0-60mph (97km/h) benchmark in just 3.5 seconds.

Other track-day specials include the radically styled Ariel Atom, reviving a great name from the past, and the equally eye-catching Lotus 340R. The slightly more practical Lotus Elise is now offered in a restyled form with two standard engine specifications – delivering 120bhp and 156bhp. Lotus has also developed the Elise concept in other directions, with a central-seat Sport Elise coupé powered by a 200bhp engine and intended for a one-make race series. A road version, the Exige, reverts to a conventional two-seat configuration and uses slightly less powerful engines of either 177bhp or 190bhp.

MG TF 160

Manufacturer:	MG-Rover (Longbridge, England)
Production years:	2002 onward
Engine location:	Mid-engined
Configuration:	In-line four-cylinder
Bore x stroke:	80x89.3m
Capacity:	1796cc
Valve operation:	Twin overhead cam, 16 valves
Fuel system:	Electronic fuel injection
Power:	158bhp at 6900rpm
Gearbox:	Five-speed manual
Driven wheels:	Rear wheel drive
Chassis/body:	Unitary steel body
Suspension:	Front: double wishbones with coil springs and anti-roll bar Rear: multi-link with coil springs and anti-roll bar
Brakes:	Hydraulically operated discs, ventilated at front
Wheels/tires:	7x16in front alloy wheels. 195/45x16 front, 215/40x16 rear tires
Top speed:	137mph (220km/h)
Acceleration:	0-62mph (100km/h): 7.6sec

Right: Audi's latest TTs feature 3.2-liter V6 engines and clever semi-automatic gearboxes.

Left: Mercedes-Benz has just announced a new SLK: enthusiasts will hope it is more involving to drive than the existing SLK.

Below: A high-revving normally-aspirated engine was the Honda S2000's big attraction.

Right: BMW's latest roadster, the much acclaimed Z4.

Supercar performance

General Motors' European brands now list an excellent sports car known in Britain as the Vauxhall VX220 (and in the rest of Europe as the Opel Speedster), and in a curious footnote to the period when General Motors owned Lotus, this new sports car was based on the Lotus Elise – but fitted with a 2.2-liter, 145bhp Vauxhall/Opel engine. In March 2003 the VX220 was given a major performance boost when it was fitted with the 200bhp turbo engine from the Astra GSi. The VX220 Turbo was claimed to top 150mph (241km/h) and hit 60mph (97km/h) from rest in less than five seconds, figures which put its performance into the supercar league. British buyers of both the Turbo and the normally-aspirated 2.2 were given a free day's driver training at Bedford Autodrome by former Grand Prix driver Jonathan Palmer's Palmersport operation.

If cars like these are just too raw for you, there's plenty of choice when it comes to sports cars that are capable of playing a practical role, too. Alfa Romeo's four-cylinder and V6 GTV and Spider models still look attractive despite being nearly a decade old, and attract such illustrious

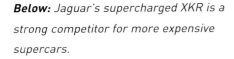

Below: Jaguar's supercharged XKR is a strong competitor for more expensive supercars.

Who Owns Whom?

The motor industry is increasingly made up of multinational corporations controlling a variety of brands. As far back as the 1960s Ford had tried to buy Ferrari, and when those negotiations failed it first built its own Le Mans car, the GT40, and then became involved with Alessandro DeTomaso's Pantera. In the 1980s there was a link with the new owners of AC. Then in 1987 Ford bought 75 percent of Aston Martin, and in 1989 it paid $1.6 billion to take control of Jaguar. Volvo is also now part of the blue oval, and there are links with Mazda, too.

Ferrari secured its future thanks to a tie-up with Fiat, which also now controls Lancia, Alfa Romeo, and Maserati. The other long-established Italian supercar manufacturer, Lamborghini, was bought by the American Chrysler company in 1988, then by a group of Indonesian investors in 1994, and finally by the Volkswagen group in 1998. During the same year Volkswagen bought the remains of Bugatti, and the group also includes Audi and Bentley – plus Seat, which may yet make a true sports car.

Lotus had early links with Ford, and later there was investment from Toyota. In the 1980s General Motors took control, and then the company passed to Romano Artioli's new Bugatti company. When that failed, a number of deals were explored to find a future for the company, and control passed to the Malaysian company responsible for Proton cars in 1996. But there are plenty of independents left: Morgan, Caterham, TVR, and others still thrive.

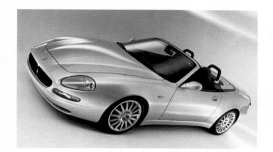

Above: *Maserati has enjoyed a renaissance under the control of Ferrari.*

customers as former Boomtown Rat, Sir Bob Geldof. Audi's TT coupé and roadster were revised shortly after launch after it was found that some drivers lost control during high speed cornering, though whether there was anything wrong with the way the TT handled is a moot point. Audi revised the TT once again in 2003, with visual detail changes and the addition of V6 engines – probably as a response to the 3.2-liter V6 now available in the small Mercedes-Benz roadster, the SLK. Supercharged 'Kompressor' four-cylinder engines of 2.0-liters and 2.3-liters (delivering 163bhp and 197bhp respectively) are fitted to two cheaper SLKs; at the other end of the range sits the SLK 32 AMG, with a 354bhp V6 engine. A new SLK debuts in 2004.

Above: *Chrysler's new Viper, the SRT-10.*

Left: *V8 power lifts the Esprit into the supercar bracket.*

Above: The latest R230-series Mercedes-Benz SL, available with six, eight, or 12-cylinder engines.

Below: TVR's latest roadster, the Tamora.

New from Honda

Amongst these revised and facelifted machines sit two genuine newcomers. The first is Honda's S2000, which offers up-to-the-minute styling and a high-revving four-cylinder engine generating no less than 237bhp (nearly 119bhp per liter) without recourse to superchargers or turbochargers. Strong sales proved that the package was right, despite which Honda announced a raft of changes for the 2004 car aimed at improving still further the S2000's handling, braking, and styling.

The other major newcomer to this part of the market is the BMW Z4 roadster which replaced the highly successful Z3 during the summer of 2003, its eye-catching sharp-edged styling quickly grabbing the headlines. Power came from 2.5-liter and 3.0-liter six-cylinder engines developing 192bhp and 231bhp respectively, and an 'entry level' 2.2-liter version (still a straight six) with 170bhp was added to the range later that year. The 3.0-liter car could despatch the 0-60mph (97km/h) sprint in less than six seconds and its top speed, as with so many modern performance cars, was electronically limited to 155mph (250km/h). Even the electric roof was fast, retracting in an amazingly swift 10 seconds. Electric power steering made its BMW debut, the steering feel being optimized by computer, while a system called Dynamic Driving Control offered sporting drivers quicker throttle response and less steering assistance at the touch of a button.

And the Z4 isn't the only sports car in BMW's extensive line-up. In 2003 the 6-series badge was revived with a 645Ci coupé, powered by a 4.4-liter V8 engine, said to achieve 0-60mph (97km/h) in 5.6 seconds (and a top speed limited to 155mph/250km/h). At the top of BMW's range lies the Z8, a retro-styled roadster with considerable presence – and immense performance, as it shares its 4941cc, 400bhp V8 engine with the M5 sports sedan. Like the Z3 (and the 750iL sedan) the Z8 made an appearance alongside Piers Brosnan in a James Bond film – this time *The World Is Not Enough*, where it sported such vital accessories as a remote start control and ground-to-air missiles. Sadly the Z8 ends up being sawn in half – to the displeasure of Q branch, no doubt.

Porsche Boxster S	
Manufacturer:	Porsche (Stuttgart, Germany)
Production years:	2001 onward (other Boxster models 1997 onward)
Engine location:	Mid-engined
Configuration:	Flat six-cylinder
Bore x stroke:	93x78mm
Capacity:	3179cc
Valve operation:	Twin overhead cam per bank, 24 valves
Fuel system:	Electronic fuel injection
Power:	252bhp at 6250rpm
Gearbox:	Six-speed manual
Driven wheels:	Rear wheel drive
Chassis/body:	Unitary steel body
Suspension:	Front: MacPherson struts
	Rear: MacPherson struts
Brakes:	Hydraulically operated ventilated discs on all four wheels
Wheels/tires:	7x17in front, 8.5x17in rear alloy wheels. 205/50x17 front, 255/40x17 rear tires
Top speed:	162mph (260km/h)
Acceleration:	0-60mph (97km/h): 5.9sec

Sports car choice

For the $132,000 budget that buyers of the Z8 needed in the United States in 2003, there were numerous other sports car options. Maserati's Ferrari V8-powered 4.2GT (successor to the 3200GT) and Jaguar's supercharged V8 XKR (developed from the XK8) offered similar power and performance to the BMW Z8, for considerably less money. The Jaguar also had its own bit of Bond-film kudos, as transport for one of 007's foes in *Die Another Day*. Chrysler's all-new Viper SRT-10 matched the Z8's performance if not its build quality and elegance. Honda's recently-revised NSX wasn't quite as quick, but had its own blend of mid-engined virtues – and would have left enough in the kitty for a Fiat Barchetta. The Lotus Esprit, now powered by the company's own V8 engine, was quick enough to keep up but almost too cheap at under £50,000 ($87,500).

BMW's arch-rival Mercedes-Benz introduced its latest SL – known internally as the R230 – in only two guises, the rapid SL500 (306bhp, 5.0-liter V8) and the even more rapid SL55AMG (500bhp, supercharged 5.4-liter V8). Since then two more engine options have been added to extend the range at both ends, with a new entry-level 3.7-liter V8 SL350 and an SL600 with 5.0-liters of twin-turbo V12 power.

If all these cars are too clever and too refined – or just too expensive – for you, then the place to go is Blackpool – the home in Britain of TVR. The Chimaera continues with a choice of 4.5-liter and 5.0-liter V8 engines, while the rest of TVR's range combines V8 and straight-six power units. The Cerbera coupé is available with a 4.0-liter six-cylinder engine or a choice of 4.2-liter and 4.5-liter V8s, while the striking Tuscan has a choice of 3.6-liter and 4.0-liter sixes. The smaller engine also powers TVR's entry-level roadster, the Tamora. TVR has also been developing its own 7.7-liter V12 engine – essentially two straight-sixes mounted at 90 degrees – for a future Speed 12 model. The most recent products to emerge from Blackpool are the 440bhp

Above left: Morgan has merged retro and modern looks for its BMW-powered Aero 8.

Below: Porsche's Boxster roadster shares much with the latest 911.

Above: A familiar shape, but the 911 continues to develop underneath.

Below: Mazda sticks with the rotary engine for its latest sports coupé, the RX-8.

T440R coupé and the Tamora-based T350 coupé. An attractive V8-engined rival to TVR, reviving the famous Jensen name, sadly did not succeed.

If you're after a more traditional look then Morgan, as ever, is the company to help. Morgan's range now starts with the Runabout, powered by the same 1.8-liter Ford Zetec engine as its stablemate, the 4/4. A special edition car to celebrate the 35th anniversary of the Rover V8-powered Plus 8 was announced during 2003, while at the top of the range sits the Aero 8, which made its debut at the Frankfurt show in 2001. Despite retaining some elements of the traditional Morgan shape, such as running boards and separate fenders, the Aero 8 has been designed to offer more effective aerodynamics than the older models. The starting point for the new model was the all-aluminum chassis of Morgan's 1997 FIA GT Championship 'GT2' class racer, which was developed into a durable road-car structure with assistance from Alcan, the Morgan being the first production car to use Alcan's advanced technology. Powering the Aero 8 is what Morgan technical chief Chris Lawrence describes as 'the best drivetrain you can get,' the 4.4-liter, 286bhp BMW V8.

During 2003 Morgan offered 15 roadgoing replicas of its works racing cars, called Aero GT Coupés. These featured bigger 4.6-liter BMW V8 engines developing 330bhp, and a carbonfiber hard top and all were finished in the team's racing colors of two-tone blue and silver.

Another marque renowned for an iconic bodyshape is Porsche, which seems to have taken the best elements from its traditional air-cooled, rear-engined 911 cars and its more recent water-cooled, front-engined 928 and 968 models. The Stuttgart range no longer offers air-cooled engines or front-engined cars, and now starts with the Boxster, a mid-engined open roadster introduced in 1997 with 2.4-liter engines but now available with either a 2.7-liter or 3.2-liter water-cooled flat-six.

The 911 had been radically revised for the 1990s to produce the '964 series' Carrera 2 and Carrera 4 models, and these had been updated and restyled for the 1994 '993 series' with the brand new multi-link rear suspension that had been developed for Porsche's stillborn sedan car project. In 1998 there was another dramatic transformation: Porsche revealed the '996 series' 911,

Chrysler Crossfire	
Manufacturer:	Chrysler/Karmann (Osnabrück, Germany)
Production years:	2003 onward
Engine location:	Front
Configuration:	In-line four-cylinder
Bore x stroke:	89.9x84m
Capacity:	3199cc
Valve operation:	Twin overhead cam per bank, 18 valves
Fuel system:	Electronic fuel injection
Power:	215bhp at 5700rpm
Gearbox:	Six-speed manual (five-speed auto optional)
Driven wheels:	Rear wheel drive
Chassis/body:	Unitary steel body
Suspension:	Front: double wishbones with coil springs and anti-roll bar Rear: multi-link with coil springs and anti-roll bar
Brakes:	Hydraulically operated discs, ventilated at front
Wheels/tires:	7.5x18in front, 9x19in rear alloy wheels. 225/40x18 front, 255/35x19 rear tires
Top speed:	150mph (241km/h)
Acceleration:	0-62mph (100km/h): 6.5sec

which shared much of its engineering – and its front-end styling – with the Boxster. Finally the air-cooled flat-six engine has given way to a water-cooled unit, to aid emissions performance and to help the 911 to pass stringent new drive-by noise regulations, where rear-engined cars like the 911 are at a disadvantage. The noise tests look for the peak noise level as the car passes – with a rear-engined car both the engine noise and the exhaust noise hit the test microphone at the same time, while a front-engined car has two separate noise sources, resulting in a lower peak. Porsche's engineers have thus had to work extra hard to get the 911 approved.

Today the 911 range includes Carrera 2 and (four-wheel-drive) Carrera 4 models with 320bhp, in coupé and cabriolet forms, plus a two-wheel-drive Targa, a four-wheel-drive Turbo with 420bhp and the magnificent rear-drive GT2 with 462bhp. Even though the 911 is still central to Porsche's range, it is now a very different motor car, and shows that there is plenty of new thinking in the sports car market. Other recent debutants prove the point. The RX-8 that Mazda first showed in concept form at the 2001 Geneva show was more than just a replacement for the rotary-engined RX-7 sports car, for instance. Instead the RX-8 is intended to offer four-door convenience in a sporting shape, with what Mazda called 'Freestyle' doors – rear-hinged rear doors with no central pillar, allowing much easier access to the rear seats. The RX-8 also introduced the RENESIS rotary engine, normally aspirated (the previous RX-7 had been turbocharged) and capable of producing up to 280bhp. Meanwhile Mazda's Japanese competitor Nissan has reintroduced the famous 'Z' line with the 350Z and Chrysler has taken advantage of its new connections with Mercedes-Benz to create the SLK-based Crossfire coupé, seen as a concept car in 2001 and a production machine in 2003. And there's more to come.

Above left: *Nissan's Z-car line is back on top form with the 350Z.*

Above: *Chrysler's Crossfire uses the Mercedes SLK platform.*

Toward Tomorrow

Above: Audi's Le Mans quattro concept car drew much praise.

Previous page: Cockpit of the latest Ferrari, the 612 Scaglietti.

Opposite below: VW's W12 engine debuted in a wild supercar concept.

Below right: Porsche's Carrera GT is a superbly crafted combination of beautiful styling and awesome performance.

It's always dangerous to speculate about the new models that might make an appearance in the next few years. But recently, sports car manufacturers have been giving us plenty of insight into their plans for the future. Soon there will be even more sports cars for enthusiasts to choose from, in all price ranges, and some of these cars will demonstrate significant new advances in technology.

Racing has always inspired fast road cars, and the current GT racing regulations have resulted in some ultra-fast, ultra-rare machines for road use. Porsche has recently added the Cayenne off-roader to its range, but of more interest to sports car enthusiasts is the mid-engined Carrera GT that is to be built alongside the Cayenne at Porsche's new Leipzig factory. Based on a stillborn Le Mans racer, the Carrera GT is constructed entirely from carbonfiber composite materials, giving it a light and strong structure. Power comes from an all-alloy 68-degree V10 engine which shows its racing heritage with a rev limit of 8400rpm and a peak power speed of 8000rpm, where it develops 612bhp. Maximum torque, a substantial 435lb ft (590Nm) doesn't arrive until the engine is spinning at 5750rpm. The Carrera GT uses ceramic brake discs, similar to those which were first seen on the 911 GT2, and extends its use of ceramics to the clutch – a first for a production car. Porsche talk about a maximum speed of 205mph (330km/h) and a 0-62mph (100km/h) time of 3.9 seconds.

GT concepts

Porsche is not the only manufacturer to be cashing in on its involvement in GT racing. At Frankfurt in 2003 show-goers were bowled over by Audi's Le Mans quattro concept, which uses

Porsche Carrera GT	
Manufacturer:	Porsche (Stuttgart, Germany)
Production years:	2003 onward
Engine location:	Mid-engined
Configuration:	V10
Bore x stroke:	96x76mm
Capacity:	5733cc
Valve operation:	Twin overhead cam per bank, 40 valves
Fuel system:	Electronic fuel injection
Power:	612bhp at 8000rpm
Gearbox:	Six-speed manual
Driven wheels:	Rear wheel drive
Chassis/body:	Carbonfiber composite structure
Suspension:	Front: double wishbone with pushrod-operated inboard coil spring/damper and anti-roll bar Rear: double wishbone with pushrod-operated inboard coil spring/damper and anti-roll bar
Brakes:	Hydraulically operated ceramic ventilated discs on all four wheels
Wheels/tires:	9.5x19in front, 12.5x20in rear forged magnesium alloy wheels. 265/35x19 front, 335/30x20 rear tires
Top speed:	205mph (330km/h)
Acceleration:	0-62mph (100km/h): 3.9sec

the twin-turbo V10 engine from the R8 racing car that won Le Mans for the third consecutive year in 2002 – already seen in roadgoing form in the Audi Nuvolari quattro GT concept car. This 5.0-liter engine develops 610bhp, and features novel 'direct injection' technology. Styling has hints of the TT, the Nuvolari, and even the Audi Avus quattro concept from a few years ago. Audi's Volkswagen group stablemate SEAT, meanwhile, revealed its own GT car, the Cupra GT, at the Barcelona Motor Show in April 2003. Ironically this uses a twin-turbo V6 engine from Audi, generating 500bhp. The Cupra GT is expected to top 180mph (290km/h).

Both the Porsche and the Audi have V10 engines, which seem to be fashionable now among the manufacturers of super-fast cars (though Volkswagen debuted a W12 unit in a sleek supercar concept some years ago). Both Audi and Porsche have chosen V10s because their engines were originally designed as racing units, but modern approaches to engine balancing have made the V10 a practical proposition as a road car layout. It remains to be seen how long it will take sports

Above: The Mercedes-Benz Vision SLR concept led to the SLR McLaren production car.

Mercedes-Benz SLR McLaren*

Manufacturer:	McLaren Cars (Woking, England)
Production years:	2004 onward
Engine location:	Front
Configuration:	V8
Bore x stroke:	97x92mm
Capacity:	5439cc
Valve operation:	Twin overhead cam per bank, 24 valves
Fuel system:	Electronic fuel injection
Power:	626bhp at 6500rpm
Gearbox:	Five-speed semi-automatic
Driven wheels:	Rear wheel drive
Chassis/body:	Carbonfiber composite structure
Suspension:	Front: double wishbone and coil spring
	Rear: double wishbone and coil spring
Brakes:	Hydraulically operated carbon ceramic discs on all four wheels, ventilated front
Wheels/tires:	9x18in front, 11.5x18in rear alloy wheels. 245/40x18 front, 295/35x18 rear tires
Top speed:	208mph (335km/h)
Acceleration:	0-62mph (100km/h): 3.8sec

* specifications to be confirmed

Bugatti 16.4 Veyron*	
Manufacturer:	Bugatti Automobiles (France)
Production years:	2004 onward
Engine location:	Mid-engined
Configuration:	W16
Bore x stroke:	86x86mm
Capacity:	7993cc
Valve operation:	Four overhead camshafts, 64 valves
Fuel system:	Electronic fuel injection, four turbochargers
Power:	1001bhp at 6000rpm
Gearbox:	Seven-speed sequential semi-automatic
Driven wheels:	Four wheel drive
Chassis/body:	Carbonfiber composite structure with aluminum subframes
Suspension:	Front: double wishbone and coil spring Rear: double wishbone and coil spring
Brakes:	Hydraulically operated carbon ceramic discs on all four wheels, ventilated front
Wheels/tires:	20in alloy wheels. 265/30x20 front, 335/30x20 rear tires
Top speed:	252mph (406km/h)
Acceleration:	0-62mph (100km/h): 2.9sec
* specifications to be confirmed	

Above right: Will this be the world's fastest car? Bugatti's Veyron is said to achieve McLaren-beating pace.

Opposite left: Bristol's Fighter supercar made an appearance in Britain at the Goodwood Festival of Speed in 2003.

car engines to acquire some of the more radical systems used in Formula 1 engines over the last few years – systems such as pneumatic valve operation, allowing the engine to run to higher operating speeds and so deliver a greater power output.

It seems odd that the Mercedes-Benz SLR McLaren will feature nothing more unusual than a large-capacity V8. The car is a joint venture between Mercedes-Benz and McLaren, which runs Mercedes-powered Grand Prix cars – all of which have V10 engines. The SLR would certainly have had more technical cachet with a V10 under the hood – even if the end result might not have been any quicker or more exciting to drive. At least performance shouldn't be in doubt, as the supercharged V8, developed by AMG, produces 626bhp – enough to make the SLR sprint to 60mph (97km/h) from rest in less than four seconds. Just as likely to raise eyebrows are the SLR's doors, which are pivoted from the A-pillars so that they open outward and upward – a modern reinterpretation of the 1950s 300SL gullwing production car and the rare SLR Competition Coupé.

McLaren-beating performance

Still more new supercars are set to emerge soon. A W12 engine was fitted to a Volkswagen concept car shown at Tokyo in 2001, and the car later set a new record for distance covered in 24 hours at the Nardo test track – 4402.8 miles (7085.7km) at an average of 183.45mph (295.24km/h). The W12 went into a luxury sedan codenamed D1, known publicly as the Phaeton, in 2003. Meanwhile a related W16 will be fitted to the Bugatti Veyron which is due to enter production in April 2004, after its debut in final production-ready form at the Tokyo Motor Show in October 2003. Volkswagen, now custodians of the Bugatti brand, claim the W16 engine will develop 1001bhp and deliver McLaren F1-beating performance, including a top speed of more than 400km/h (249mph) and a 0-60mph (97km/h) time of less than three seconds.

Ferrari is due to replace the 456M early in 2004 with a new all-aluminum V12 car, the Pininfarina-styled 612 Scaglietti. Using light alloys for the spaceframe chassis and the bodywork gives the 612 Scaglietti a 132lb (60kg) weight advantage over the 456M, despite bigger overall dimensions, while at the same time providing a 60 percent increase in structural rigidity.

Performance improves as a result of the lower weight, the 540bhp output of the 65-degree V12 engine driving the 612 to a claimed 196mph (315km/h). Handling improves, too, thanks to a lower center of gravity. The gearbox is mounted in unit with the differential at the back of the car, improving the weight distribution, while electronically controlled traction control and stability systems enhance the car's basic dynamics. In addition to the engineering, it's a good-looking machine: the scalloped sides are said to recall a special-bodied 375MM built by Scaglietti for film director Roberto Rossellini, as a gift to his wife – movie star Ingrid Bergman.

In Britain, the enigmatic Bristol company has followed up its stark Speedster with the new gullwing Fighter, powered by a V10 Chrysler engine related to that in the Viper. The Fighter made its public debut at the Goodwood Festival of Speed in the summer of 2003, alongside Ford's new GT, which brings back the iconic styling of the 1960s Ford GT40 with modern technology and road manners.

The expanding Aston Martin marque, another outpost of the Ford empire, is soon to go into production with two new cars. A concept called AMV8 Vantage appeared early in 2003, and this will be the forerunner of a new entry-level V8 model (known internally as AM305). More recently Aston Martin has revealed the 2+2 DB9 – successor to the DB7, which has become the biggest-selling car in Aston Martin's 90-year history. Like the later versions of the DB7, the DB9 will use a version of the Aston V12 engine, production of which was planned to move from Cosworth Technology in Britain to a new factory at Cologne in Germany in 2004. Production of the car is also based at a new location, at Gaydon in Warwickshire.

Ferrari 612 Scaglietti*	
Manufacturer:	Ferrari (Maranello, Italy)
Production years:	2004 onward
Engine location:	Front
Configuration:	V12
Bore x stroke:	89x77mm
Capacity:	5748cc
Valve operation:	Twin overhead cam per bank
Fuel system:	Electronic fuel injection
Power:	540bhp at 7250rpm
Gearbox:	Six-speed semi-automatic
Driven wheels:	Rear wheel drive
Chassis/body:	Aluminum alloy spaceframe and body panels
Suspension:	Front: double wishbone and coil spring
	Rear: double wishbone and coil spring
Brakes:	Hydraulically operated discs on all four wheels
Wheels/tires:	Alloy wheels
Top speed:	196mph (315km/h)
Acceleration:	0-60mph (97km/h): 4.8sec
* specifications to be confirmed	

Above: *Ferrari's 612 Scaglietti is attractive – and quick.*

Above: *Bristol's stark Speedster apes the front-end styling of its 1950s sedans.*

Above: Ford relives its past glories with the GT.

Though the production version of the AMV8 Vantage is intended to be cheap for an Aston, it's still way beyond the reach of most of us. A little more affordable is the replacement for the Honda NSX, which industry insiders believe will be revealed in 2006 and will be similar to the Honda Sports Concept shown by the company at the Tokyo Motor Show in 2003. Even more affordable will be the new Mercedes-Benz SLK, which is due soon to answer criticism that the old model was too staid in its appearance and its road manners. The new model shares plenty of styling cues with its potent big brother, the SLR McLaren, and is expected to offer a wide variety of engines ranging from a 143bhp supercharged four to a 476bhp, 5.4-liter V8. There will also probably be a straight-six diesel.

As the development of the SLK suggests, sports cars in the future will use a wider variety of power units – and recent concept cars from some manufacturers demonstrate the same trend. Jaguar's R-D6 coupé concept, unveiled at the Frankfurt show in 2003, uses a new 2.7-liter twin-turbo V6 diesel – challenging ideas about the kind of power units that are suitable for a sporting

Right: Latest from Aston Martin is the four-seat DB9, which will be built at a new factory in Warwickshire, England.

brand like Jaguar (and preparing the way for Jaguar's X-type diesel production car). Peugeot's 2002 RC concept, a 2+2 mid-engined sports car, was presented in gasoline and turbodiesel forms. Mazda's Kusabi (from the Japanese meaning either 'wedge' or 'making way for something new') is a lightweight sports car powered by a 1.6-liter common-rail diesel engine and is said to make even city driving fun. Mazda has also recently shown the Ibuki ('adding vigor') and Roadster Turbo concepts, which hint at the possible direction for future Miata and RX-8 models. The RX-8 itself also appeared at the Tokyo Motor Show in October 2003 in a hydrogen-fueled form, demonstrating that the RENESIS rotary engine is particularly well-suited to running on hydrogen, needing little modification.

Left: Honda's HSC hints at what an NSX replacement might be like.

Below: Aston Martin's vital small sports coupé will be based on this impressive AMV8 concept.

Electrifying sports cars

Hybrid powertrains, combining electric motors with gasoline or diesel engines, are also being developed for sports cars. The benefit of a hybrid is that the electric motor can power the car at low speeds and in city centers, helping to reduce noise and improve city air quality. When more performance is required out on the open road, the gasoline or diesel motor kicks in – at the same time charging the electric motor's batteries for the next low-speed run. Toyota's Compact Sports

Right: R-D6 concept blends classic Jaguar styling cues with modern thinking.

Below: Peugeot RC concept cars were presented in gasoline- and diesel-engined forms.

and Specialty concept car displayed at the Frankfurt show in 2003 is one of the latest examples, with an electric motor driving the front wheels and a 1.5-liter gasoline engine driving the rear wheels, Toyota using a more powerful electric motor to reduce the amount of time the car relies on its gas engine.

Another hybrid concept is Subaru's B9 Scrambler, first seen at the Tokyo show in 2003, which uses an electric motor up to 50mph (80km/h) and then turns to gasoline power. The Scrambler promises to combine sports cars and off-roaders, as it has four-wheel drive and variable-height air suspension, which should give it impressive off-road performance and what Subaru calls the 'agility of a motorcycle.' This duality of purpose is a strong theme in recent concept cars: Hyundai, for instance, showed its Clix 'fun activity vehicle' in 2001, a cross between coupé, roadster, and sports-utility vehicle. Four-wheel drive is likely to continue – particularly in cars from Audi, Porsche, and Subaru – but front-wheel-drive sports cars seem unlikely to become common for the moment. SEAT did, however, release an attractive front-drive sports car concept called Tango, in 2001.

Motorcycle themes have already influenced sports car design. As far back as 1998 Renault released the Zo concept, which included exposed chassis frame sections like a motorcycle (and another innovative engine, this time a direct-injection gasoline unit). Since then cars like the Ariel Atom and Lotus 340R have developed this motorcycle styling influence, which is particularly suited to the stark, no-nonsense track day machines which have become popular in recent years. But Dodge's Razor concept in 2002 proved that a no-frills driver-centered sports car could still have a neatness of line.

Above *Future sports cars will offer a wider range of engine types: this experimental Mazda RX-8 runs on hydrogen.*

Below: *This could be the shape of the next Miata: Mazda's Ibuki concept car.*

Right: Toyota's Compact Sports and Specialty concept has an electric motor driving the front wheels and a gasoline engine driving the rear wheels.

Above: Hyundai's Clix 'fun activity vehicle' dates from 2001.

Outside influences

It is likely that influences from outside the motor industry will continue to play their part in sports car styling – whether they come from motorcycles, aircraft (the Subaru Scrambler has a 'wing and fuselage' face recalling its parent company's aircraft heritage), or even chronograph watches, which influenced the instruments in Aston Martin's AMV8 Vantage and Jaguar's R-Coupé. The Jaguar also reveals influences from modern room design in its innovative use of traditional materials. Further innovations will aid passenger comfort and driver control: adjustable pedals, used by Marcos since the 1960s, made a reappearance on Volkswagen's Concept R sports car (and Jaguar's production XJ sedan).

Below: Aircraft design influenced the styling of the Subaru B9 Scrambler.

The 'Might Have Beens'

Sports car history is littered with great ideas for cars that somehow never quite got off the ground. But the 1970s seem to have been a particularly poor decade for new launches. Always full of bright ideas, MG had proposed replacing its aging range with a mid-engined car code-named ADO21, but British Leyland management opted instead to approve Triumph's 'Bullet' prototype for production as the TR7. But Triumph didn't get everything its own way. An ambitious plan to create a range of sporting cars around a prototype called 'Lynx' never came to anything, the prototype itself now residing in the British Motor Industry Heritage Trust collection at Gaydon in Warwickshire.

At one stage Aston Martin looked likely to take over MG, and a William Towns-restyled MGB was created – but just one was built. Aston's twin-turbo gullwing Bulldog supercar also looked promising, but again there was only ever one car made.

The Panther Six and, later, the Solo and Solo II all had some merit but never really succeeded, and Vauxhall's interesting Equus sports car never came to anything. More recently Bertone and Pininfarina have created pretty sports cars for motor show stands, without attracting production contracts for them. MG's EX-E and Alfa Romeo's Nuvola were more sporting might-have-beens that could have been production successes. There are many more. Fortunately plenty of sports cars have reached production in recent years – and there are many more just around the corner.

Above: One of the most attractive 'might have beens,' the Alfa Romeo Nuvola.

Innovation in aerodynamics

Aerodynamics, too, will be a major influence in the styling of future sports cars, as designers try to obtain the greatest grip and stability at high speeds, while reducing drag still further to improve performance and reduce fuel consumption. Active aerodynamic systems, such as those already seen on cars from Porsche, McLaren, Lamborghini and others, will also help marry good looks with efficient aerodynamic performance. The Mercedes SLR McLaren even incorporates a flip-up airbrake that improves stability during high-speed braking, a backward glance to the air-braked 300SLR racing cars of the 1950s.

Left: Renault's 1998 Zo concept featured exposed chassis members and a direct-injection gasoline engine – both ideas which have since reached production.

Above: SEAT's Tango concept was front-wheel drive – still rare among sports cars.

Above: In a corner the outside wheels of the Mercedes F400 Carving concept car lean in like a motorcycle.

Right: VW's Concept R roadster brought back the idea of using adjustable pedals – which Marcos had used as far back as the 1960s.

In recent years many manufacturers have looked backward for inspiration in their cars' styling. Often the results have been exciting blends of old and new styles, but the 'retro' approach can only have a finite life. Attractive though they are, retro-styled cars like BMW's Z8 roadster and Jaguar's S-type sports sedan borrow from the past rather than contributing to the future, and their time will soon be up. Stylists of the future will have to make statements of their own, understanding a brand's heritage and representing it with new ideas rather than recycling old ones. Styling concepts like Jaguar's R-Coupé will have to take sports cars in new directions and help to identify a true style for the 21st century.

Improvements in brakes will be aimed at greater efficiency, less susceptibility to fade in prolonged hard use, better wear resistance, and lighter weight. Lotus has already used aluminum metal matrix composite (MMC) discs on the Elise, which are light in weight and wear slowly. Ferrari's Enzo uses carbon/silicon discs which are virtually wear-free and offer excellent retardation, even when cold. The latest models from Mercedes and Porsche have brake systems using ceramic technology. Computer-controlled anti-lock braking systems are now commonplace, many of them offering electronic brake force distribution (EBD) for even more effective retardation. Emergency brake-assist systems are also becoming more widely used to ensure optimum braking efficiency.

New types of transmission will also be seen in sports cars, and the semi-automatic gearbox operated either by a conventional center lever or by paddles behind the steering wheel will gain greater and greater popularity. At present some of these systems offer disappointing gearchange quality or unimpressive gearchange speed, but the newest systems show that these drawbacks can be eradicated. Part of the solution will be wider use of electronic 'drive by wire' throttles, where the engine is sent an electronic signal from the gas pedal rather than being directly connected to it by a mechanical linkage. These systems allow the engine and transmission to adapt better to the driver's requirements so, for instance, the engine can modulate throttle opening while the transmission is changing gear to improve the gearchange quality.

Electronic control of the throttle and electronic power steering systems (in place of the hydraulic systems which are currently more common) will also allow engineers to offer a driving experience tailored to each driver. The throttle response and the steering feedback can be

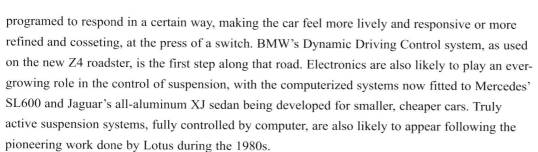

Above: *Cadillac celebrated its centenary in 2002 with the V12 Cien sports car.*

Left: *Vauxhall, too, celebrated 100 years with a sports car – the Lightning.*

programed to respond in a certain way, making the car feel more lively and responsive or more refined and cosseting, at the press of a switch. BMW's Dynamic Driving Control system, as used on the new Z4 roadster, is the first step along that road. Electronics are also likely to play an ever-growing role in the control of suspension, with the computerized systems now fitted to Mercedes' SL600 and Jaguar's all-aluminum XJ sedan being developed for smaller, cheaper cars. Truly active suspension systems, fully controlled by computer, are also likely to appear following the pioneering work done by Lotus during the 1980s.

Engineering changes

Innovative solutions to suspension design may also play a role in the sports car of the future. The Mercedes-Benz F400 Carving leans its outside wheel into corners like a motorcycle, and a development of this system may give the next generation of sports cars greater stability and grip.

Even the structure of the sports car is likely to change over the next few years. We will see greater use of aluminum and carbonfiber, and much greater use of structural adhesives as the technology for using them in production improves and there is greater awareness of modern repair techniques within the motor trade. The result will be sports cars which combine great strength and stiffness – essential for careful control of the suspension, necessary for good handling – with light weight which promotes good acceleration and braking.

All these advances mean that even mainstream sports cars are at the forefront of developing automotive technology. In the 1970s sports cars were increasingly seen as antiquated, and written off as irrelevant because of the new wave of sports sedans and hot hatchbacks. But the inherent appeal of a true driver's car shone through, and now sports cars are being shown off by their manufacturers as shining examples of the technology they bring to their cars. When Cadillac celebrated its centenary in 2002, it did so with a rakish mid-engined V12 sports car called Cien, not with a sober limousine, and Vauxhall's centenary a year later was celebrated with its own 240bhp sports car, the VX Lightning. No longer old-fashioned and irrelevant, sports cars now blend cutting-edge technology with up-to-the-minute style – and the panache that they've never been short of.

Index

Page numbers in *italics* refer to illustrations

Abarth 86, 87
AC Shelby Cobra *8-9*, 81, 102-3, *104*, 150
aerodynamics 12-13, 58, 189
Alfa Romeo 7, 48, 156, *170*, 172-3, 189
  6C 1750 *26*, 30, 83
  8C 2300 27, 30
  1750 Spider Veloce 82-3, 127, 130
  Duetto 82, 83
  Giulietta 81, 126
  Montreal 126-7
  racing *26*, 30, 82
  TZ 81-2
Allard *45*, 46, 61
Alpine 7, 86, 125
Aston Martin 7, 14, *18-19*, 105, 173, 189
  AMV8 Vantage 183-4, *185*, 188
  Atom *43*, 44
  DB1 44, 55
  DB2 55-6, 59
  DB3 *55*, 56, 60, *61*
  DB4 59, 73, 99
  DB4GT 99, 100
  DB5 99, 123
  DB9 183, *184*
  DBS 99-100, *101*
  racing 33, 55-6, 59-60
  Ulster 30, 33
  Vanquish 166, 167-8
Audi 180-1
  TT 153, *154*, 156, 173
Austin-Healey 7, 14
  100 65-6, 68
  3000 66-7, *70-1*, 79-80
  Sprite 68, 69, *74*, 75, 79
Austin Seven *33*, 34-5, 60
Auto Union 10, *11*, 40

Bentley 7, 173
  3.0-liter 24, 27-8
  4½-liter *24*, 28, 29
  6.0-liter 'Speed Six' *25*, 29
  racing 10, *23*, 27-9
BMW 7, 40, 42-3
  328 *35*, 36-7
  507 58, *59*, 120
  Dixi *34*, 35
  M1 *123*, 124
  racing 37, *123*, 124
  Z1 16, 140, 142
  Z3 *155*, 156, 174
  Z4 *172*, 174, 191
  Z8 174, 175, 190
Bristol 43, *47*, 100, 183
Brooklands 25, 28, 31
Bugatti 157, 173, 182
  EB110 *158*, 159, 160
  Type 13 28, 31
  Type 35 29, 31
  Type 35A 29, 31
  Type 57 *29*, 32

Cadillac Cien 191
Campbell, Sir Malcolm 12, 29
Caterham Cars 173 *see also* Lotus
  21 *156*, 158
  Seven 156, 158, *168*, 170
Chapman, Colin 60-1, *63*, 87-8, 89, 123, 138, 158
Chevrolet Corvette 7, 61-4, 104-6, *107*, 138-9, *141*, *147*, 149
Chrysler 177
  Viper 149, 150-1, *173*, 175
Cizeta Moroder *159*, 160

Daimler SP250 Dart *74*, 75
Datsun
  240Z 117, 119-20

280ZX *117*, 120
De Tomaso Pantera *122*, 124, 173
DeLorean 137
Dodge 105, 187 *see also* Chrysler

Ferrari 7, 14, 15, 93, 164
  166 48, 60
  250/275LM 92, 100
  250GT 60, *62*, 73, 92, 100
  250GTO 92, 101
  288GTO 136, *137*
  365GT Berlinetta Boxer *123*, 125, 159
  365GTB/4 Daytona 98, 99, 125, 159
  410 Superamerica 60, *62*
  512BB 123, 125
  612 Scaglietti *178-9*, 182-3
  Dino 206 *95*, 125
  Dino 308GT4 *124*, 125
  Enzo 164-5
  F40 136, *138*, 159, 160
  Ford and 94-5, 173
  racing 48, 60, 92-3, 99
Fiat 7, 29, 30, 125, 173
  124 Spider 83, *85*, 130
  850 Spider 83, 110
  Barchetta 166, 170, 175
  X1/9 *14*, 15, 16, 126, *127*, 130, 132
Ford
  Ferrari and 94-5, 173
  GT 183, *184*
  GT40 15, 95-7, 100, 173, 183
  Mustang GT-350 102, 104, *106*, 150
  Streetka *166*, 168
  Thunderbird 63, *64*
Frazer Nash *11*, 12, 42, 43

Grand Prix racing 10, *21*, 23, 30, 92, 160

Healey Silverstone 46, 49
Honda 87, *185*
  NSX *153*, 156, 175, 184
  S2000 *171*, 174
Hyundai Clix 187, *188*

Iso Rivolta 100-1, *102*

Jaguar 44-5, 84, 173, 184-5 *see also* Swallow
  C-type 13, *53*, 55, 56, 100
  D-type *12*, 13, 58-9, 73, 100
  E-type 7, 13, 72-3, 75, 79, 89, 110, *114*, *115*, 117-18
  R-D6 coupé 184, *186*, 188, 190
  racing *12*, 13, 45, 54-5, 56, 58-9, 73
  XJ-S *115*, 118
  XJ220 159, 160
  XK8 *152*, 156
  XK120 *12*, 44, 45, *53*, 54-5, 63, 66, 72, 100
  XK150 59, *61*, 72, 75
  XKR 156, *172*, 175
  XKSS 59, 60
Jensen 176
  Interceptor 100, *101*
  Jensen-Healey 119, 123

Lamborghini 7, 14, 173, 189
  Countach *121*, 124, 159, 160
  Diablo *158*, 159, 160, 166
  Gallardo 165, 167
  Miura 15, *90-1*, 93-4, 99, 124, 159
  Murciélago *165*, 167
Lancia 7, 173
  Beta Montecarlo 126
  Fulvia *83*, 84
  Stratos 125
Le Mans 37, 43, 92, 150, 161
  AC 102, *104*

Aston Martin 55-6, 59
  Bentley 10, *23*, 27-9
  Ford 95-6, 173
  Jaguar 13, 54, 56, 58-9, 73
  Mercedes-Benz 56-7, 58
  MG 68, 78
  Porsche 53, 180
Light Car Company Rocket 157, 158-9, 160
Lotus 60, 173 *see also* Caterham Cars
  Cortina 7, 14, 84, 88
  Eclat *120*, 123, 136, *139*
  Elan 13, 16, 84, 88-9, 123, 139-40, 141
  Elise *156*, 157-8, 168, *169*, 170, 172, 190
  Elite 13, 61, 63, 87, *119*, 123, 136
  Esprit 120, 123, 136, 139, *160*, *173*, 175
  Europa 89, 123
  Excel 136, *139*
  Seven 61, *63*, *121*, 123, 158

Marcos Mantis *144-5*
Maserati 7, 79, 173
  Bora *108-9*, 124
  Merak *122*, 124
Mazda 173
  Miata (MX5) 7, 16, 142-3, 157, *168*, 170, 185
  RX-7 *134*, 135, 142, *154*, 156, 177
  RX-8 *176*, 177, 185, *187*
McLaren F1 159, 160-1, 182, 189
Mercedes-Benz
  35hp *20*, 21-2
  190SL 57, 87
  230SL 87, *88*
  300SL 56-7, 58, 63, 73, 79, 87, 159, 182
  F400 Carving *190*, 191
  R107 SL 131-2
  R230 SL *174*, 175
  racing 10, *20*, 21-3, *25*, 29, 56-7, 58
  SLK 17, *171*, 173, 177, 184
  SLR McLaren 181, 182, 184, 189
  SSK *26*, 29
MG 7, 189
  C-type Midget *31*, 33-4
  J-type Midget *32*, 34
  K-type Magnette *32*, 34
  M-type Midget 11, 31, 33
  Metro 6R4 141, 151-2, 156
  MGA 69, 77, 78, 111
  MGB 16, *76*, 77-9, 83, 111, *114*, 116, 122, 142, 151
  MGB GT V8 *113*, 114, 116
  MGC *79*, 119
  MGF 16, *17*, 155, 156-7, *162-3*, 170
  Midget 16, *74*, 75, 110, 116, 119, 122, 142, 151
  P-type Midget 12-13, 34, 40
  racing 10, *31*, 34, 68, 78
  RV8 16, *150*, 153-4, 156
  TC *10*, 11, *38-9*, 41-2, 64, 67, 68
  TD 64, 67-8
  TF 64, 68-9
Mille Miglia *26*, 30, 37, 57
Mini Cooper 7, 14, 84
Mitsubishi 3000GT *152*, 156
Morgan 40, 173
  4/4 *47*, 49, 115, 176
  Aero 8 *175*, 176
  Plus 4 49, 65, 115
  Plus 8 *113*, 176
Moss, Sir Stirling *54*, 55, 60, *61*, 65
Murray, Gordon 159-60, 161

Nissan 177
  200SX *133*, 134
  300ZX *133*, 134-5

Panoz AIV *148*, 150

Panther 121, 140, 189
Peugeot RC 185, *186*
Pomeroy, Laurence 22, 23, 24-5
Pontiac Fiero 132-3
Porsche 180, 189
  356 13, 49, 52-3, 84, 111
  550/1500RS *52*, 53
  911 7, 13, 14, 84-6, 111-12, 113-15, 125, 136, 146-8, 176-7
  911 Targa *110*, 111
  914 15, 110, 111-12
  924 112, 135
  928 *111*, 112-13, 115, 135-6, 176
  944 *134*, 135
  959 136, 159
  Boxster 175, 176, 177
  racing 53, 114, 180
  Speedster 53-4, *136*

rallying 7, 46, 64-5, 66-7, 84, *85*, 118
  Jaguar *53*, 54
  Lancia 125-6, 141
  MG 78, 141
Reliant 7, 141, *143*
Renault Zo 187, *189*

safety legislation 7, 15, 16, 106, 110, 121, 161
Segrave, Sir Henry 12, *21*, 23
Shelby, Carroll 81, 102, *103*, 148, 150
Shelby Series 1 *148*, 151
Smart Roadster 167, 168-9
Subaru B9 Scrambler 187, *188*
Sunbeam *21*, 23
  Alpine 64-5, 66, 80-1
  Tiger 81, 102, 150
supercharging 24, *25*, 29, 114, 173, 175
Swallow *see also* Jaguar
  Austin Seven *33*, 34-5
  SS Jaguar 100 *34*, 35, 45

Tourist Trophy races 11, 25-6, *30*, 33, 45, 60
Toyota 87, 173
  Compact Sports and Specialty 186-7, *188*
  MR2 7, *15*, 16, 132, 133-4, 170
  Supra *134*, 135
Triumph 7, 13, 14, 65
  GT6 *75*, 76
  Spitfire 75-6, 119, 122, 142
  TR2 66-7
  TR3 *50-1*, 67, 79
  TR4 *78*, 79
  TR5 *78*, 79, 80, 83
  TR6 80, *116*, 119
  TR7 118, 120-2, 189
turbocharging 112, 114-15, 143, 168, 175
TVR 7, 121, 173
  350i *128-9*
  Cerbera *151*, 155, 175
  Chimaera *151*, 155, 175
  Griffith 150, 154-5
  S *131*, 154
  Tamora *174*, 175
  Tuscan 89, 154, 175

Vauxhall 40, 189, 191
  C-type 'Prince Henry' *22*, 23-4, 25
  E-type 30/98 *22*, 23, 24-5
  VX220 *169*, 172
Volkswagen 165, 166, 173, 181, 182
  Concept R 188, *190*
  Golf GTI 7, 16, 157
  Porsche 914 15, 110, 111-12
Volvo P1800 73

Westfield *156*, 158, 170